CW01668412

IN CAMERA
SNOWDON

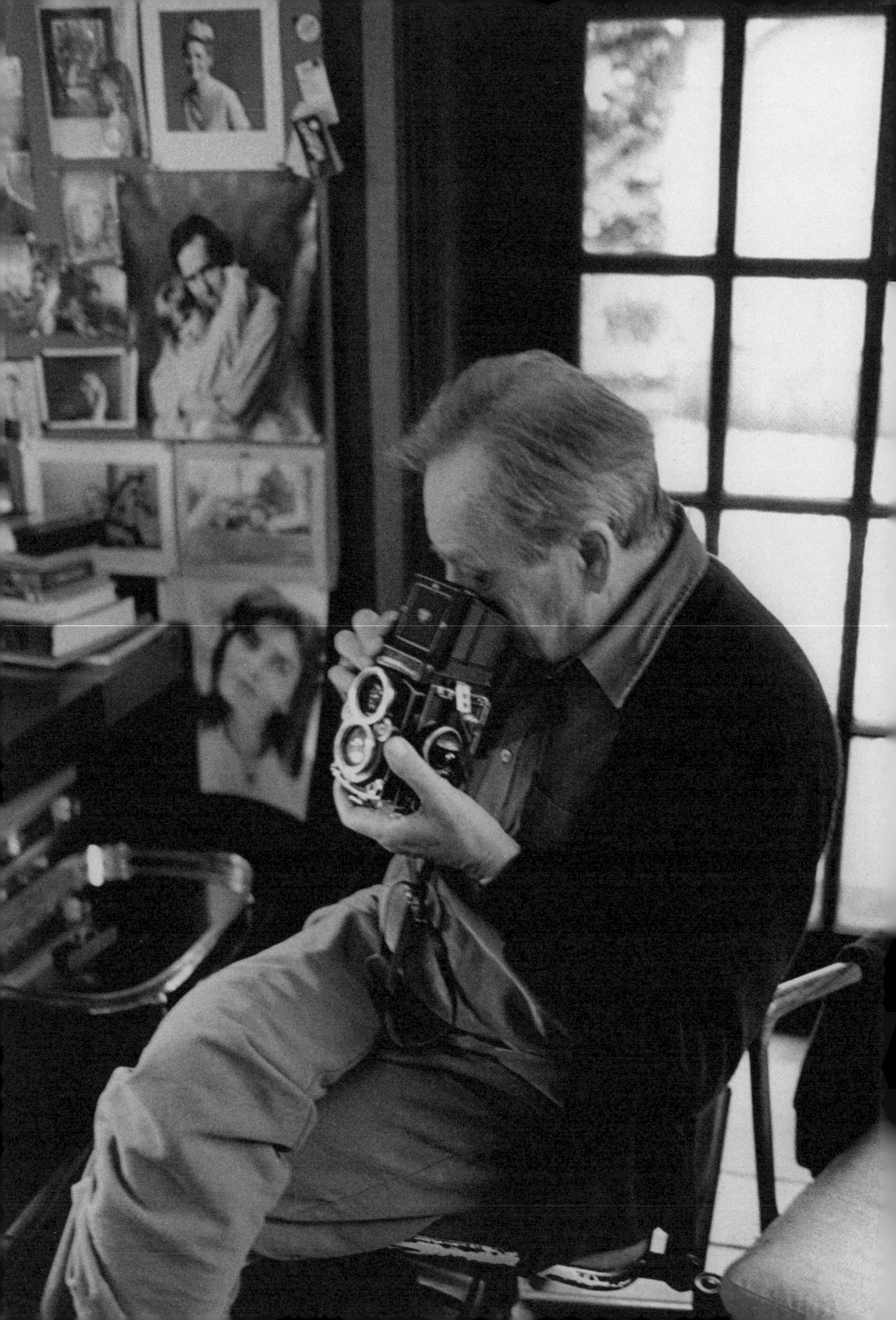

IN CAMERA
SNOWDON

ROBIN MUIR

Published on the occasion of the exhibition

In Camera: Snowdon and the World of British Art
Pallant House Gallery, Chichester
29 September 2007–27 January 2008

Curator: Robin Muir

First published in 2007 by
Pallant House Gallery
9 North Pallant
Chichester
PO19 1TJ
United Kingdom
www.pallant.org.uk

Paperback
ISBN-10 1-869827-04-X
ISBN-13 978-1-869827-04-5

Designer: David Wynn
Editors: Harriet Wailling and Edwina Vine
Editorial Support: Frances Guy

Titles set in Didot by Linotype
Body set in Foundry Sterling, generously supplied
by The Foundry, London, www.foundrytypes.co.uk
Printed in the United Kingdom by Selsey Press Ltd

Supporter of the Collection 2007
Bonhams 1793

Supporter of the Gallery 2007
UBS

Supporter of the Exhibition
METrO

Frontispiece
Snowdon, Kensington, 2007
by Paolo Roversi

Contents

Director's Foreword 7
Stefan van Raay

Curator's Acknowledgements 9
Robin Muir

In Camera
Snowdon, Private View and
'The Lively World of British Art' 11
Robin Muir

Photographs 31

Chronology 165

Director's Foreword

Many of the photographs by Snowdon in this publication have been taken in the inner sanctum of artists' studios: the very private, sometimes secret rooms or spaces, 'Camera', where the alchemy of creation takes place.

The title of this exhibition 'In Camera: Snowdon and the World of British Art' suggests that we not only get a glimpse into these private spaces but also of the personalities and characters, as if he opens a door for us into the psyche of his subjects. And that is a great achievement.

Work by 35 British artists in this exhibition is represented in the collection of Pallant House Gallery, which apart from the sheer quality of Snowdon's work itself, was another reason to mount 'In Camera'. Visitors can trace many art works by these artists in the other rooms of the Gallery, sometimes even works which are a backdrop to the photographs.

The suggestion for this exhibition came from Anna Harvey, Editorial Director of New Markets for Condé Nast International who introduced us to Robin Muir, curator of the Vogue Photographic Archive. We are most grateful to her. It has resulted in a creative, professional and happy co-operation between Robin Muir, whose concept this exhibition was, and the Gallery's staff, in particular Harriet Wailling and David Wynn.

The contribution of Victoria Charlton was invaluable; she was instrumental in bringing the exhibition to Pallant House Gallery. In addition to Bonhams, Supporter of the Collection 2007, and UBS, Supporter of the Gallery 2007, we would like to thank Camera Press and Metro Imaging for their support of the exhibition.

Most of all, we thank Lord Snowdon, who agreed to this venture; a celebration, we hope, of his enduring talent as an astute observer.

Stefan van Raay
Director

Curator's Acknowledgements

My first debt of gratitude is to Lord Snowdon who readily agreed to this exhibition of his photographs some time ago and who did not get cold feet half way through. This is the second time we have worked on an exhibition together, the first his retrospective at the National Portrait Gallery, London, in 2000, during the early stages of which he showed me the boxes of transparencies and negatives for *Private View*. These had lain unexamined, for the most part, since 1964 and I wish there had been room here to show more of the astonishing outtakes and variants that never made it to the finished book.

A second debt is owed to all the editors and art directors of magazines and newspaper supplements, who commissioned the photographs, in particular the late Mark Boxer, the second editor of *The Sunday Times Colour Section*, whose role in the history of British magazine publishing deserves wider acknowledgement. His art director Michael Rand lent several key items, for which I extend my thanks. Snowdon took his first photograph for *Vogue* in 1956 a relationship that has now survived over half a century. I would like to thank Brett Croft, Jooney Woodward, Jeb Crowell, Bonnie Robertson and Paul Dyer of the Condé Nast Library for their help on an almost daily basis.

Camera Press, Lord Snowdon's syndication agents, have given Pallant House Gallery and me nothing but unstinting help. And I would like to thank in particular Anne Golding, who sourced all the material for the exhibition and this catalogue. I also thank her colleagues, Roger Eldridge, Daryl Bradford and Jacqui Wald. Steve MacLeod and Jason Tasker at Metro Imaging made superb prints from the material Camera Press supplied.

I am no less grateful to Victoria Charlton, who has contributed greatly to the process of bringing Snowdon's photographs to Chichester, and to Anna Harvey of Condé Nast International who first identified Pallant House Gallery as the ideal venue.

For all their practical help, I would also like to thank Frances and Rodolphe von Hofmannstahl; John Backham; Chris Beetles and Giles Huxley-Parlour (The Chris Beetles Gallery, London); Sir Peter Blake; Philippe Garner; Suzanne Hodgart; Paul Lyon-Maris; Paolo Roversi and Studio Luce, Paris; Trevor Rush; and, not least, Lynne Wilson at Snowdon's studio in London.

It has been a pleasure to work with Stefan van Raay and his staff at Pallant House Gallery, who richly deserve the accolades showered upon it and them: Elaine Bentley, Andrew Churchill, Frances Guy, Nick Higbee, Edwina Vine and Simon Martin. I would like to thank in particular, Harriet Wailling for her tireless help, both editorial and marketing, and David Wynn for his catalogue design.

Robin Muir
West Sussex, August 2007

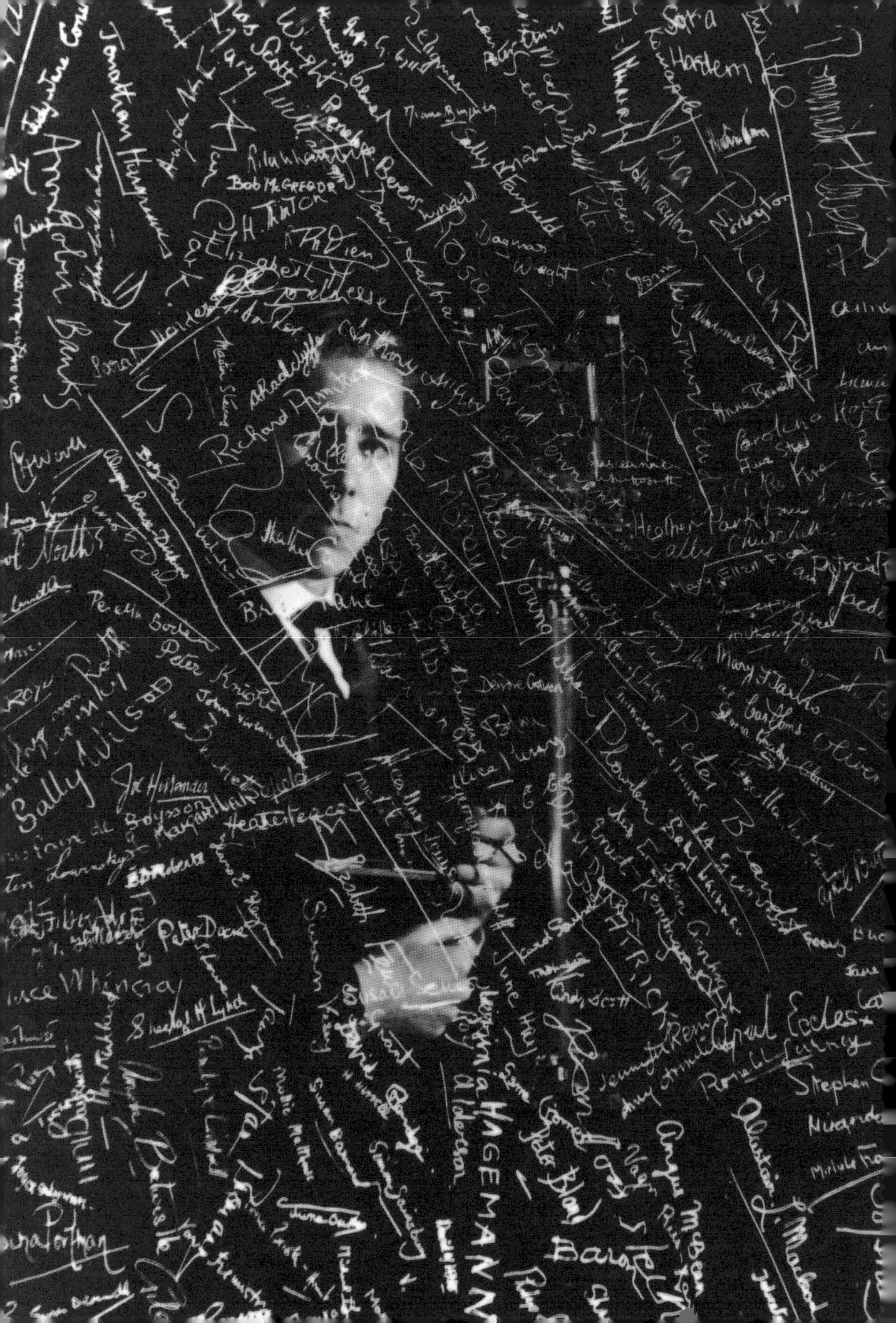
Bob McGREGOR
Peter Knight
Heather Park
Sally Churchill
Stephen

In Camera
Snowdon, Private View and 'The Lively World of British Art'

> *'Just what has turned London into one of the world's three capitals of art? Who did it, and how? And what kind of people are they?'*
> (Private View, 1965)

This exhibition derives much of its content from the book *Private View*, published in 1965. Having posed these questions in its foreword, the authors Bryan Robertson, John Russell and Lord Snowdon attempted to answer them in several hundred photographs, and column upon column of densely-packed text.

Their response required a wealth of pictures not just of painters and sculptors and their works – 'Enormously, and above all, the artists matter' – but also of a battery of establishment figures and facilitators cast in supporting roles; all vital to the energy, initiative and ambition of an art capital in the ascendant. A preamble in monochrome to the stars in full colour, they include the directors of the National and the Tate Galleries; the Principals of the Slade and the Royal College of Art; the London art scene's leading picture dealers and its *eminences grises*; the art world's foremost scholars, critics and theorists; auction house chairmen; eminent patrons and benefactors, public servants, foundry men and frame-makers. The writer Colin McInnes praised the book's 'constant delights', adding that Snowdon's 'visual observations are often as trenchant, if not more so, as those of Robertson and Russell'.[1]

Self-portrait through 'visitors' looking-glass,
Pimlico studio, 1956

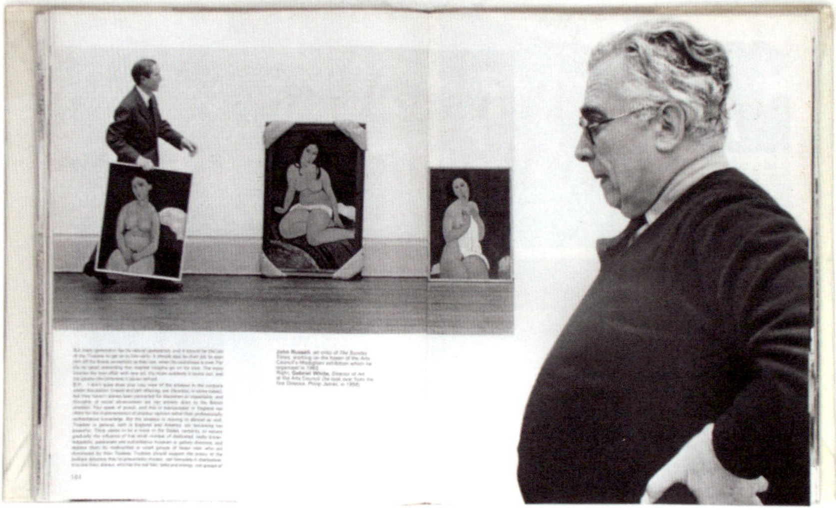

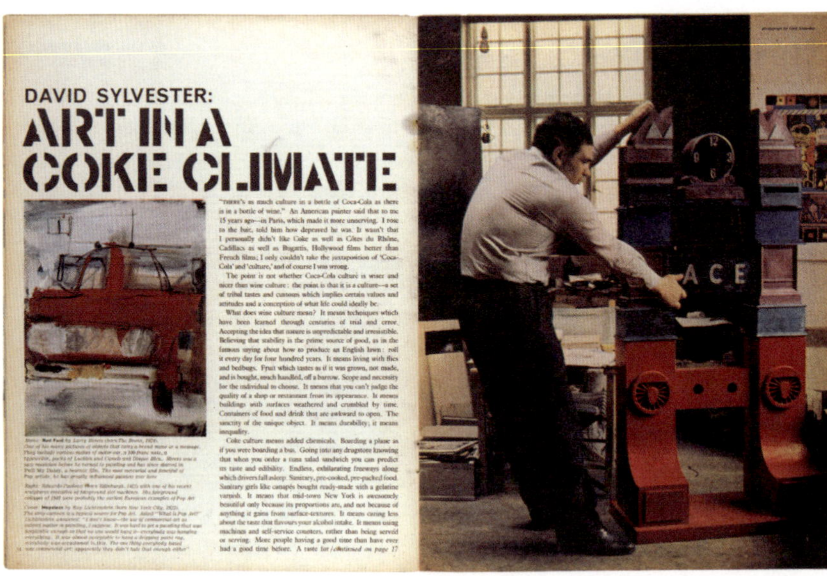

Top From *Private View*: John Russell with Modigliani and Gabriel White, Director of Art, the Arts Council, 1963
Above David Sylvester, 'Art in a Coke Climate', *The Sunday Times Magazine*, January 26, 1964

The most trenchant perhaps, the Director of the Courtauld Institute and Keeper of the Queen's Pictures scrutinising a transparency of a Picasso painting. Sir Anthony Blunt's notoriety could not, clearly, have been envisaged by the photographer, but the finesse of light and shadow distorting the subject's face to emphasise an inscrutable stare into space has lent it a subsequent – and very particular – resonance.

The three who shared authorship of *Private View* were equally distinguished and included John Russell, the insightful art critic of *The Sunday Times,* and Bryan Robertson, Director of the Whitechapel Gallery, London, who was admired as much for his curatorial, as for his organisational skills. Photographs of the two art historians were included in the book, Robertson by virtue of office and Russell as a leading exhibitions organiser, but its *spiritus movens* was the third and youngest author. Snowdon was by 1965 one of Europe's most well-known photographers, though he would always claim that where expertise was concerned, he was far from its best: 'Most photographers of my age started taking photographs because they failed at something else...For me photography is a way of recording things because I can't draw'.[2] The *Daily Express* put it another way: 'His secret may be this: that he is the only photographer in the world more nervous than his sitters...'[3]

For Snowdon *Private View* had been a Herculean task. In three weeks in October 1963, for example, he photographed Peter Lanyon in Cornwall; Elisabeth Frink, Prunella Clough, Derek Boshier, Patrick Caulfield, Patrick George and Peter Blake in or around their London studios; John Piper in the graveyard of St. Anne's, Limehouse; L.S. Lowry at Leather Lane Market, Clerkenwell; Sir Anthony Blunt at the Courtauld (twice); John Pope-Hennessey in his Campden Hill study; Kenneth Clark at home in Albany, Piccadilly; the art historian Professor Ernst Gombrich at the Warburg Institute and the directors of Agnews and Christie's; as well as undertaking several commissions for *The Sunday Times Magazine.*

The finished book featured 81 artists and around the same number again of satellite figures. It took Snowdon to St. Ives, the West Country and the northern Home Counties, but London was its focus. As the painter Jack Smith observed, amplifying an original Bryan Robertson *aperçu*, 'the wilderness starts ten miles from the centre of London in any direction'[4]. With London a putative 'art capital' of the world, John Russell estimated that the authors had 'travelled a thousand miles' within its environs and that 'fixed ideas about London dropped away one by one'.[5]

Much anticipated, *Private View* was the publishing sensation of the year, prompting one critic to declare that 'it is already the "Debrett" of art – if you are not in it, you are "out"'.[6] But adding a note of caution in *Apollo*, Anthony Powell disregarded the authors' opening questions to ask one of his own: 'Will our great-grandchildren turn over these pages with roars of laughter or with hushed respect?'[7]

Private View was Snowdon's third book, following two projects in black-and-white, both published in 1958: *Malta*, a collaboration with Sacheverell Sitwell, and the self-motivated *London*. In the second, as Tony Armstrong-Jones, he wrote that his photographs were intended 'to make ordinary people react – to laugh or to see something they hadn't taken in before...but not to wince.'[8] This self-appraisal would be repeated over the years, almost as a mantra, not just because he believed it to be true, but also because it neatly forestalled criticism of any perceived 'lightness' in his work. About his fashion photography – he had started at *Vogue* in 1956 – he was at his most self-deprecating, admitting to an in-built inclination to artifice: 'I was determined to have fun for myself and hopefully for the reader too'.[9] This was reflected in a playful debunking of the vocabulary of 'high fashion' achieved mostly by incongruous locations, extravagant props and a judicious use of nylon thread to stabilise a toppled champagne glass or a collapsing house of cards. 'The only thing that can be said', Snowdon recalled, 'is that the photographs didn't imitate the elegant pictures by Irving Penn which I admired so much...'[10]

His subsequent engagement by *Queen* (from 1957) was prompted by this disarming, off-the-cuff approach to photography, one he had always been keen to display. *Queen*'s art director, Mark Boxer, recalled that he commissioned Armstrong-Jones precisely 'to cover events like Henley or the Chelsea Flower Show in a less conventional way',[11] or in the photographer's own words 'with a slight sense of ridicule'.[12]

The photographs for *London* had been made on a small handheld 35mm Leica camera and without artificial light 'because this seems to me', he explained, 'the only way a photographer can hope to keep himself out of the scene'[13]. Keeping himself out of the scene had been a priority in a career, concomitant with fashion and *Vogue*, as a theatre photographer. A miniature camera allowed him to photograph rehearsals unobserved and closer to the *mise-en-scène* than had been traditional. He would impose this protocol with small and medium format cameras on *Private View* too, remarking that 'the best work of any photographer is that in which he is most absent and the subject most present'.[14]

Though generally well received, the photographic establishment did not initially hail *London* as a *succès d'estime*. The *British Journal of Photography* excoriated it for the graininess of the illustrations, its informality of tone and for the impertinence that blurred, badly framed images could constitute a document: 'a recital of squalors... marked by squalid photography'.[15] The book's unconventional structure also came in for criticism: chapter headings were anomalous and enigmatic and layout juxtapositions, conceived by Mark Boxer, irreverent. Naturally, these dissident qualities made it compelling to a generation of young British photographers, and it has since been recognised as a classic of reportage: 'a landmark in promulgating a crisper 35mm vision of the landscape', according to one commentator.[16]

In *London*, the art world featured obliquely, as it had so far in Snowdon's oeuvre. The only painter approached for the book, and photographed on the first day of 1958, was John Bratby. His unkempt presence in a low-lit bedroom, looming over his infant son's cot and dangling a cigarette, was the first significant portrait of a British painter Armstrong-Jones had made. Bratby basked in establishment esteem – he had represented Britain at the Venice Biennale in 1956 and would shortly be elected an Associate of the Royal Academy – but it was his downbeat personal demeanour and circumstances, not the colourful subject matter of his paintings, that chimed with the metropolitan romance of *London*. Along with fellow painters and Royal College of Art contemporaries Derrick Greaves, Jack Smith and Edward Middleditch, Bratby was part of a putative loose-knit group of social realists 'The Kitchen Sink School'. The term was derived from an article in *Encounter* by David Sylvester and partly suggested by Smith's *Mother Bathing Child* (1953), but Bratby, to his irritation, became its public face.[17] Despite the 'life and exultation' evinced by Sylvester in Bratby's paint-encrusted works, Bratby the man was by most accounts uncompromisingly uncouth; 'an only-partly engaging slob, a proto-beatnik' was one assessment.[18] As such and in domestic disharmony, Armstrong-Jones recognised Bratby as a manifestation of London's artistic/bohemian underbelly, a vital part of the city's allure. The fleeting crepuscular snapshot – far from his good-natured photographs for *Vogue*, *The Sketch* and *Queen* – remains a significant moment in the development of his portraiture. The painter's shambling presence also acts as a coda to *London* and to the decade too. The fifties, as more than one photographer noted, were black-and-white; the sixties were vibrantly coloured. Armstrong-Jones' all-but-unobserved scrutiny of subject and casual approach to photography's constraints, anticipates the tactics he would use for *Private View*. When the huge art book appeared, several commentators remarked on Snowdon's reluctance to be experimental but none could fail to notice that British art was, as the subtitle to the American edition put it, a 'Lively World' and displayed in glorious colour.

From *London*: The Last Presentation,
Buckingham Palace, 1958

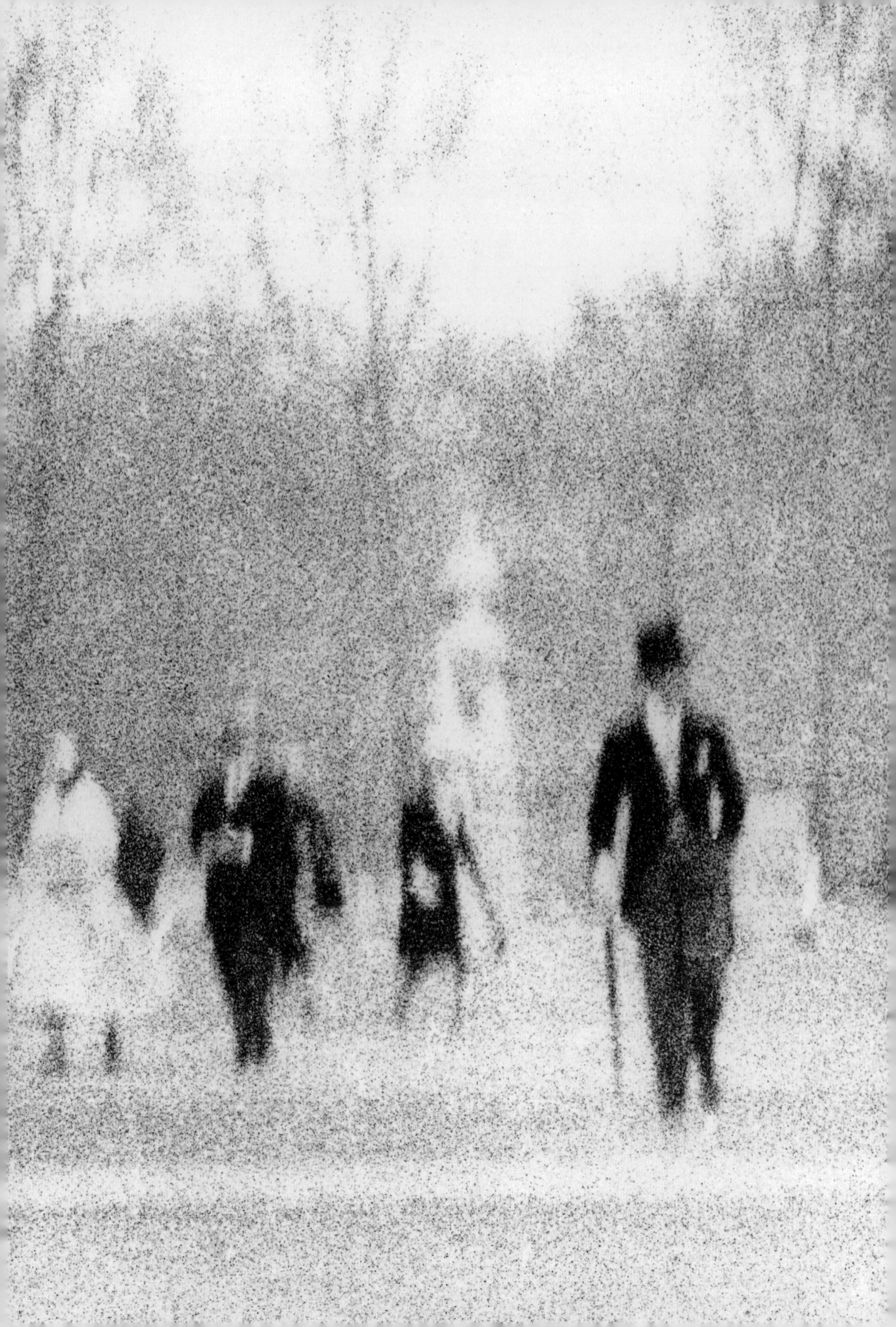

Private View was made in the interstices of Snowdon's career, both as a photographer and as a public figure. In 1960 he had married Princess Margaret Rose, daughter of George VI and sister to the Queen. Tony Armstrong-Jones became the Earl of Snowdon, and much else besides his by-line changed. As a photographer his marriage closed as many doors as it opened. The anonymity that had allowed him to operate from a studio and flat in *mondaine* Pimlico and a riverside base in unfashionable Rotherhithe and to walk unrecognised between the two ended. On his part the contract with *Vogue* was not renewed; the magazine recalled, wistfully, that where its young star was concerned 'the ordinary was the last thing we expected – or got'.[19]

It was no longer possible to treat him as just another photographer with a job to do, no matter how much he wished it so. His own fame surpassed, occasionally overwhelmed, that of his sitters. Interviewed for *Vogue* in 1963, Cecil Beaton reflected upon the advances photographers had recently made: 'When I began, a photographer had no sort of social position at all...but now [they] can go anywhere'.[20] That they were no longer regarded as inferior tradesmen had as much to do with Armstrong-Jones' elevation as it did the democratizing, swinging sixties. In the light of the duties and responsibilities commensurate with marriage to the reigning monarch's younger sister, it is striking that – after an initial hiatus – Snowdon's photographic productivity increased.

The spur was the planned colour supplement to *The Sunday Times* newspaper. The magazine, known until February 1963 as *The Sunday Times Colour Section*, was the brainchild of Roy Thomson, *The Sunday Times'* new owner, and Dennis Hamilton, his paper's new editor. At the suggestion of Mark Boxer, the supplement's acting editor, Snowdon was announced as 'artistic adviser' in 1961. His extraordinary photographs for the magazine, from portrait to landscape to social document, remain some of the best he would ever make and rebuffed an assumption among the paper's rivals that his appointment was a publicity stunt. Snowdon was phlegmatic about his obvious predicament:

> *Taking up photography after a break of two years wasn't a problem for me; I hadn't stopped using a camera. But a reportage photographer needs total anonymity and must blend into the background like a chameleon. This ability is totally lost if your face becomes known through television and the press...It's not that I'm instantly recognizable, but particularly at seaside resorts, where people are sitting around using their eyes, I'm often accosted if I have a camera in my hands. They say: 'am I right?' or 'I've got a bet with my daughter you aren't....'*[21]

The nebulous advisory role was anyway quickly forgotten but not before Snowdon had redesigned the interior of Roy Thomson's office. He hung it with paintings he thought the proprietor might approve, such as Sidney Nolan's antipodean landscapes, and examples by younger British artists of whom Snowdon felt the owner of a new and dazzling publication should be aware.

The first issue appeared on 4 February 1962 and was received by *The Sunday Times'* competitors with bewilderment and derision in equal measure. It was, inevitably, an undertaking motivated purely by commercial considerations. In the years before television could be transmitted in colour, the supplement attempted to seize the initiative – and the larger market share – in full colour quality advertising. In this respect it was not a disappointment, generating huge revenues at its outset. After its first year it had increased the paper's readership by 100,000.

Consequently, the annual editorial budget was almost limitless and Boxer's position one of great influence, though he carried about him an air of irresponsibility. Although the advertising occasionally threatened to subsume the content, Boxer maintained an editorial policy of lengthy, well-written articles and commissioned photography that came close to the hybrid of the *New Yorker* and *Queen* he had sought. Coverage of the fine arts was paramount.

British contemporary artists, London-based in particular, were emerging from the long shadows cast by American Abstract Expressionism and French 'Art Informel'. The historian Martin Harrison has identified 'a predilection', admittedly not exclusive to British painting in the 1950s, 'for pulsating colour, a luminescence that may relate to the flickering waves of incandescent and neon lighting...a reaction to wartime "blackout" restrictions as well as to contemporary dullness'.[22] In its quest for innovation, the new *Sunday Times* supplement would alight upon anything pulsating with colour and was drawn, ineluctably, to the iridescence of new British painting. The inaugural issue carried 'Pioneer of Pop Art' by John Russell, a profile of Peter Blake, shortly to have his first one-man show. Patrick Ward took the accompanying colour portrait, not the new magazine's 'artistic adviser'.

Similar features on the unexplored galaxy of British art followed during 1962 and early 1963. A study by Snowdon of sculptor Lynn Chadwick as a modern day Hephaestus wielding an incandescent acetylene torch was syndicated to American *Vogue*. An occasional series – 'Painting Now' – focused on young British artists whose fame had yet to match their promise. These included Michael Andrews, profiled by David

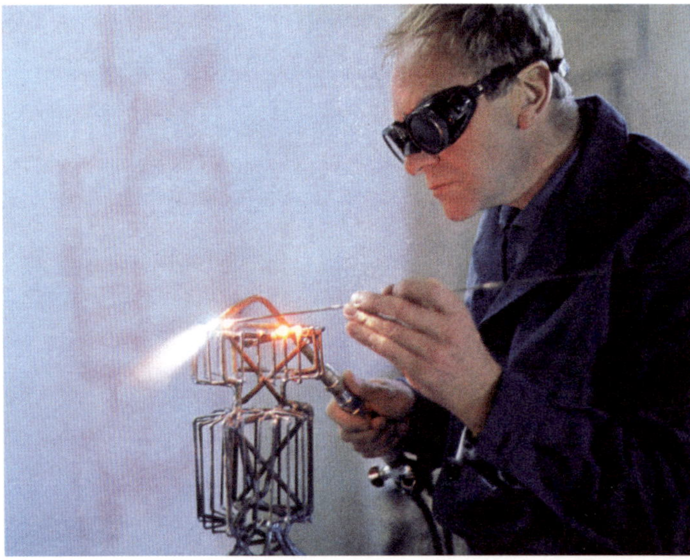

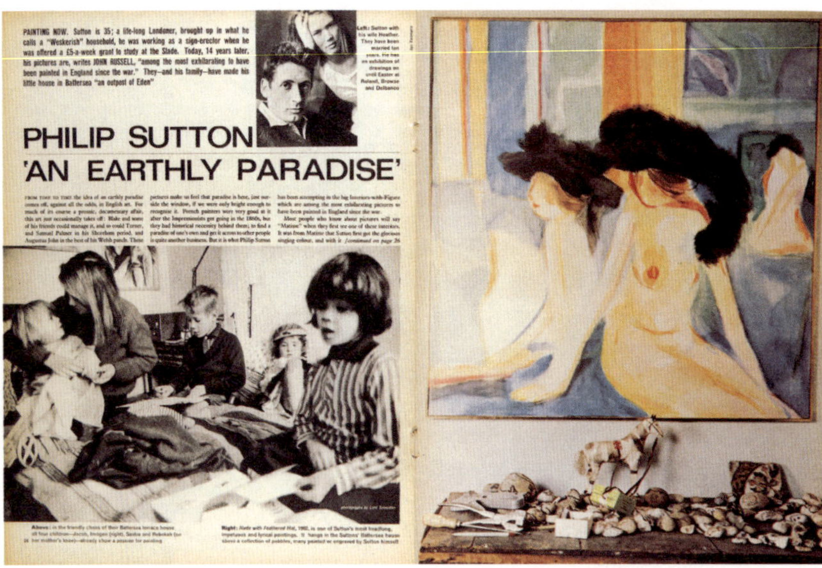

PAINTING NOW. Sutton is 35; a life-long Londoner, brought up in what he calls a "Weskerish" household, he was working as a sign-erector when he was offered a £5-a-week grant to study at the Slade. Today, 14 years later, his pictures are, writes JOHN RUSSELL, "among the most exhilarating to have been painted in England since the war." They—and his family—have made his little house in Battersea "an outpost of Eden"

Left: Sutton with his wife Heather. They have been married ten years. He has an exhibition of drawings on until Easter at Roland, Browse and Delbanco

PHILIP SUTTON 'AN EARTHLY PARADISE'

FROM TIME TO TIME the idea of an earthly paradise comes off, against all the odds, in English art. For much of its course a prosaic, documentary affair, this art just occasionally takes off: Blake and some of his friends could manage it, and so could Turner, and Samuel Palmer in his Shoreham period, and Augustus John in the best of his Welsh panels. These pictures make us feel that paradise is here, just outside the window, if we were only bright enough to recognise it. French painters were very good at it after the Impressionists got going in the 1860s, but they had historical necessity behind them; to find a paradise of one's own and get it across to other people is quite another business. But it is what Philip Sutton has been attempting in the big Interiors-with-Figure which are among the most exhilarating pictures to have been painted in England since the war.

Most people who know about pictures will say "Matisse" when they first see one of these interiors. It was from Matisse that Sutton first got the glorious singing colour, and with it (continued on page 26

Above: in the friendly chaos of their Battersea terrace house all four children—Jacob, Imogen (right), Saskia and Rebekah (on her mother's knee)—already show a passion for painting

Right: Nude with Feathered Hat, [illegible], is one of Sutton's most headlong, impetuous and lyrical paintings. It hangs in the Suttons' Battersea house above a collection of pebbles, many painted or engraved by Sutton himself

Top From *Private View*: Lynn Chadwick, Gloucestershire, 1962

Above John Russell, 'Philip Sutton: an Earthly Paradise', *The Sunday Times Colour Magazine*, March 31, 1963

Sylvester, R.B Kitaj (Ohio-born but London-based) by Bryan Robertson and 'Philip Sutton: An Earthly Paradise' by John Russell. [23] A Snowdon portrait, subsequently published in *Private View*, accompanied each.

For the issue of 2 June 1963, Boxer felt confident enough to initiate 'British Painting Now', a 12-page survey of the state of British art. A new art director, Michael Rand, commissioned the photographs from Snowdon. The survey was initially conceived in two parts to reflect 'British Painting in the Sixties', an exhibition organised for the Contemporary Art Society in two London venues. Established names could be found at the Tate Gallery and emerging names at the Whitechapel (under the auspices of Bryan Robertson). However, before publication, both parts were knitted together to make one discursive appraisal. David Sylvester provided an essay 'Dark Sunlight', which would give the magazine extra lustre by proving controversial.

This commixture of old and new, established with emergent, the nearly-forgotten with the promising, was the germ of *Private View*. Of the senior painters, the magazine selected four. Sir William Coldstream, a trustee of both the National and Tate Galleries and an admired educationalist, was an establishment figure *ne plus ultra*, his unobtrusive and genial appearance providing a contrast to the bearded bohemianism of his 'Euston Road' colleague Victor Pasmore. The two, both naturalistic painters, went together, the magazine considered, 'like Flanagan and Allen' (that is, until Pasmore discovered abstract painting). An abstract painter from the start, William Scott held a probably unique position in British art, a link between pre-war Parisian high gesture and transatlantic abstract expressionism. He had known Emile Bernard, correspondent of Gauguin and Van Gogh, and was later among the first to make personal contact with Jackson Pollock, Mark Rothko and Willem de Kooning. Also with links to pre-war movements, though mostly literary, was Robert Medley, by 1963 head of the painting department at the Camberwell School.

The younger figures included Harold Cohen, a leading light of new abstractionism. Sylvester admired him especially for his technique as much as the bold canvasses he produced: 'the paint may be put on thickly or thinly, but either way it is put on matter-of-factly without showmanship or over subtlety…' [24] Not shy of showmanship, David Hockney was caught in the street by Snowdon sporting a gold lamé jacket and swinging a matching shopping bag. Two further, more conventional portraits for the magazine, showed him gold-jacketed in front of the recently completed *A Domestic Scene, Los Angeles* (1963); in the other, smoking a cigar in a red cardigan, next to a figure from the life-sized and probably uncompleted *The Hypnotist* (1963). The last figure to be photographed for the piece was Frank Auerbach in his studio in Camden Town. Snowdon would return there twenty years later for *Vogue*. On both occasions he marvelled at the painter's tiny, self-contained milieu, making still life vignettes of, among other things, Auerbach's paint-encrusted domestic utensils. Patrick Kinmonth, Snowdon's *Vogue* collaborator, found the studio 'as adapted to him as the room of a blind man, leaving [Auerbach] free to concentrate on the unknown'. [25] In 1982, Snowdon, more out of necessity than lack of imagination, positioned Auerbach in almost exactly the same spot next to a wall of pinned-up reproductions of Rembrandts and Francis Bacons, which had over the two decades hardly changed.

But the figure that loomed out of 'British Painting Now', in by far the most expressive photograph, was Francis Bacon. Snowdon photographed him emphasising a point by raising his arms aloft (while leaving it undocumented how they might have come crashing down). Barely a year younger than Coldstream and Pasmore but somehow occupying a middle ground between the old and new schools, Bacon was, as Auerbach's pin-ups indicated, the 'painter's painter'. As would subsequently be revealed, he was a favourite of Sylvester too: 'He isn't a pro, ready to have a go at what is asked of him, but a Gentleman, playing the game to divert or torment himself...' [26]

David Sylvester's essay was entertaining and consciously provocative from its opening line: 'British painting always inclines to have a somewhat forced, unnatural air, like ladies' cricket or hip clergymen...' [27] Using Bacon as an example, he endorsed the 'purity' of the amateur, unable or unwilling to accede to the demands of the gallerists' bottom-line, and motivated only by an almost primordial compulsion to create. The other approach atrophied British art as a foreign virus might a healthy body: 'Professionalism', Sylvester maintained, 'seeks to make the difficult look easy and covers up traces of the strain'. The vagaries of commercialism made a *reductio ad absurdam* of the painter's skill, forestalling 'obsession' and turning art into 'overly aesthetic' exercises or 'mere decoration'. [28]

Condemnation was quick to follow. The following week the paper published a letter signed by a dozen artists, including Peter Blake, Anthony Caro, Robyn Denny, R.B. Kitaj and Eduardo Paolozzi, as well as one featured in the previous week's piece, Harold Cohen. It ended on a statement of defiance: 'Mr Sylvester seeks to drag British art back into the suffocating club atmosphere of amateurism and dilettantism at a time when, for the first time in this century, a generation of artists has deliberately taken up a position outside and against it'. [29] Sylvester had, against the odds, galvanised interest in new British art. The magazine was quick to exploit the situation and Sylvester's next piece, 'The Art of the Impossible' attempted to explain to the casual weekend reader, the dark, obfuscating complexities of Francis Bacon's paintings. [30]

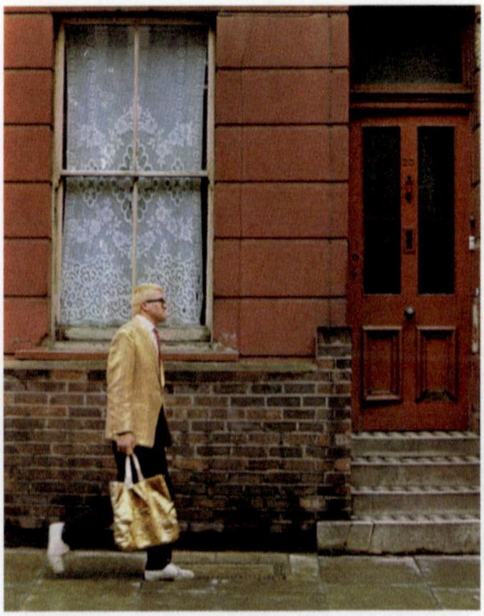

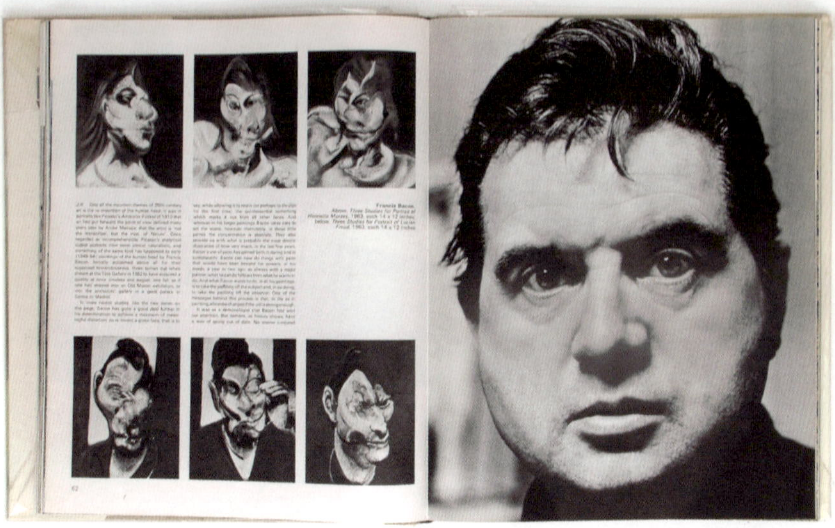

Top From *Private View*: David Hockney, Paddington, 1963
Above From *Private View*: Francis Bacon,1963

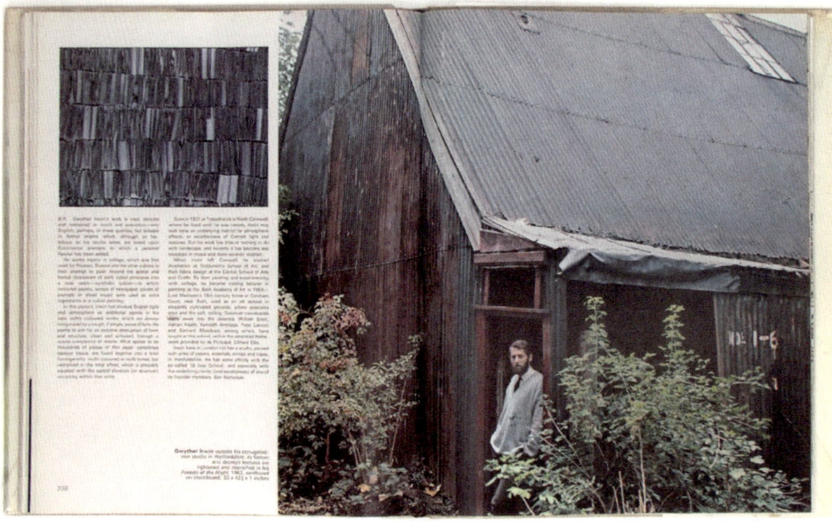

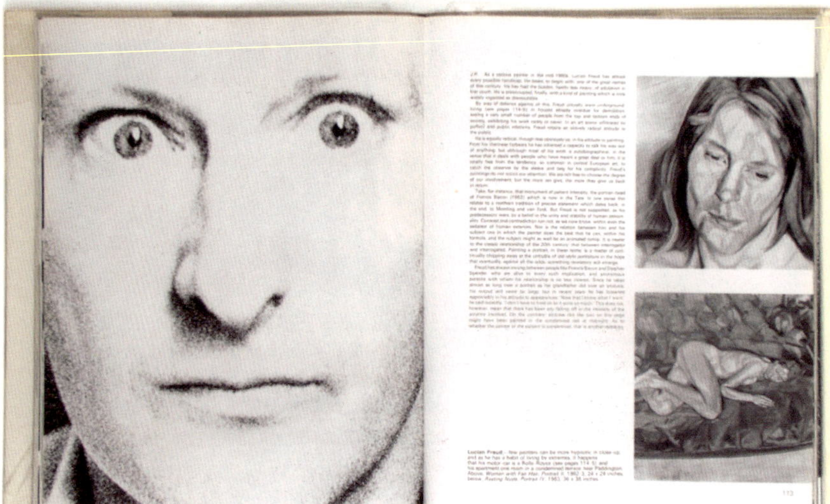

Top From *Private View*: Gwyther Irwin, Hertfordshire, 1963
Above From *Private View*: Lucian Freud, 1963

In the summer of 1963 a decision was made to continue the survey of British artists in book form. Its basis in a succession of popular magazine articles led certain reviewers to pronounce it 'merely modish' or with 'the virtues one expects of weekend colour journalism'.[31] There was truth in this, especially concerning the last section of the book 'The New Generation'. Since many of the photographs *had* originated in magazines, the designer Germano Facetti devised the layouts to be self-contained double-page spreads – a magazine convention – with a portrait of the artist and examples of his or her work. The grid was not rigid and allowed for 'full-bleed' whole page pictures opposite smaller ones at any given size, an imperative for a book containing several hundred photographs. Often aware of what might be placed opposite his portrait in the final spread, Snowdon made eye-catching devices that also owed much to the conceits of contemporary magazine design. The busts, trophies and tailors' dummies assembled by Peter Blake in his garden, suggested the arrangement of figures and items of *On the Balcony* (1957/8); the corrugated iron roof of Gwyther Irwin's studio reflected the intense vertical striations of *Forests of the Night* (1963); a pointillist headshot of Richard Hamilton was in clever imitation of the artist's style. And so on to great effect.

With *Private View*, Snowdon succeeded in the calm unenforced intimacy that had so far characterised the best of his work. 'I don't want people to look at a photograph but *into* it', he told one interviewer as he was making the *Private View* pictures.[32] The subject was allowed to expand or shrink into his own private world as it suited him while Snowdon 'agile as a dragonfly powered by Boeing' manoeuvred dexterously around with the minimum of disturbance.[33] As he wrote retrospectively in *Personal View* (1979):

> *It worked well for me because the artists were usually as engrossed in their work as I was, and their studios were quiet and controlled… When I started photographing artists it was relatively fresh to me. I tried to echo the mood of their work in my photographs. I would happily alter the colour of my transparencies afterwards to match the colour of the paintings to get a tighter link.*[34]

Snowdon's success with artists arose too out of an identification with – and an admiration for – what they were able to do and, perhaps, what he could not. Photographers took photographs, as he reminded anyone who cared to listen, because they could not paint. To pre-empt any accusations of undue reverence there were occasional exercises in pure fun: the Tate's Sir John Rothenstein cast as a pixie on a polythene toadstool: Barbara Hepworth as predatory mantis on a Cornish rock; David Sylvester scuttling away with a Soutine; and in a scenario that infuriated its subject,

Lucian Freud strolling past a Bentley, which the caption assumed was his (he denied it vehemently) [35]. In *The Observer*, John Richardson was astute: 'Confronted with the solemn spectacle of the English art establishment the two authors genuflect. Not so the photographer: more often than not Lord Snowdon puts out his tongue...' [36] While he could be mischievous, he could be boundlessly sympathetic too. Helen Lessore sitting alone in the gloom of the West End gallery she had directed for years and would shortly lose is justly regarded as one of Snowdon's finest photographs.

Another book published in 1965, far less conventional and co-art directed by Mark Boxer, was *David Bailey's Box of Pin-ups*. Bailey was *Vogue*'s star photographer, and from an East London working-class background, the polar opposite of Snowdon's. *Pin-ups*, a book of monochrome portraits, celebrated the 'triumphant classlessness' of the decade, the example nonpareil being the photographer himself. A boxed collection of thirty-six loose-leaf, sheet-fed photogravures, *Pin-ups* identified the members of a new 'Pop' meritocracy of models and milliners, magazine art directors and pop stars. The four Beatles, David Hockney and Michael Caine stayed the course but *Pin-ups* chiefly memorialised the transient. Unlike Snowdon, Bailey was fascinated by the tinsel of celebrity – 'a bright, brittle quality, the more appealing because it tarnishes so soon' – and sprinkled it purposefully upon the undeserved and the unforgivable. [37] Among the latter, the East End gangster twins Ronnie and Reggie Kray. Bailey's friend Terence Donovan, Cecil Beaton enjoying a revival, and Snowdon, represented photography's fashionable elite. However, the proximity of the Queen's brother-in-law to two of London's most powerful underworld figures caused controversy. Francis Wyndham, who knew Snowdon well, had written the biographical notes, and the observations of this shrewd friend give an insight into Snowdon's state of mind on the eve of publication of *Private View*. 'So whatever happened to Tony Armstrong-Jones?' he asked. While acknowledging Snowdon's attitude to life and art is 'essentially theatrical' and admiring his lack of pretension, 'classlessness', 'quick responsive mind' and revealing that 'snob' was his strongest term of abuse, Wyndham admitted that Snowdon was:

> *Impatient, impulsive, nervously energetic; he is fascinated by every form of mechanical gadget; his indignation at inferior design is genuine and ferocious. Responding to the look and feel of things, he is superficial and sensual in the literal and honourable meanings of these words. Lord Snowdon needs constant reassurance and hates criticism. He likes people who like him, but if they do so for the right reason – himself.* [38]

The year 1965 and the publication of two very different photographic books was something of a watershed for a generation of British photographers. As Martin Harrison has identified it, 'the desire...to present photographs in book form – that is outside the context of magazines – portended one of the most significant changes in photography'.[39] Congratulating Snowdon on the success of his beautiful book, the Queen with wry humour wondered if she ought to consider acquiring a coffee table.

Published by an Edinburgh based firm, typeset in London, printed in Lucerne and bound in Künzelsau, West Germany, the arrival of *Private View* was accompanied by a succession of events commensurate with a potential landmark. The launch party was attended by many of the artists and art world luminaries featured in it. At 11 by 13½ inches and containing nearly 400 photographs, it weighed 5½ lbs (more with the robust slipcase for the American market). Priced at 7 guineas it was not a bestseller. This was not for lack of effort (or hyperbole) on the part of the distributor. The Oxford don Quentin Bell, an occasional reviewer for *The Listener*, received a fulsome encomium from W.H. Smith: 'Through the keen eyes', it read, 'of brilliant observers (who have access to the studios of the great from which the public, of course, are rigorously barred) we can begin to see more clearly what modern art is...' He considered that *Private View* might in time be remembered as much as a social document as a record of the state of British Art.[40]

There were of course omissions from *Private View*, most glaringly Scottish artists working in their native land but who showed down south, and English painters, such as Robin Philipson, who had chosen to remove themselves north. But the authors had never left it in any doubt that London was at the nucleus of the British art explosion. Others overlooked included many Royal Academicians, as well as William Gear, Ruskin Spear, Gillian Ayres (her husband Henry Mundy appeared), Bryan Kneale and Alan Reynolds, whom Bryan Robertson himself had called 'the golden boy of post Neo-Romanticism in England'.[41] John Bratby did not merit inclusion, nor his colleagues Derrick Greaves and Edward Middleditch (Jack Smith, however, had dumped the kitchen sink and now appeared, on the evidence of *Private View*, as a conceptual painter of pictographic motifs). Ben Nicholson, then in Switzerland, declined to be photographed but allowed examples of his work to be published.

If one can judge from critical reaction and its aftermath, it is likely that with the publication of *Private View* Snowdon had reached a turning point. He began to be regarded as a photographer again, and a brilliant and incisive one, not a status-enhanced personality wielding a small camera. Branching out into design, he had conceived (with Cedric Price and Frank Newby) a modernist aviary for London Zoo and joined the panel of the Arts Council. His work continued for *The Sunday Times Magazine*, becoming bolder in tone and scope, in his words, 'more serious and, if necessary, un-prepossessing'.[42] This relates, for the most part, to his photo-essays on what the magazine would call 'matters of social concern': the plight of the homeless, children under stress, caring for the mentally ill and the vicissitudes of old age. They are now regarded as solemn classics of British social reportage.

In late 1970, Snowdon renewed contact with *Vogue*. An early assignment was a sitting with Bryan Kneale at the Royal Academy, a *coup de foudre* of two superimposed prints. And Snowdon's encounters with artists would be a feature of the magazine (and its American sister edition) throughout the next three-and-a-half decades. The list of sitters remains an impressive one, which ranged internationally and across disciplines, from Dubuffet to De Kooning, Baselitz to Beuys, Kokoschka to Christo, Oldenburg to Rauschenberg, Stella to Schnabel (the latter unknowingly under a small table he was raising for his wife to lean on).

It might be presumptuous to suggest that a sitting with Snowdon has something of the air of 'a rite of passage' but no acknowledged 'Young British Artist' has yet passed the opportunity by. Rachel Whiteread, Matt Collishaw, Damien Hirst, Mark Wallinger and Gary Hume were taken between 1990 and 1997. Fiona Rae and two London-based Germans, Juergen Teller and Wolfgang Tillmans, between 2001 and 2003. Jake and Dinos Chapman more recently in 2005. Snowdon admits to being baffled aesthetically just twice by modern art. Firstly, when photographing the extremely wealthy art collectors of the Ruhr whereupon an earnest dealer revealed a block of concrete in which his artist had encased a brand new Volkswagen. The second occasion was a sitting in 1991 in New York with Neo-Conceptualist Robert Gober, whose beeswax facsimiles of disembodied, trouser-clad human legs mystified him greatly.

When *Private View* was published in the United States, with its descriptive subtitle 'The Lively World of British Art', American *Vogue* quoted Snowdon widely. His carefully chosen words then reflected what he had ever since hoped to accomplish:

> *As a photographer one meets people without barriers; there is no defence. There are two points I believe in: the photographer is secondary, and photographs must not be impressive, they must capture a moment and move the reader only through mood.*[43]

In the end, perhaps there is no greater praise for a photographer than that willingly given by a sitter raked by his lens. Especially if the subject is not known for communicating much to the world in anything other than layers of accreted paint. In October 1965, on seeing his likeness in *Private View* the reticent Frank Auerbach wrote to the equally reticent Lord Snowdon, 'I feel that I have been very well treated'.[44]

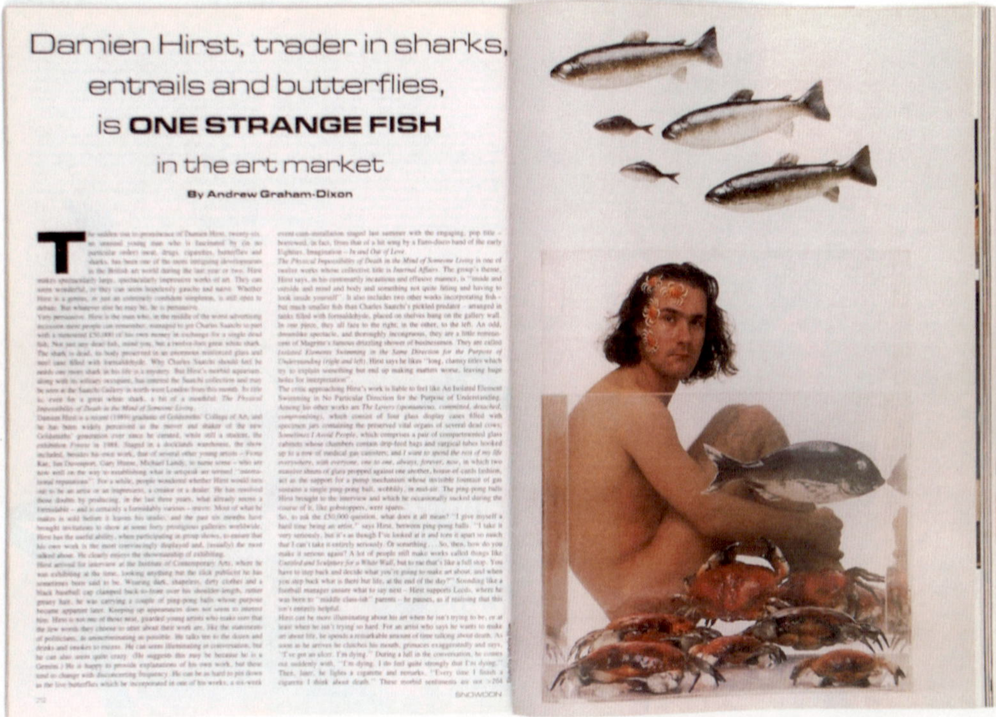

Andrew Graham-Dixon, 'One Strange Fish', *Vogue*, March 1992

Endnotes

[1] Colin MacInnes, 'A Nation of Artists' *New Statesman* 15 October, 1965
[2] Snowdon, *Sittings* (Weidenfeld & Nicolson, 1983) p.17
[3] Undated cutting from the *Daily Express* c.1958
[4] Jack Smith, quoted in Noel Barber, *Conversations with Painters* (Collins, 1964) p.111
[5] John Russell, 'The Adventure of Making Private View' *Vogue* (U.S.) 15 November 1965
[6] G.S. Whittet, 'Private View, Publicly Reviewed' *Studio International* November 1965 p.189
[7] Anthony Powell, 'Snapshots and Slogans' *Apollo* December 1965 p.517
[8] Tony Armstrong-Jones, *London* (Weidenfeld & Nicolson, 1958) unpaginated
[9] Snowdon, *Personal View* (Weidenfeld & Nicolson, 1978) p.66
[10] Snowdon, *Personal View* op.cit. p.66
[11] Mark Boxer, 'British Photography 1955-1965: My Part in its Downfall' quoted in *British Photography 1955-65: The Master Craftsmen in Print* (Photographers'Gallery, 1983) p.9
[12] Snowdon, *Personal View* op.cit. p.50
[13] Armstrong-Jones, *London* op.cit. unpaginated
[14] Ainslie Ellis, 'The Vibrant Eye' *The British Journal of Photography* unpaginated
[15] Stuart Black, 'London' *The British Journal of Photography* 19 December 1958 unpaginated
[16] Martin Harrison, *Young Meteors: British Photojournalism 1957-1965* (Jonathan Cape, 1998) p.56
[17] David Sylvester, 'The Kitchen Sink' *Encounter* December 1964 p.61
[18] Martin Harrison, *Transition: The London Art Scene in the Fifties* (Merrell, 2002) p.86
[19] 'Tony Armstrong-Jones and his View of Fashion for Vogue' *Vogue* April 1960 p.145
[20] Cecil Beaton, quoted in 'Beaton by Bailey, Bailey by Beaton' *Vogue* May 1963 p.97
[21] Snowdon, *Personal View* op.cit. p.98
[22] Harrison, *Transition* op.cit. p.18
[23] See 'Michael Andrews' *The Sunday Times Colour Magazine* 29 July 1962; 'R.B. Kitaj: A Fantastic Conspiracy' *The Sunday Times Colour Magazine* 10 February 1963; 'Philip Sutton: an Earthly Paradise' *The Sunday Times Colour Magazine* March 31 1963
[24] David Sylvester, 'Dark Sunlight' *The Sunday Times Magazine* 2 June 1963 p.13
[25] Patrick Kinmonth, 'Frank Auerbach: Face to Face Darkly' *Vogue* February 1983 p.103
[26] Sylvester, 'Dark Sunlight' op.cit. p.10
[27] Sylvester, 'Dark Sunlight' op.cit. p. 8
[28] Sylvester, 'Dark Sunlight' op.cit. p. 10
[29] Roy Ascott, Peter Blake, Antony Caro, Bernard Cohen, Harold Cohen, Robyn Denny, R.B. Kitaj, Richard Smith, William Turnbull, Brian Wall, Eduardo Paolozzi, Anthony Benjamin 'Amateurs in Art', letter to *The Sunday Times* 9 June 1963
[30] David Sylvester, 'The Art of the Impossible' *The Sunday Times Magazine* 11 July 1963
[31] Reyner Banham, 'A Particularly Soft English Hardback' *New Society* 21 October 1965 p.26
[32] Ellis, 'The Vibrant Eye' op.cit unpaginated
[33] Russell, *Vogue* (U.S.) op.cit. p.168
[34] Snowdon, *Personal View* op.cit. p.98
[35] See *Queen* October 20 1965 editorial
[36] John Richardson, 'The Art Set' *The Observer* 17 October 1965 p.54
[37] Francis Wyndham, *David Bailey's Box of Pin-ups* (Weidenfeld & Nicolson, 1965) unpaginated
[38] Wyndham, *David Bailey's Box of Pin-ups* op.cit. unpaginated
[39] Harrison, *Young Meteors* op.cit. p.144
[40] Quentin Bell, 'Private View' *The Listener* 21 October 1965 p.634
[41] Bryan Robertson, quoted in Michael Harrison, *Alan Reynolds* Kettles' Yard, Cambridge 9 August – 21 September 2003
[42] Snowdon, *Private View* op.cit. p.138
[43] Snowdon, quoted in 'Private View' *Vogue* (U.S.) 15 November 1965 p.85
[44] Frank Auerbach, letter to Lord Snowdon, October 10 1965

Photographs

John Bratby (1928–1992)

At home, Blackheath, 1958
London

Bratby was not the first painter of reputation to sit for Tony Armstrong-Jones (as Snowdon then was), but his unkempt presence looming over his infant son Jason's cot with a lit cigarette made the most striking impression. Taken with a small camera and in low light, it appeared in Armstrong-Jones' book *London* (1958). Along with Derrick Greaves, Jack Smith and Edward Middleditch, Bratby was part of a loose-knit group of social realists the 'Kitchen Sink School'. Bratby the man was, by most accounts, uncompromisingly uncouth. As such, and in domestic disharmony, he was a cipher for London's artistic/bohemian underbelly, a vital part of the city's allure. Armstrong-Jones' crepuscular snapshot – far from his good-natured photographs for *Vogue*, *The Sketch* and *Queen* – remains a significant moment in the development of his portraiture.

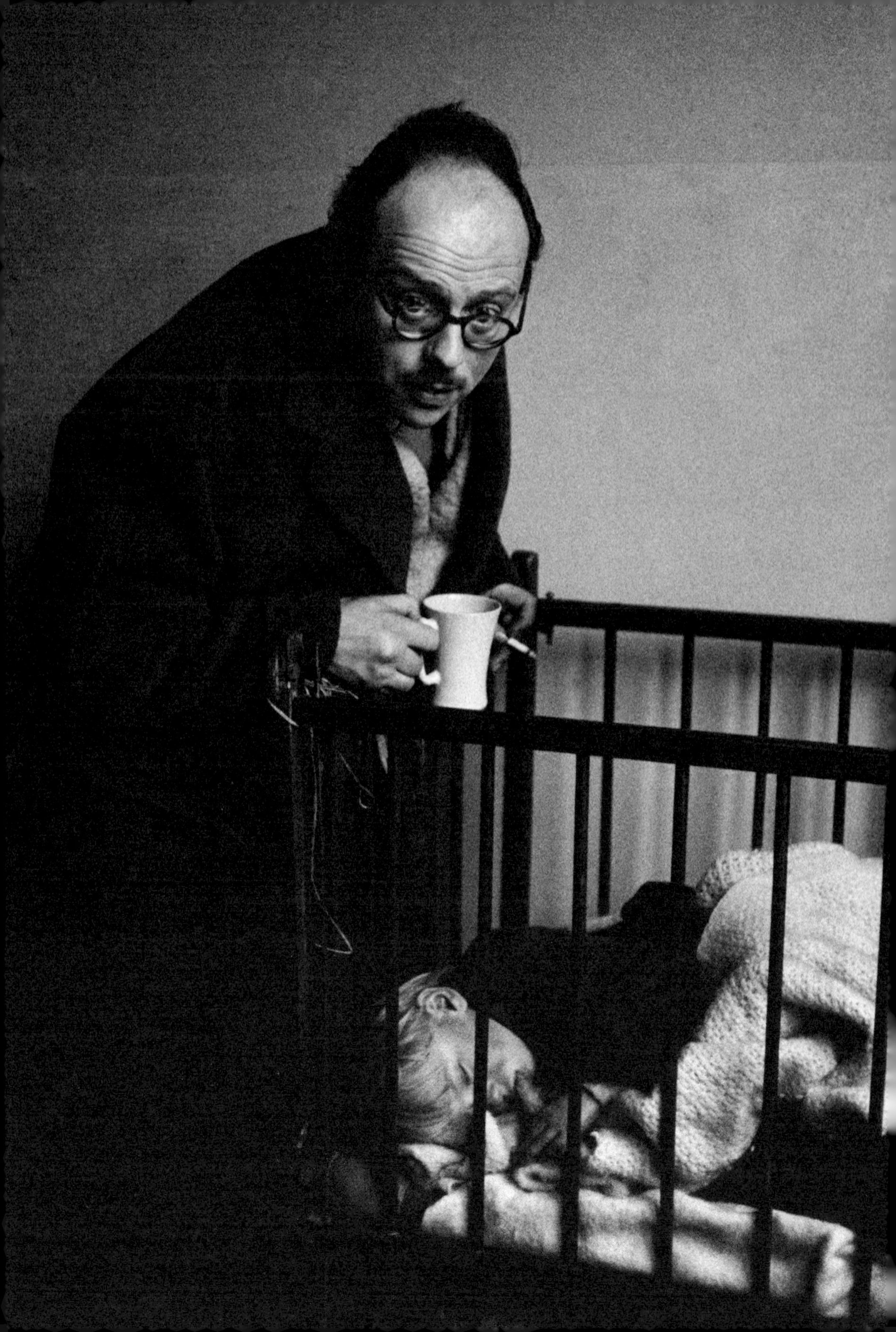

Michael Andrews (1928–1995)

In his studio, Islington, 1962
The Sunday Times Magazine

Andrews studied at the Slade under William Coldstream. One of his diploma paintings, *A Man Who Suddenly Fell Over* (1952), was acquired by the Tate Gallery from his first one-man show at the Beaux Arts Gallery, London. In 1957 Andrews helped to re-decorate the Colony Room, a drinking club in Soho, London, overseen by Muriel Belcher. Several years later he made two group portraits *The Colony Room I* and *II* (both 1962) in which many habitués appeared including Lucian Freud, Bruce Bernard and Francis Bacon, as well as the proprietrix herself. *The Colony Room I*, still on the easel here in Andrews' studio, now forms part of the permanent collection at Pallant House Gallery.

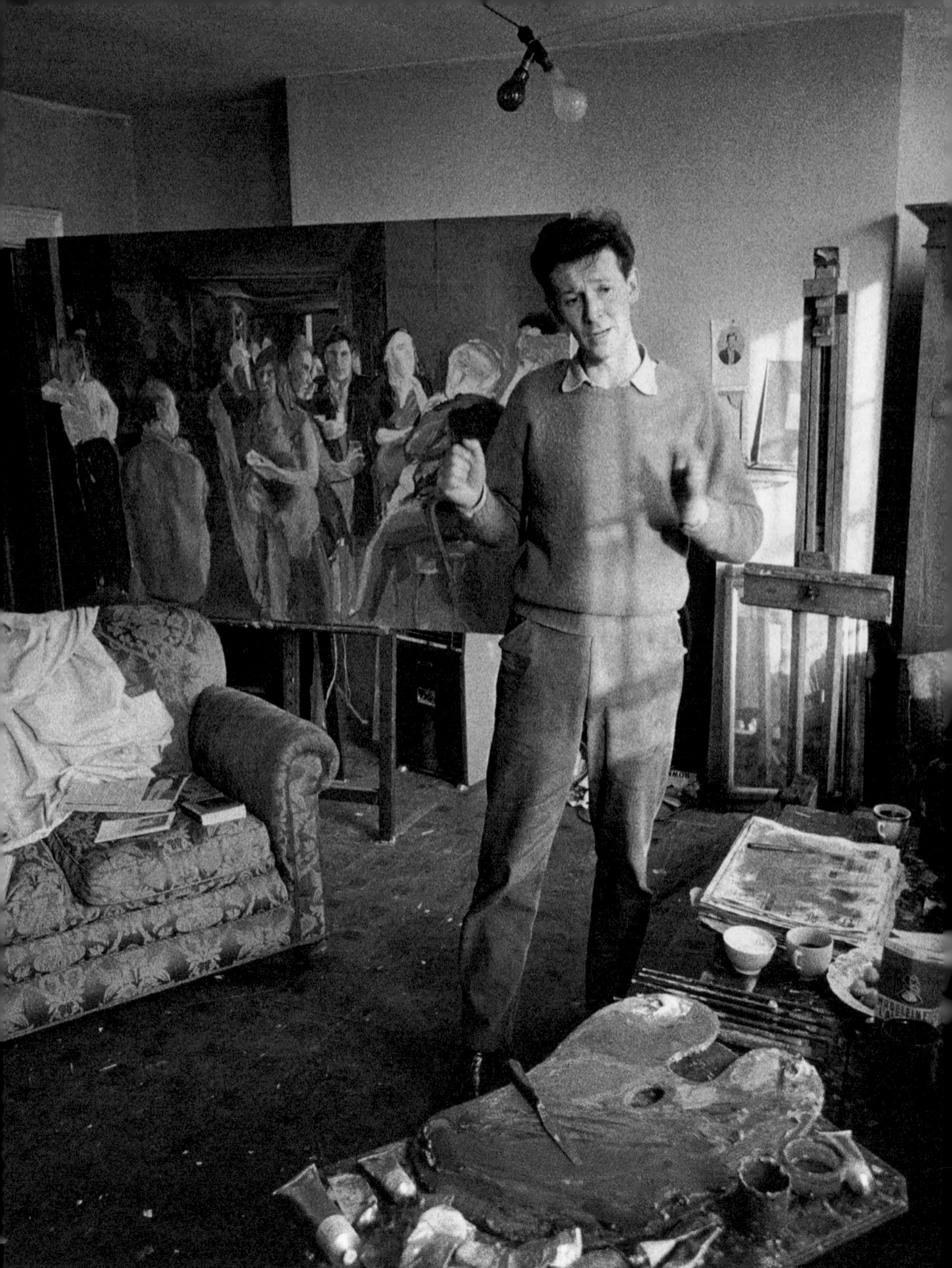

R.B. Kitaj (b.1932)

With his wife Elsi and son Lem, Dulwich, 1962
The Sunday Times Magazine

A former itinerant merchant seaman, R.B. Kitaj sprang to prominence in the 1960s, a leading Pop artist and appropriated by Britain as one of her own, although he originally came from Cleveland, Ohio. He originated the notion in 1976 of a 'School of London', which, though he did not define it, came to include himself, Bacon, Freud, Auerbach, Kossoff and Andrews, all of whom – bar Kitaj – had shown work at the Beaux Arts Gallery. His honorary English status was arguably cemented by his election to the Royal Academy in 1991. Later he told *Vogue* in a rare interview that 'one thing led to another and England became a habit. Over the years, I've tried to leave but I've given up now.' However, after the death of his second wife and disgusted by the ferocious criticism that greeted some new work, a few years later he did leave. Snowdon photographed Kitaj and his family on a wintry morning in Dulwich, south London. Kitaj bought a house there and bicycled to the Royal College of Art each day. 'In the first few days', he recalled some thirty years later, 'there was this funny looking kid with big glasses and short black hair, making the most beautiful drawing. "I'll give you five quid for that". He said, "Done." We've been like brothers ever since.' This was David Hockney.

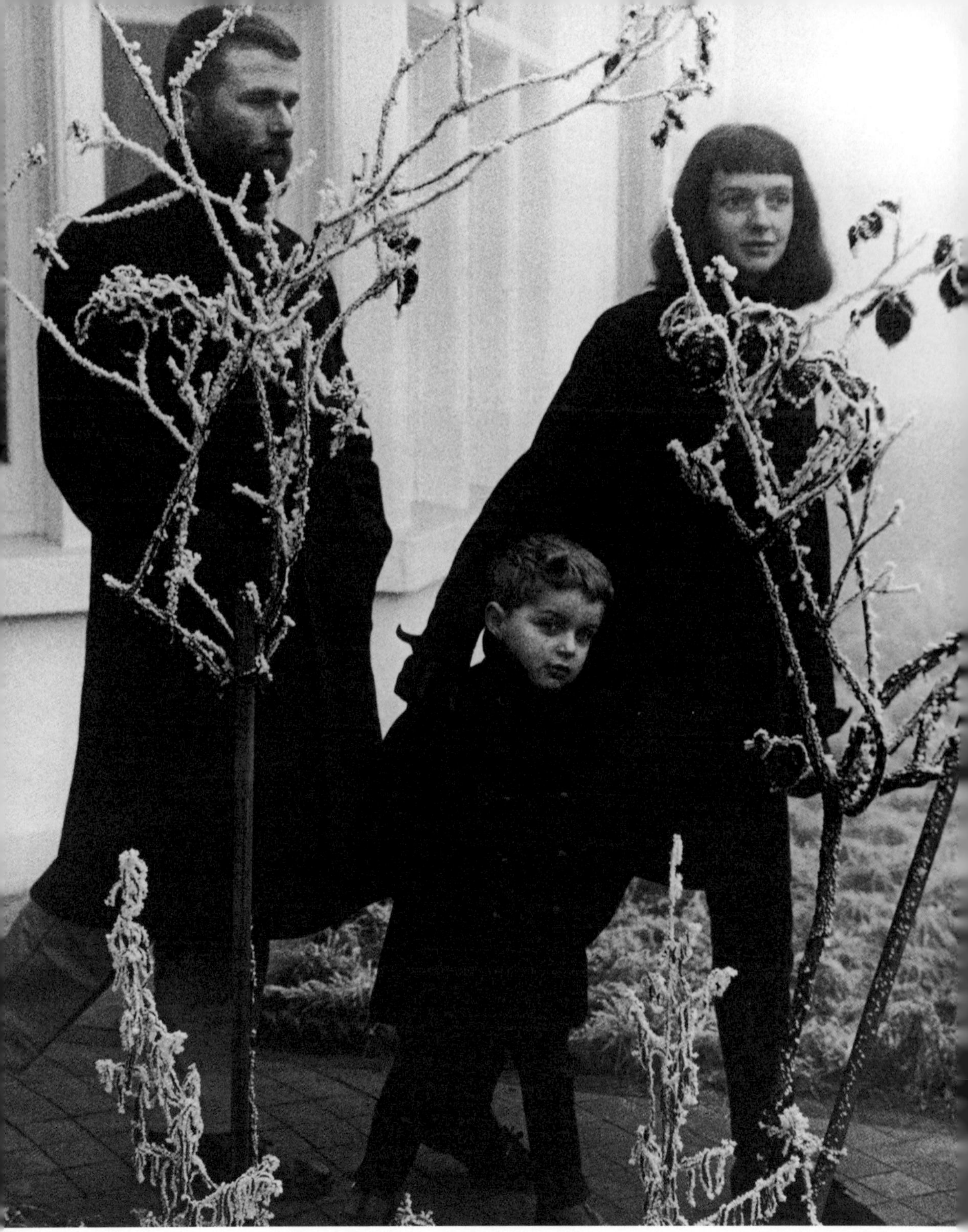

Francis Bacon (1909–1992)

In his studio, South Kensington, 1963
The Sunday Times Magazine

This portrait of the painter stands almost alone in the imagery of Bacon, as it depicts the dazzling smile described by his many biographers but which eluded most photographers. This was the only portrait of his friend that the critic David Sylvester chose to display in his home. Bacon's relationship with photographers and photography was ambivalent. When he died in 1992, his studio was sealed off. There had been a time when it might rattle with the sound of approaching photographers. Here, having negotiated the narrow staircase, they would make their way towards, as one commentator colourfully put it: 'the naked light-bulb hanging on its despairing flex'. Over the years, their number included the well-known, such as Snowdon, Irving Penn, Bill Brandt and Cecil Beaton; the lesser known, such as John Deakin and Douglas Glass; and gifted amateurs, such as Bruce Bernard and Dan Farson. The now-famous studio floor-space was littered with the accumulation of thirty years. This consisted, for the most part, of the painter's 'working documents': paint-accreted photographic prints, half-tone reproductions of photographs and film stills taken from newspapers and magazines and other mass-media imagery.

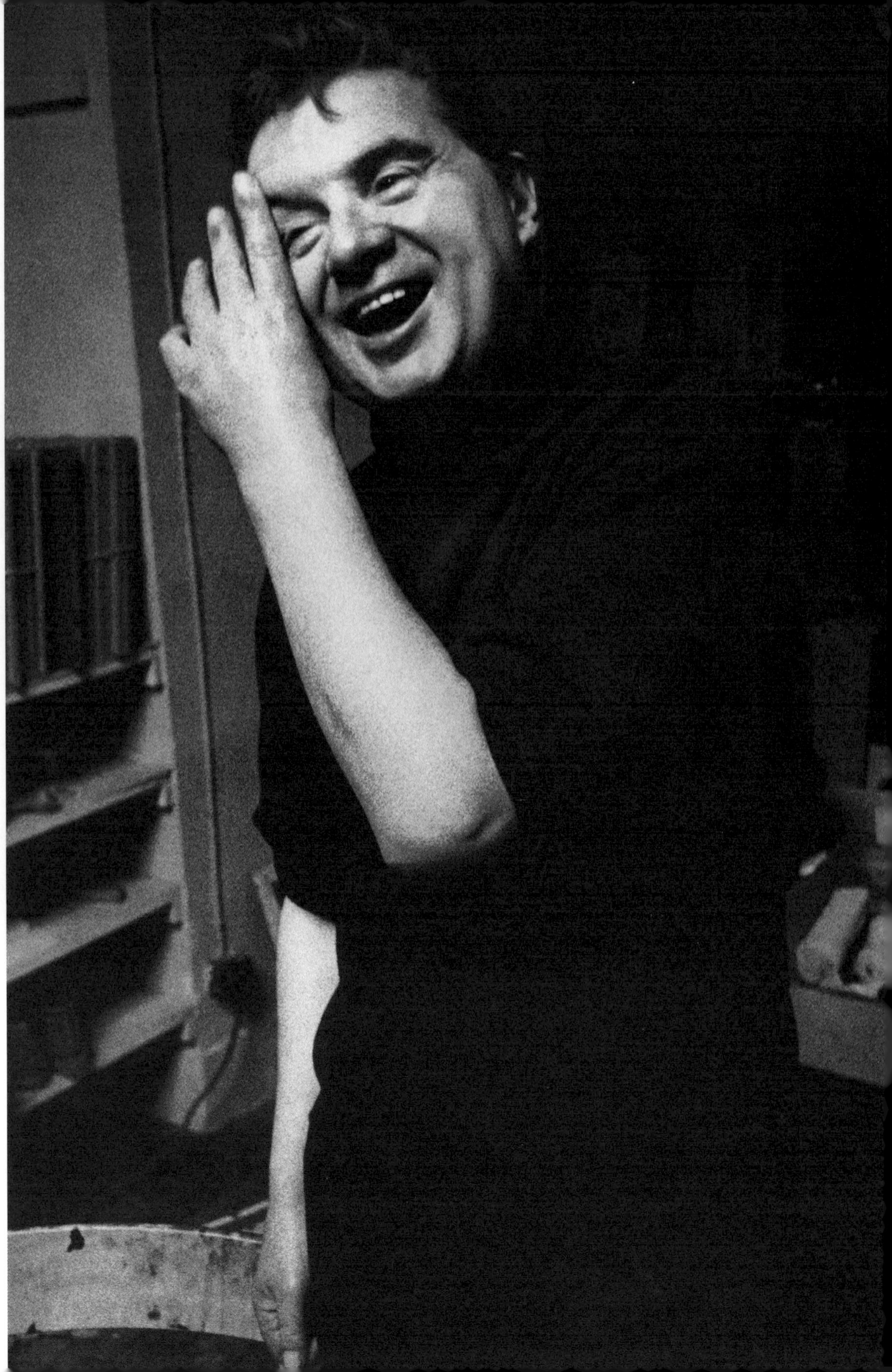

William Coldstream (1908–1987)

In his studio at the Slade School of Art, 1963
The Sunday Times Magazine

A variant of this photograph was used for the cover of *The Sunday Times Magazine* in June 1963, an issue devoted to established and emerging British painters. The critic David Sylvester provided an essay 'Dark Sunlight' in which he argued that, although British painting could be elegant, 'there's virtually always something incomplete about it, something tentative, something unfulfilled'. He made a case for William Coldstream and Francis Bacon as Britain's leading painters, and readers were introduced to 25-year-old Royal College of Art graduate, David Hockney. Coldstream was a trustee of both the National and Tate Galleries, a director of the Royal Opera House, Slade Professor of Fine Art at London University and an admired educationalist. A painter of meticulous portraits, Coldstream worked painstakingly from life, often measuring out height and distance with a paintbrush or, as here, a plumb-line and produced barely three or four paintings a year.

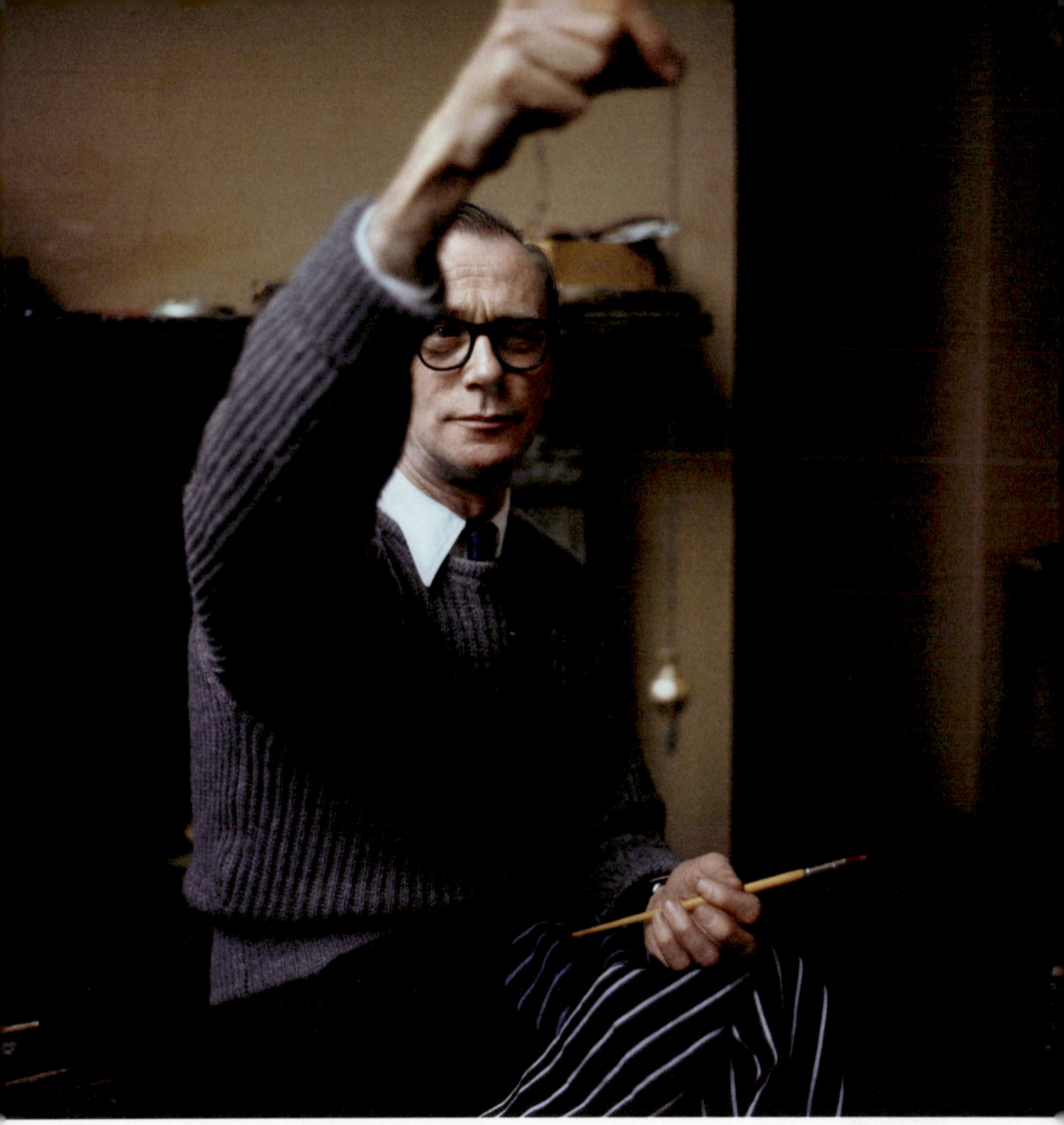

Jack Smith (b.1928)

At home, Brighton, 1963
Private View

Bryan Robertson marvelled in *Private View* at the prodigious talent and output of a man still only in his thirties: 'Jack Smith has so far achieved the most truly monumental body of work to come from any artist of his generation in England.' Smith started painting at 14 and then studied at the Royal College of Art from 1950 to 1953 and painted in a naturalistic style, mostly scenes of domestic life. His *Mother Bathing Child* (1953) gave rise, by way of an article written by David Sylvester, to a genre, the 'Kitchen Sink School'. As well as Smith, this group comprised, for the most part, John Bratby, Derrick Greaves, Edward Middleditch (none of whom enjoyed the epithet). Out of them, only Jack Smith was included in *Private View*, not for his neo-realism but for his abstract studies of visual perception. Snowdon's portrait of the artist – in a milieu more associated with his former style – was taken while Smith tackled another preoccupation: the development of a 'language' of painted pictographs.

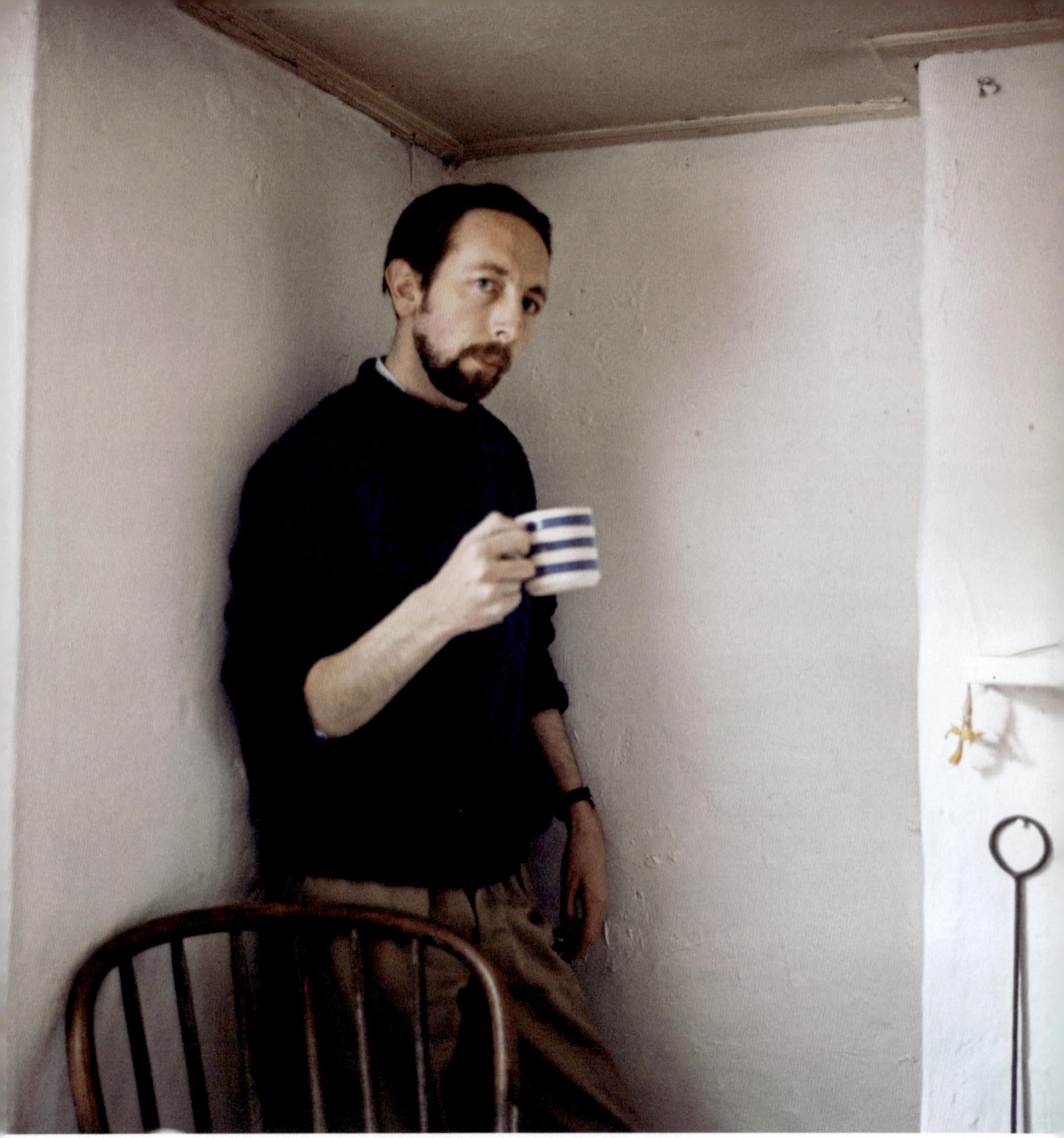

William Scott (1913–1989)

In his studio, Chelsea, 1963
The Sunday Times Magazine

Born in Greenock the son of a sign writer, and brought up in Northern Ireland, Scott attended Belfast College of Art and the Royal Academy Schools. His pre-war paintings were influenced by French Post-Impressionism. During the war, he served in the same artillery regiment as Carel Weight and their far-seeing commanding officer relieved both men of duties on Sundays in order to paint. *Vogue* called his later work 'the purest, most frank and forthright of his generation'. His still-life from the fifties and sixties, for which he is best known, are spare, simple in composition, and focused mostly on kitchen utensils and staple foodstuffs. They paved the way for an *oeuvre* that became increasingly abstract. He was among the first Britons to meet and respond to the work of Americans such as Pollock and Rothko. He was awarded the CBE in 1966 and given a retrospective at the Tate Gallery in 1972.

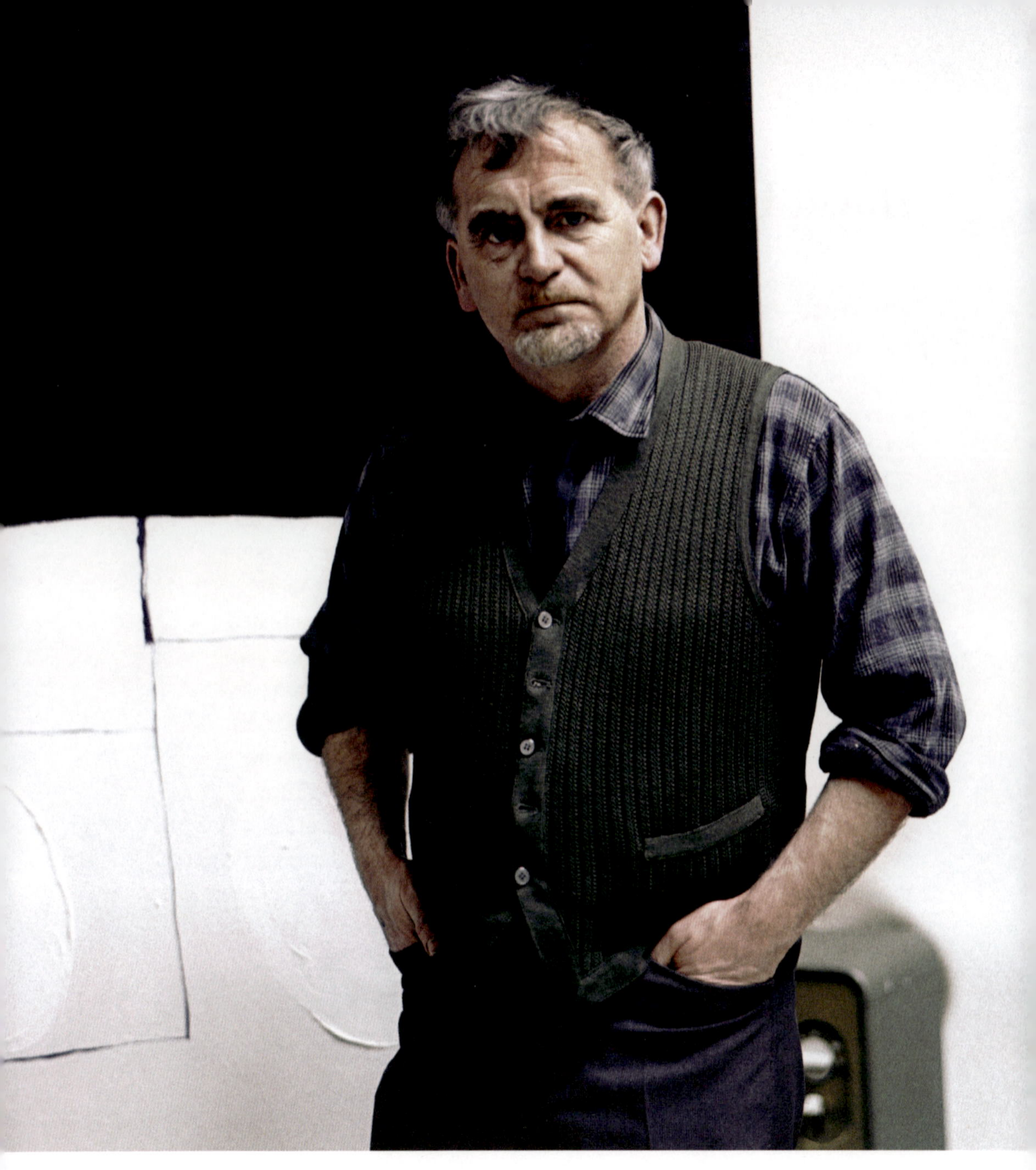

David Hockney (b.1937)

In his studio, Paddington, 1963
The Sunday Times Magazine

As Bryan Robertson pointed out, though the glowing tip of Hockney's cigar forms the maximum point of intensity in this famous portrait, 'it has a rival in the subject of the painting behind him'. This was the recently completed *The Hypnotist* (1963), which was yet to leave his Paddington studio. Already blonde-haired, Hockney's distinctive and raffish personal style and his emblematic spectacles set him apart from his first wave Pop Art contemporaries. Edward Lucie-Smith had already declared him the best young British painter of his generation, his success 'the most meteoric since Augustus John or at the very least Stanley Spencer'. Ahead of him lay California and its swimming pools, later opera and stage sets, *Mr and Mrs Clark and Percy*, dachshunds, Polaroid film collages and research into the properties of lenticular devices, but for now he stands, insouciantly smoking a cigarette, near a large canvas. By 1963 Hockney had already explored many of the imperatives to future success. For *The Rake's Progress*, a suite of sixteen etchings updated from Hogarth's London to contemporary New York, he cast in the title role a thin, bespectacled *ingénu*, who reinvents himself in a kinder climate by bleaching his dark hair blonde...

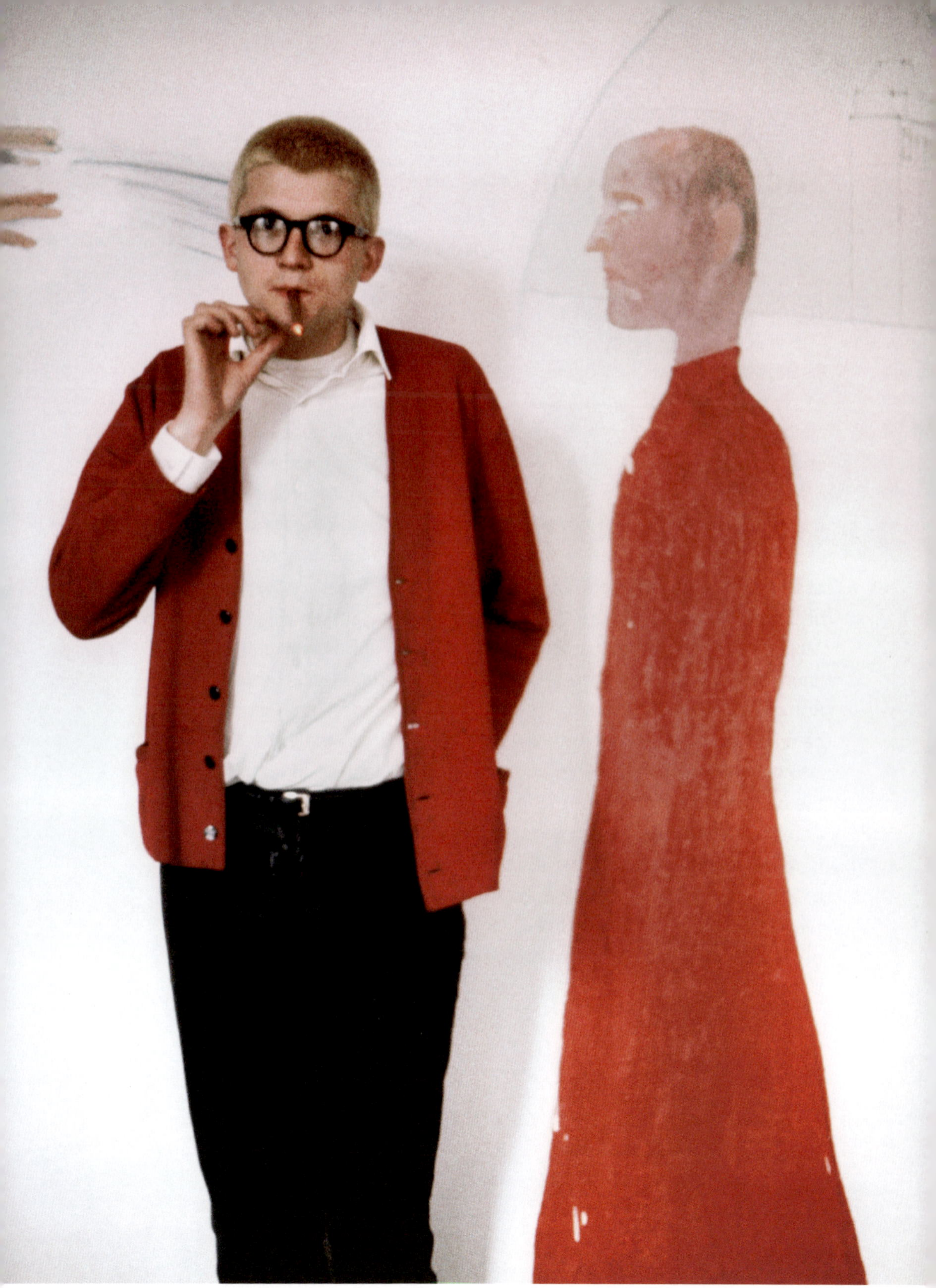

Victor Pasmore (1908–1998)

At home, Blackheath, 1963
The Sunday Times Magazine

Perhaps John Russell was overemphasising it when he wrote that Victor Pasmore's abandonment of landscape painting in favour of abstractionism, was 'one of the few more controversial happenings' England had witnessed 'since John Henry Newman left the Church of England and became a Roman Catholic', but in avant-garde circles the decision was undoubtedly a *cause-celèbre*. Pasmore had first experimented with figurative painting, becoming a leading light of the 'Euston Road School'. So linked were the naturalistic styles of Coldstream and Pasmore that in the forties, *The Sunday Times Magazine* reported their names went together 'like Flanagan and Allen', figureheads in the fight to repel the advances of continental Surrealism. But in the late 1940s, influenced by Ben Nicolson and Naum Gabo, he reintroduced elements of three-dimensional Constructivism into post-war British art. This continued into the 1950s and for the pioneering exhibition *This is Tomorrow* (1956) he contributed a Constructivist sculpture in collaboration with Erno Goldfinger. In 1959, he was awarded the CBE (and the CH in 1982) for services to the fine arts, not least for his inspirational Bauhaus-inflected teaching syllabus at Durham University, a model adopted by other higher education arts establishments.

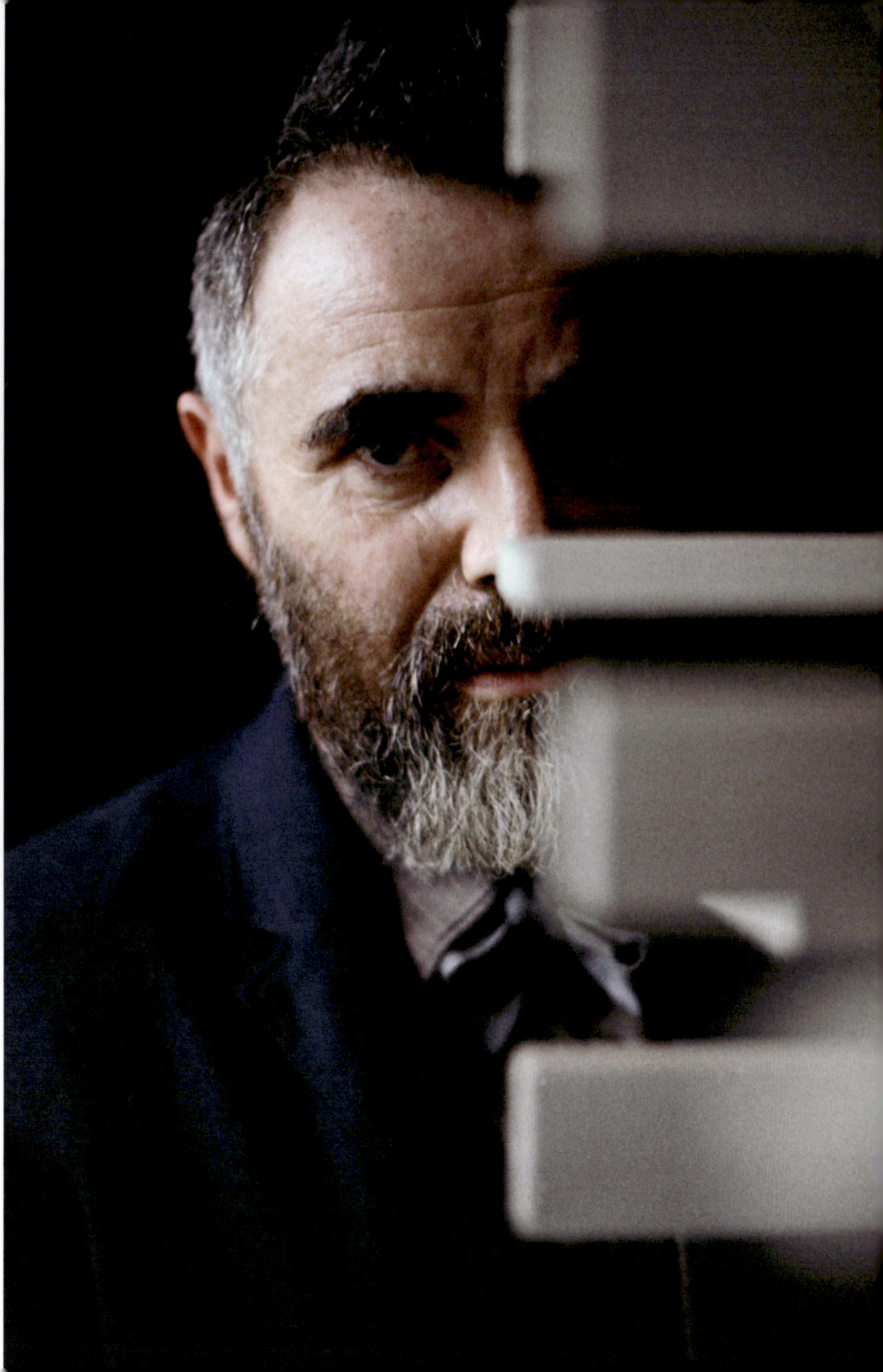

Richard Smith (b.1931)

In his studio, the East End, 1963
Private View

It seemed entirely appropriate that Richard Smith's first substantial one-man show was held in New York in 1961. His influences are derived almost entirely from America of the 1950s: the artists Jasper Johns and Mark Rothko in particular, and its vibrant and seductive commercial culture in general. He had encountered both when on a scholarship that allowed him to live and work in New York at the crucial moment between 1959 and 1961, making him also the first of his Pop contemporaries to go there. He was attuned likewise to the imagery of mass media, especially American magazines, whose production values were strong and whose use of colour printing was up-to-the-minute. Corporate branding, commercial insignia and emblems, the packaging of commodities, all engaged him greatly: 'the communication media are a large part of my landscape', he told one interviewer, and 'My interest is not in the message so much as in the method'. His experiments with asymmetrically-shaped canvasses developed into three-dimensional artworks. *Piano* (1963) referred to the advertising imagery of cigarette packets and, set against the rectangle of the canvas, the cigarette carton jutted out to meet the floor at an angle.

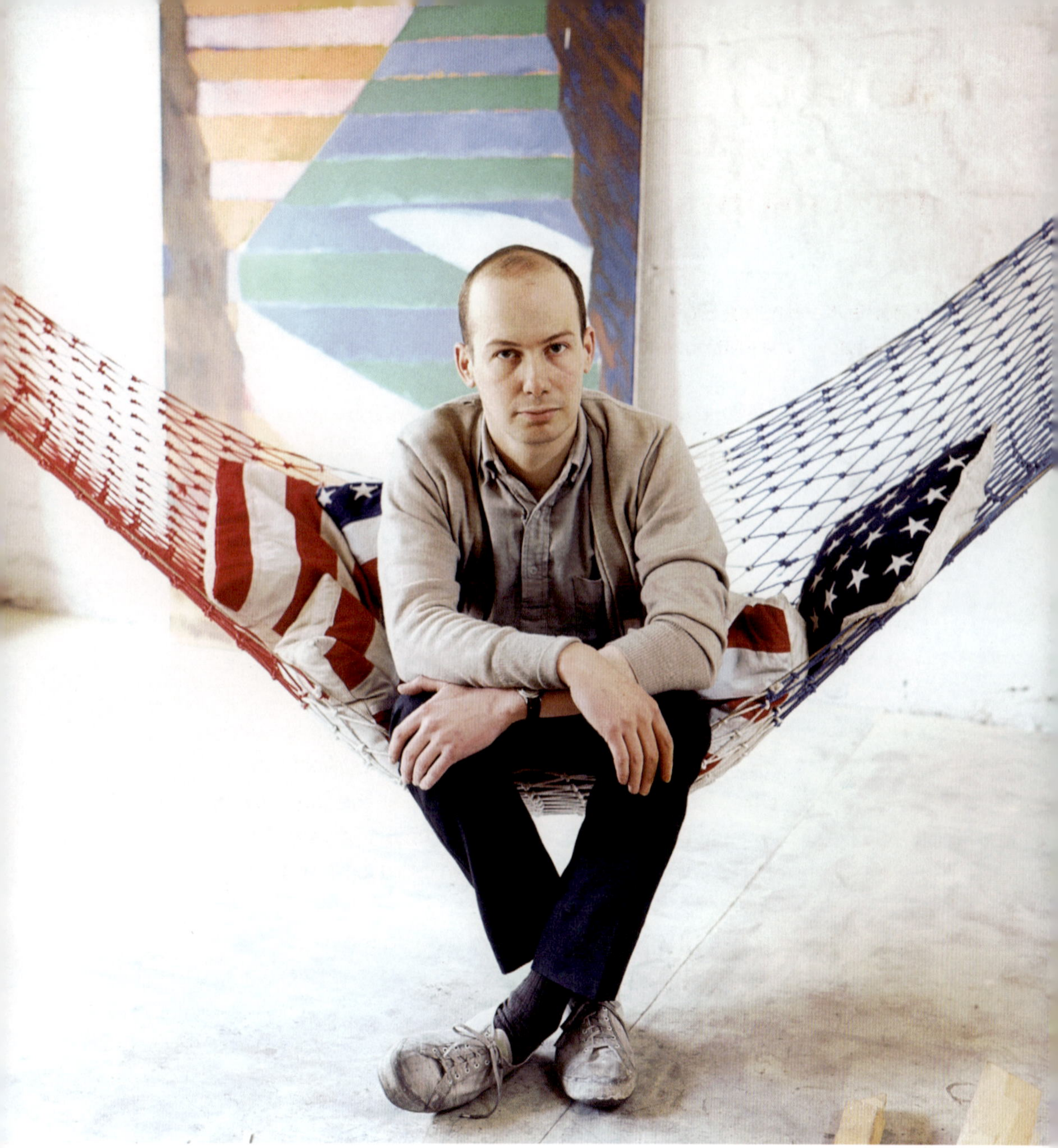

Joe Tilson (b.1928)

At home, Kensington High Street, 1963
The Sunday Times Magazine

'There is a sense in which Joe Tilson's work needs no explanation', wrote John Russell, 'When Tilson makes a giant keyhole and puts the word 'KEY' underneath, only someone very stupid would fail to get the point. Equally, if this was the only point of the picture we should quickly move on'. Russell is referring to *Key-Box* (1964) a 6-foot-tall construction of paint on wood. The accent on 'make' is vital, for Tilson was a carpenter and joiner for several years before studying at St Martin's School of Art, and subsequently the Royal College of Art. The Marlborough Gallery gave him his first solo show in 1962. Forty years later, he was the subject of a major retrospective at the Royal Academy. His early paintings were influenced by Abstract Expressionism, which he had encountered first hand at the Tate Gallery in 1956 but, responding to nascent homegrown 'Pop Art', he came to use his carpentry skills to create vibrant wooden constructions and painted reliefs. *Private View* showcased some of Tilson's larger pieces, including *Joy-Box* (1962); work which the authors – in the nicest possible way – considered, would 'stop a train if he wanted it to'.

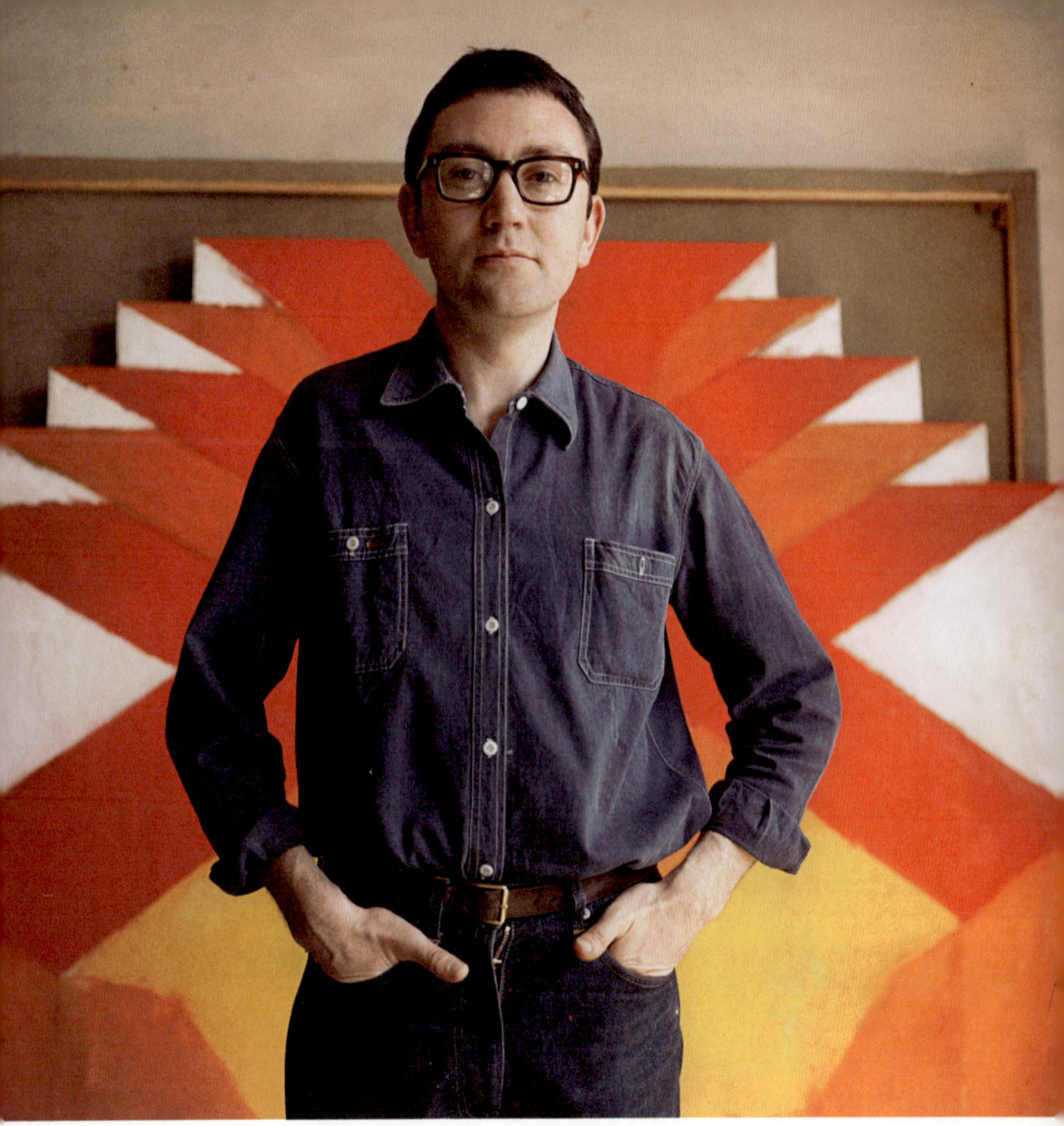

Lucian Freud (b.1922)

In the street, Paddington, 1963
Private View

The photographer John Deakin, who knew Freud well during the fifties and sixties, once wrote of the painter's curious appeal: 'When I said that only the bad ones grumbled at my portraits, I should have excepted Lucian Freud, whose work I admire so much. But perhaps his grumbles were just part of his act; he is such a strange fox-like person...' As the leading painter of portraits of his generation, Freud was awarded the Order of Merit in 1993. He had been made a Companion of Honour ten years previously. He was born in Berlin and took British citizenship in 1939. During the 1940s he was hailed by the writer and critic Herbert Read as 'the Ingres of Existentialism'. By 1963, when this portrait was taken, he had begun to work on one of the themes for which he is best known, the female nude. John Russell observed that 'as a serious painter in the mid-1960s, Lucian Freud has almost every possible handicap. He bears, to begin with, one of the great names of this century. He has had the burden, hardly less heavy, of adulation in his first youth. He is preoccupied, finally, with a kind of painting which is now widely regarded as disreputable'.

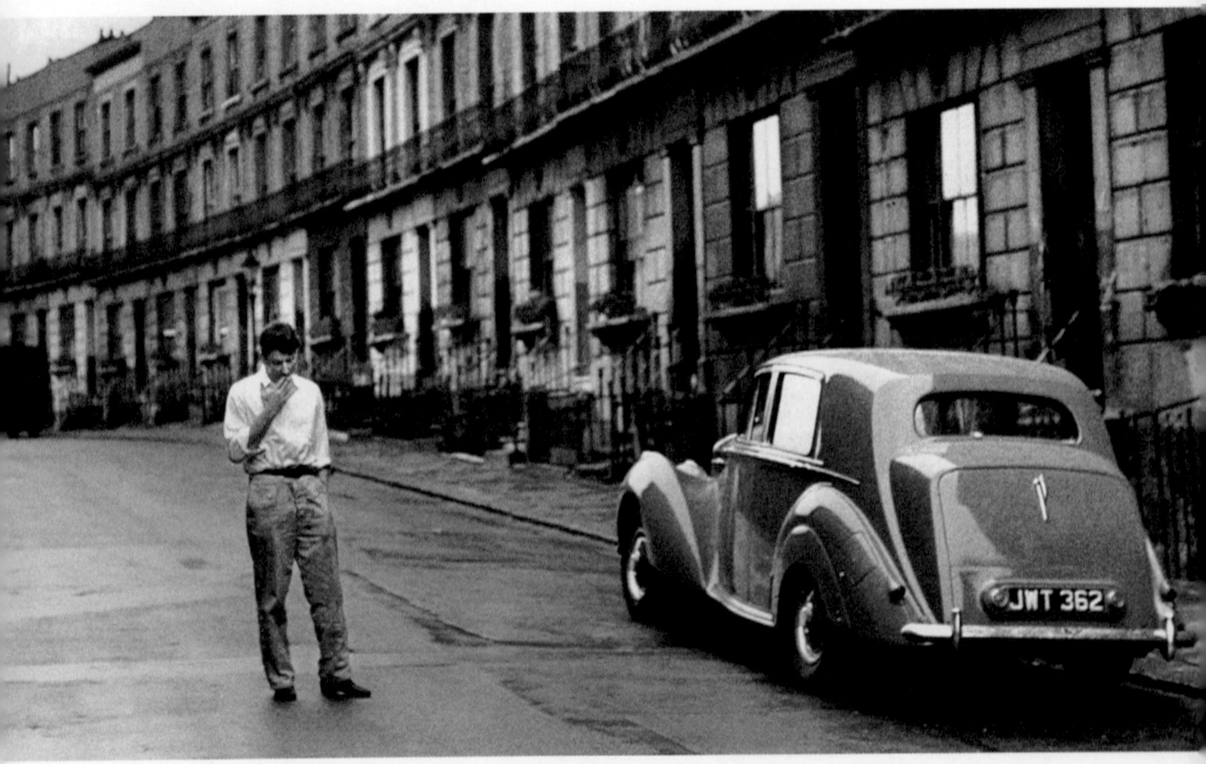
JWT 362

Eduardo Paolozzi (1924–2005)

In his studio, Chelsea, 1963
The Sunday Times Magazine

Born in Leith, the son of Italian immigrants, Paolozzi studied briefly at Edinburgh College of Art before moving to London. Influenced at first by Surrealism, his early collages and sculptures (incorporating images from popular culture and utilising found objects) were among the first expressions of British Pop Art, of which he is considered a father figure. With Paolozzi, as far as sculpture was concerned, carving and modelling went out; construction out of wood and scrap metals came in. Dragging his sculpture *Ace* (1962) out of his studio for an exhibition, the authors of *Private View* endorsed a criticism of one of these 'machine edifices'. Bryan Robertson admonished the artist for a 'possible weakness in [his] talent: a tendency to design rather than to compose in either mental or physical depth, and thus to produce intelligent design jobs rather than sculpture'. This may have been prompted by an inherent precondition of what Paolozzi called his 'industrial collages': where the artist, interested only in the concept, is removed from the construction which is left to assistants.

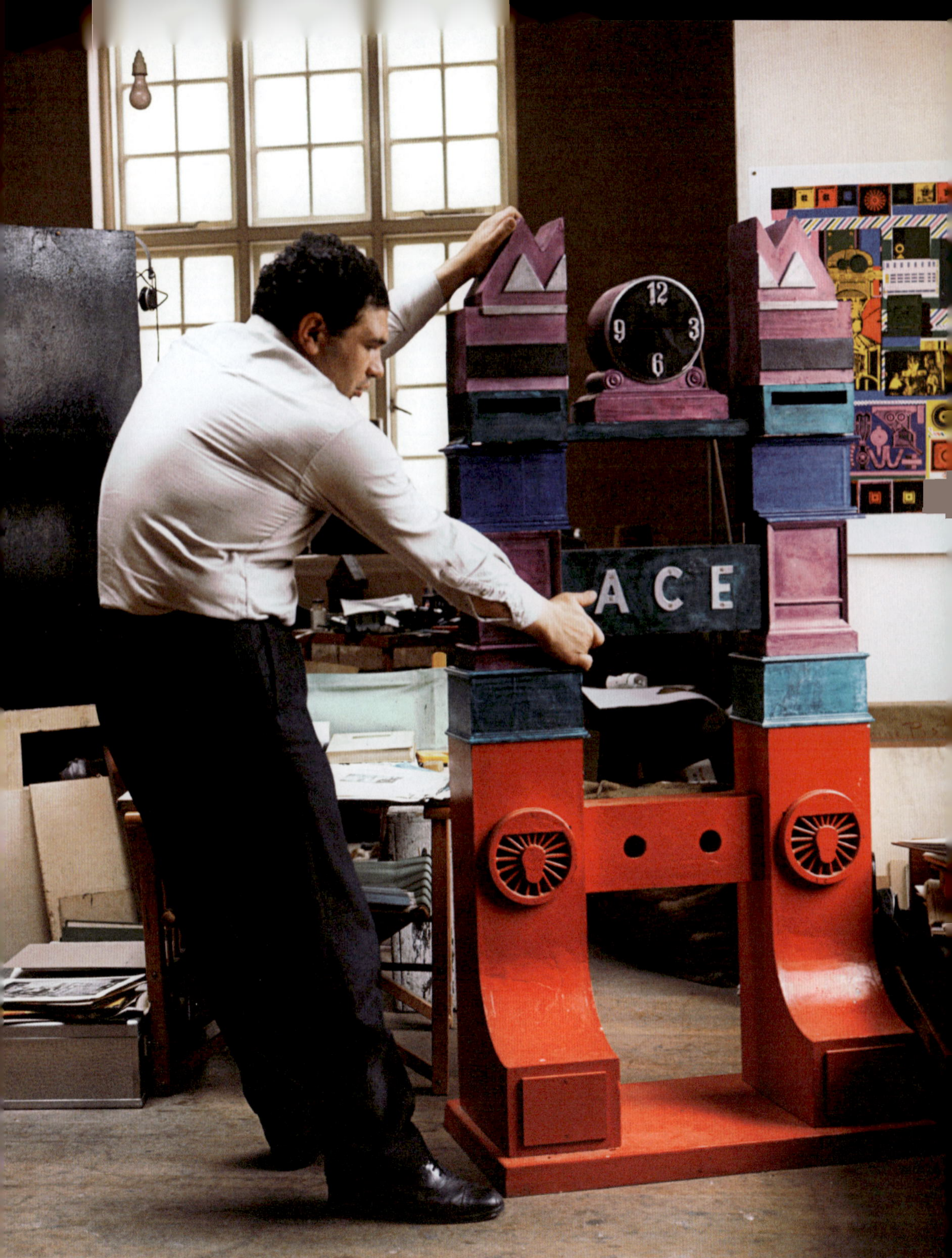
ACE

Adrian Heath (1920–1992)

In his studio, Fitzrovia, 1963
Private View

As a thriving artistic bohemia, Fitzrovia was, by the 'Swinging Sixties', a pale shadow of its former incarnation. One of the few who found its eighteenth-century architecture and abundance of cafés and pubs conducive to work was Adrian Heath. Initially influenced by the figurative work, if not the proximity, of the 'Euston Road School' (Euston Road was a very short stroll from Fitzrovia) he then took as his own departure point the example of Victor Pasmore and went objectively abstract. Heath had studied at the Slade until the outbreak of war. He joined the RAF and from 1942 to 1945 was a prisoner-of-war in Germany, where he met and taught Terry Frost. An astute commentator on the development of abstract art, in 1954 he wrote of his own paintings: 'The thing of interest is the actual life of the work: its growth from a particular white canvas or board... the problem is to exercise some logical or objective control on its gradual evolution'. In 1969 he was artist-in-residence at the University of Sussex.

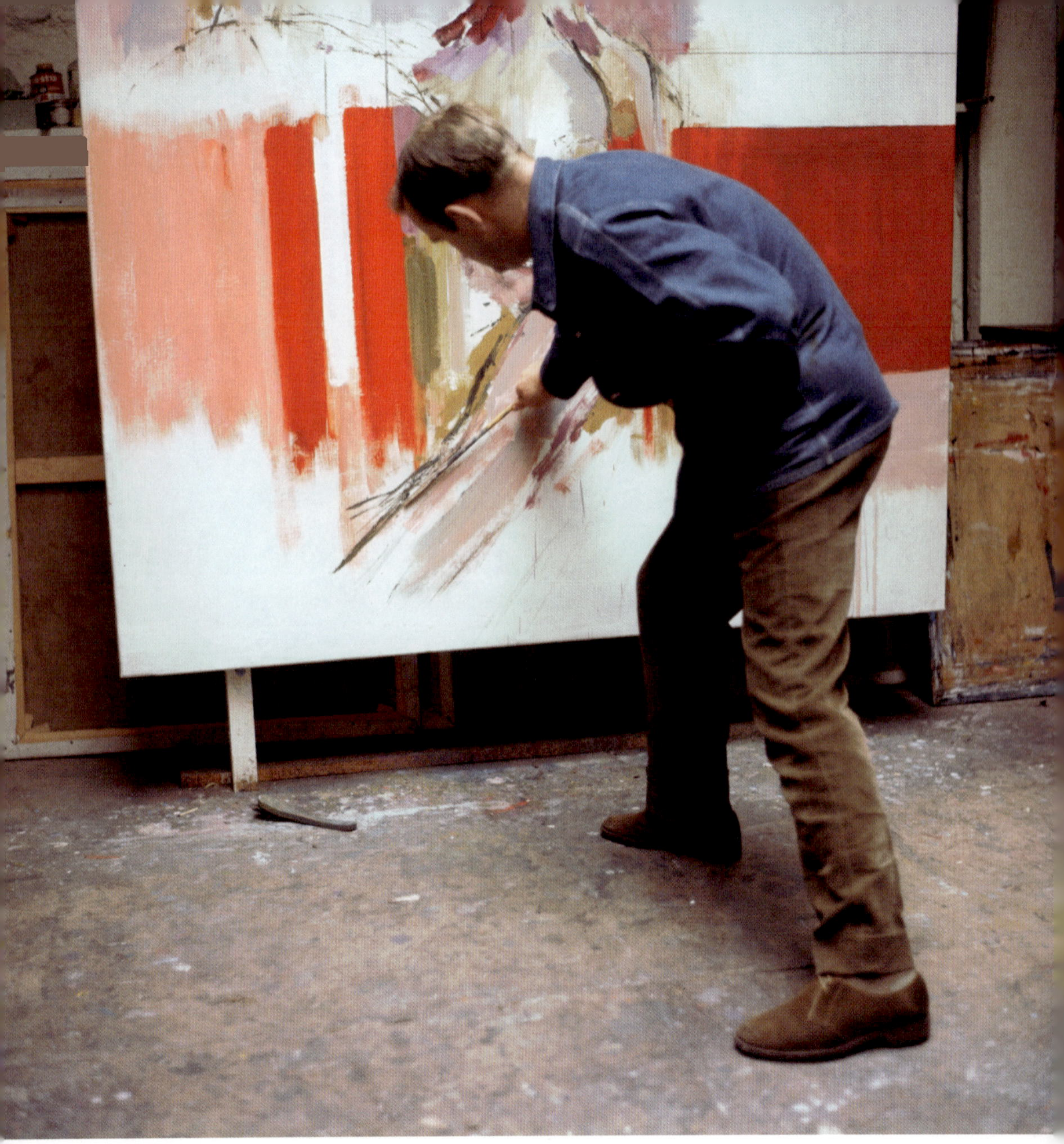

Patrick Procktor (1936–2003)

At home in Marylebone, 1963
Private View

Patrick Procktor achieved the rare distinction of appearing three times in *Private View.* A tall, gregarious and much-loved figure on the London art scene, Dublin-born Procktor had a colourful early life. Straitened family circumstances led to a fractured higher education and at 18, as a National Service inductee, he joined the Navy and learned Russian fluently enough to be an interpreter on his discharge. Painting in his spare time, he enrolled at the Slade in 1958. His first solo show in 1962 was a commercial and critical success and this led to his inclusion in *New Generation 1964* at the Whitechapel. His bold figurative style was in thrall to the Pop Art sensibility of the day, but in time he made quieter more meditative works often in watercolour. Always at the centre of an extrovert circle which included David Hockney and Francis Bacon (though not at the same time), he was at ease in the worlds of theatre and fashion too. He counted as friends the fashion designer Ossie Clark, the balletomane Richard Buckle and the renegade playwright Joe Orton.

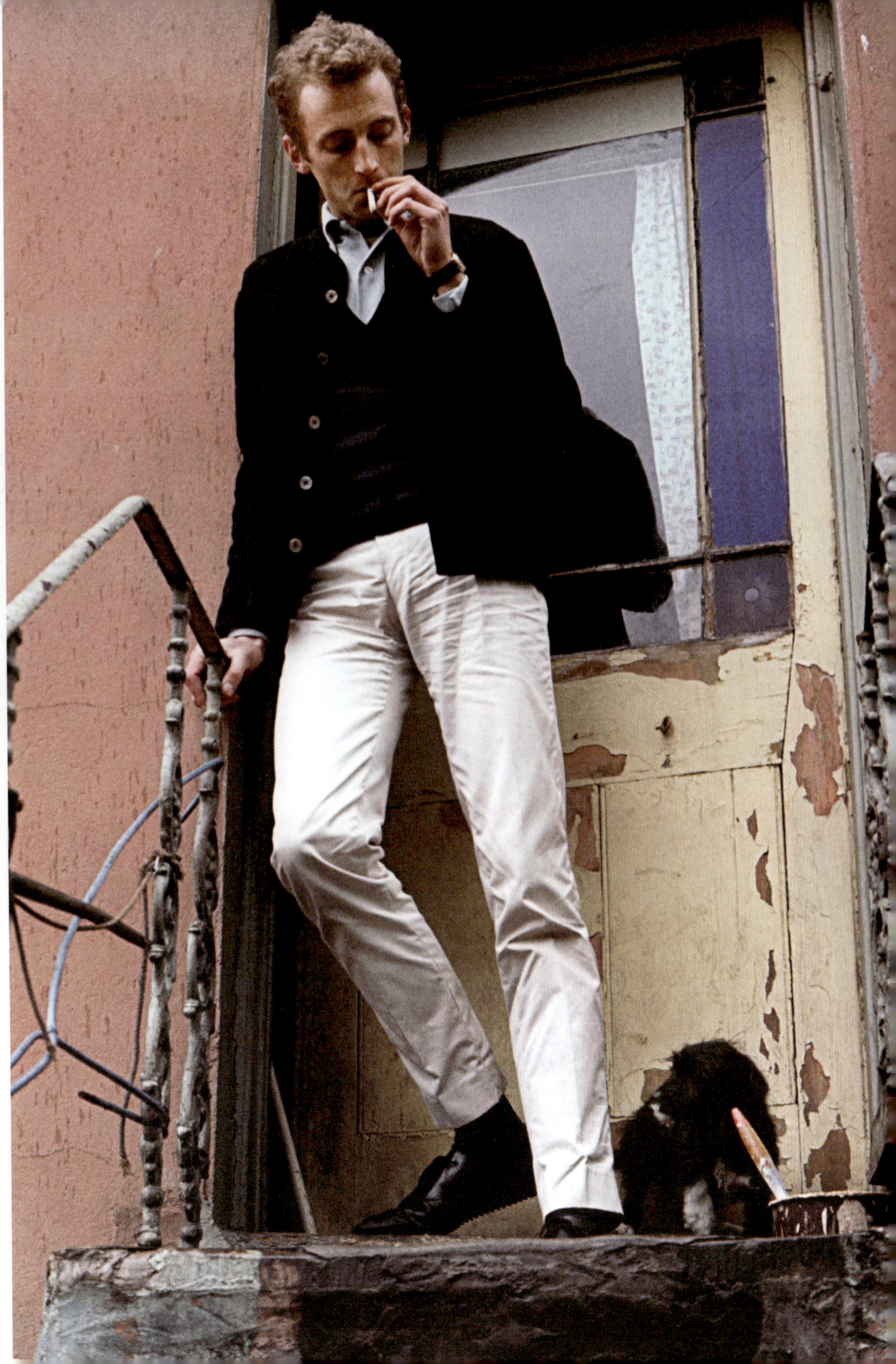

Helen Lessore (1907–1994)

The Beaux Arts Gallery, Mayfair, 1963
Private View

Helen Lessore took over the Beaux Arts Gallery in Mayfair in 1951 on the death of her art dealer husband. A well-regarded painter herself, she sublimated her own creative inclination in favour of others. The list of painters she launched was remarkable: Craigie Aitchison, Michael Andrews, Frank Auerbach, David Kossoff, Euan Uglow among many others, all then unknown. But her enthusiasm was for what she termed 'The Great Tradition' of realism and she gave shows and much time to Jack Smith, Derrick Greaves, Edward Middleditch and John Bratby. Known popularly as the 'Kitchen Sink School' for their unsentimental scrutiny of urban life, they were also known as the 'Beaux Arts Quartet'. These four represented Britain at the Venice Biennale in 1956 and two years later, Lessore was awarded an OBE for her contribution to the fine arts. Snowdon's portrait of the much-loved art dealer and patroness assumes an extra poignancy, as not long afterwards, she was forced to close the gallery. The escalating commercialism of the West End art world did not much interest her.

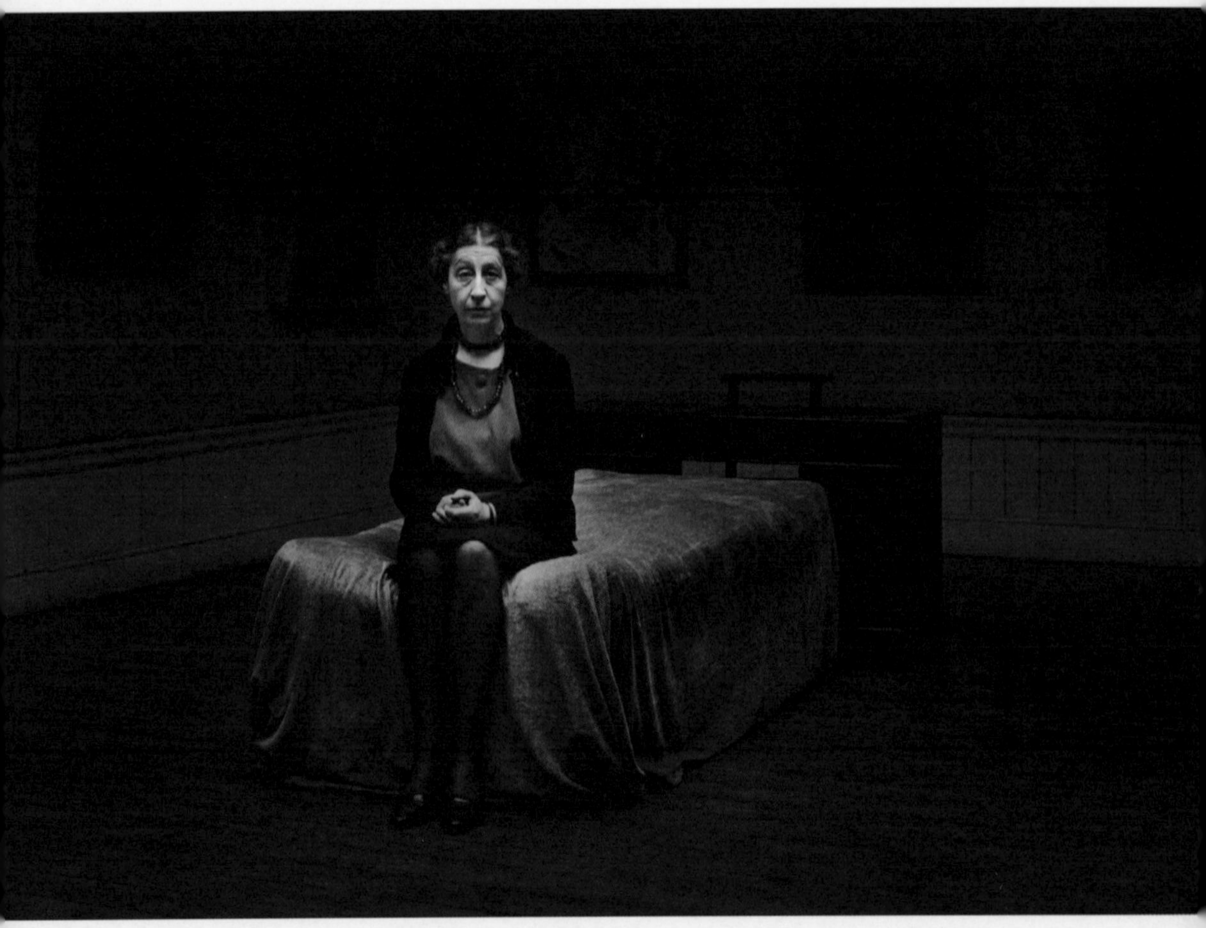

Anthony Caro (b.1924)

The Whitechapel Gallery, 1963
Private View

At the opening of his show of recent work at the Whitechapel Gallery, Anthony Caro stands before *Early One Morning* (1962), an aluminium and steel structure. Open, linear and brightly painted it was typical of the forms and shapes he began to conceive in the early 1960s. The exhibition was pivotal to the ever-upwards trajectory of British sculpture and it made Caro's reputation. His outlook had changed in 1959 when on a Ford Foundation grant-aided visits to New York, he encountered the critic Clement Greenberg and the metal constructions of David Smith, as well as the paintings of Kenneth Noland. This led to his first abstract, welded sculpture *Twenty-Four Hours* (1960), made of found steel. Caro was knighted in 1987 and awarded the Order of Merit in 2000, the first sculptor to receive it since Henry Moore. A major retrospective at the Tate Gallery opened in 2005. Interviewed for it, he said 'somebody asked me recently: "What happens to your sculpture once you've made it?" It's important that it has a showing. If I finish it, photograph it, then put it in store, it's only half the story. People may like it, or criticise it. But it has to go out into the world. I am seldom interested in the placement or context of my work. For one thing, I rarely take on commissions, making massive things that are going to stay there permanently. My sculptures move around more like paintings'.

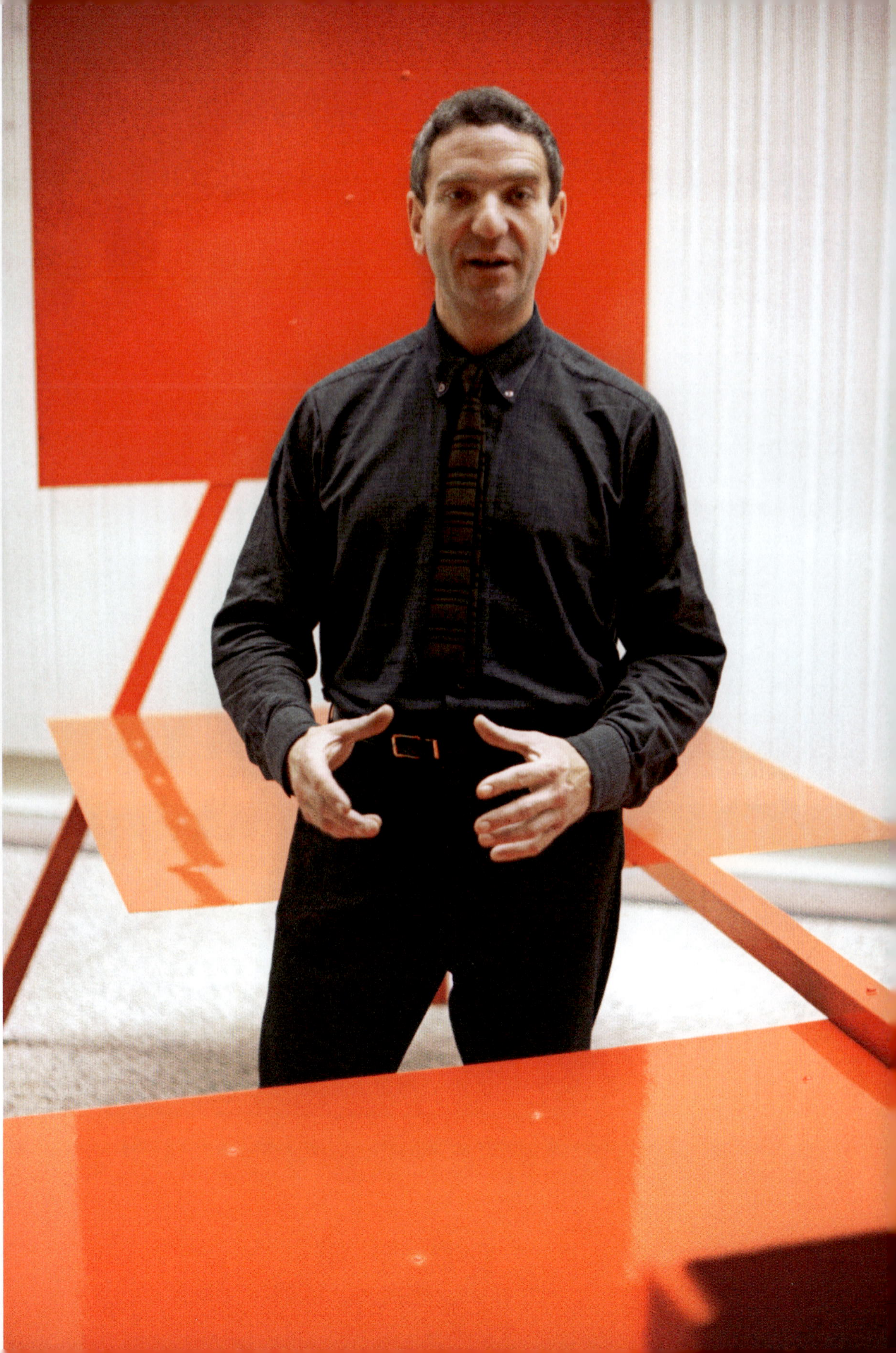

Paul Huxley (b.1938)

In his studio, Hammersmith, 1963
Private View

'Paintings today', Paul Huxley was quoted in *Private View*, 'should be about question-making not story telling or recording... Painting can only be enlightening by posing questions and making reconnaissance trips rather than by supplying answers. We become more wise by not knowing...' In paintings such as *Untitled No.98* (1968) Huxley questioned the viewer's capacity for correct perception: three diminishing triangles gave the canvas an almost three-dimensional feel but several bands of colour reminded the viewer of the painting's inherent flat plain. Alongside David Hockney, John Hoyland, Patrick Procktor and Bridget Riley, Huxley showed at the Whitechapel Gallery's *New Generation 1964* to great success; 'one of the most incisive and certain intelligences at work' concluded Bryan Robertson, its curator. Huxley is no stranger to Pallant House Gallery, not least for the wall painting he conceived in 2001. He was appointed Professor of Painting at the Royal College of Art in 1986 and became Professor Emeritus in 1998.

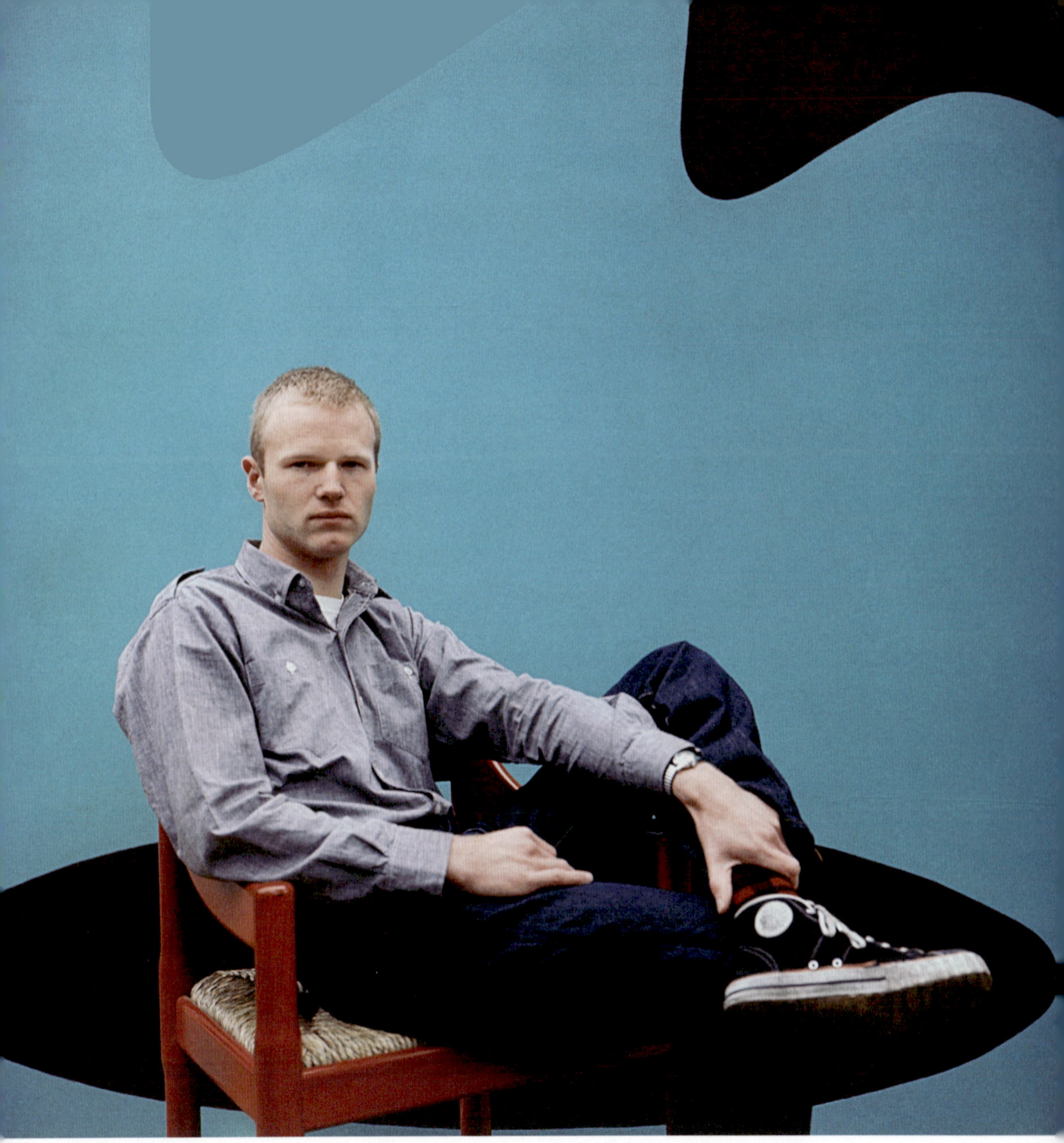

David Sylvester (1924–2001)

The Tate Gallery, 1963
Private View

By the 1960s the polymathic David Sylvester was a much read commentator on art, not least because of his association with *The Sunday Times Magazine*, which brought his cogent words into wide circulation. He is best known for his association and deep friendship with Francis Bacon, which culminated in the publication, in 1975, of the transcripts of their conversations, but he contributed equally to modern interpretations of the work of Giacometti and Magritte (the latter's five-volume catalogue rasionné took Sylvester nearly 25 years to complete). As an exhibitions organiser he was in a class of his own (his first in 1951 was a show of Henry Moore, whose secretary he had briefly been). Snowdon's photograph showed him re-arranging an Arts Council exhibition of Soutine. He is carrying a portrait of Madame Castaing. Though a brilliant raconteur – his in-depth knowledge encapsulated free-form jazz, cricket, football and sci-fi films – he was also a master of the emphatic *longueur*. Accompanying him on a car journey from London to Brighton, Snowdon asked Sylvester a relatively simple question. Not a word passed between either until Brighton loomed. Then the reply came: 'Yes'.

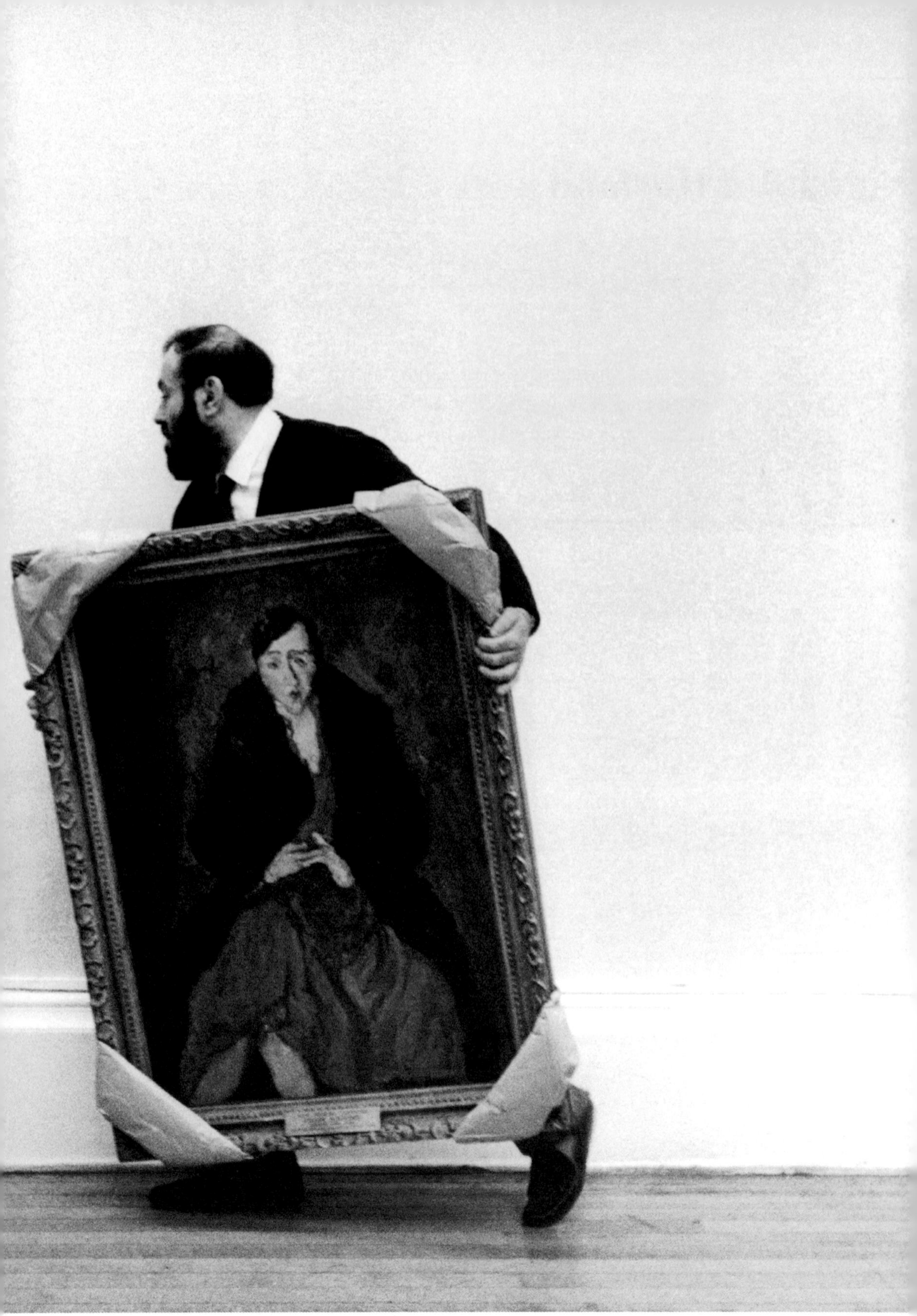

John Hoyland (b.1934)

With his son Jeremy, at home, London, 1963
Private View

Bryan Robertson was impressed with Hoyland's maturity as a painter. He had graduated only a few years previously from the Royal College of Art but was 'a serious thinker – and originator', who had worked 'convincingly on a large scale.' His earliest work accentuated the geometric possibilities of abstraction before yielding to sinuous, organic shapes. In the year after this portrait, and before *Private View* was published, Hoyland embarked on a bursary trip to New York. Here he was exposed to the work of Helen Frankenhalter and Kenneth Noland and he added to his repertoire of ideas elements from 'Colour Field' painting. Also in 1964 he held his one-man show at the Marlborough Gallery. Two retrospectives of his work have been held in London: at the Serpentine in 1989 and ten years later in 1999 at the Royal Academy. In that year he was appointed Professor of Painting at the Royal Academy Schools. He had been elected to the Academy in 1991. Next to the vividly coloured abstract *21-8-63* (1963), Bryan Robertson concluded by telling readers that 'Hoyland is a true inventor'.

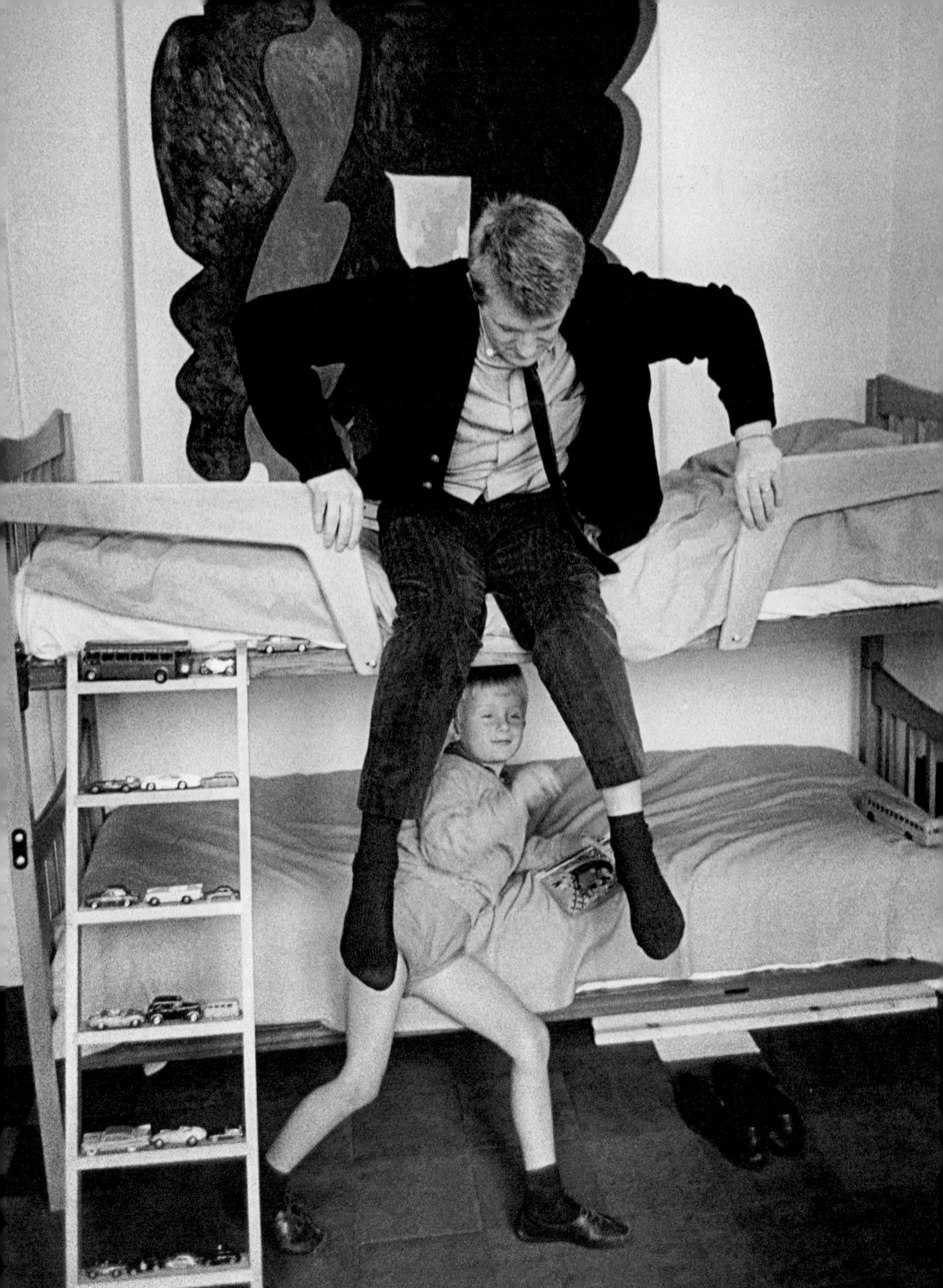

John Piper (1903–1992)

St Anne's, Limehouse, 1963
Private View

Chief among the romantic painters who came to prominence in the 1940s when Britain was at peril, John Piper was passionate about the preservation of Britain's heritage and the threat to its disappearing ecclesiastical architecture in particular. He designed in the post-war years the Baptistery window in the resurrected Coventry Cathedral (he was also instrumental to the rebuilding projects for St Anne's, Soho and Liverpool Cathedral). Snowdon showed him at work in the churchyard of St. Anne's, Limehouse, famous for its Hawksmoor tower. But as the authors of *Private View* remarked, Piper defied easy categorization. He was a painter of abstracts and a stage designer much called upon from 1943 onwards. John Russell's thumbnail sketch was as apposite as it was charming: 'Piper at sixty-one is what he always was: erect and accessible, with the looks of an affable Montezuma, the loping irregular gait of an Olympic champion limbering up for the hop, step and jump, and an awareness of absolutely everything around him that makes him, in an unassertive way, one of the most intelligent men in England...'

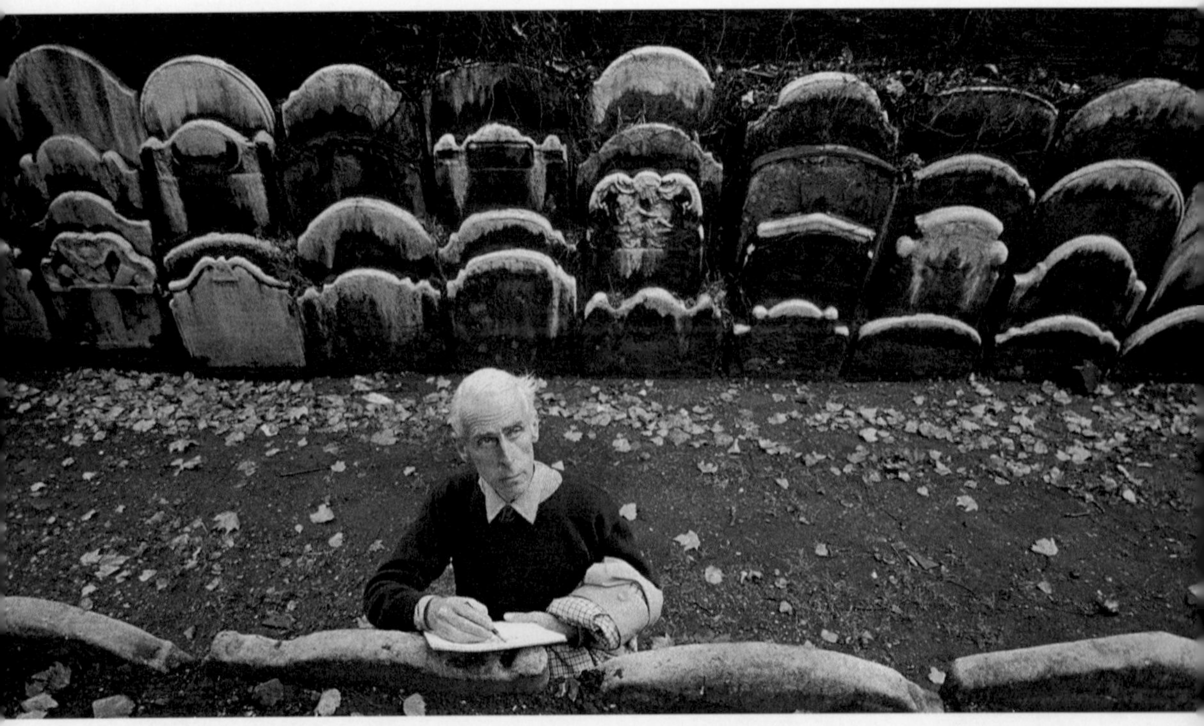

L.S. Lowry (1887–1976)

Leather Lane Market, Clerkenwell, 1963
Private View

Lowry studied painting and drawing part-time for a total of 20 years (1905–25) and he was, for nearly half a century, employed by the same Manchester property firm. For his idiosyncratic and well-loved paintings, he drew inspiration from what surrounded him on a daily basis: coal mining pitheads, factories and mills, rows of terraced cottages. At first they were naturalistically rendered but in time became more impressionistic, suggesting the shift to and fro of hundreds of people from home to factory gate under skies, either leaden or made so by the smog of industry. 'A country landscape is fine without people', he once remarked, 'but an industrial one without people is an empty shell. A street is not a street without people... it is as dead as mutton'. Apart from the industrial scenes populated by his 'matchstick' figures, he made rural landscapes, harbour views and seascapes, as well as the occasional emotionally-charged portrait. Lowry was not interested in the accolades or trappings of success. He lived modestly and holds the record for the most establishment honours declined in one lifetime, including an OBE, a CBE, a knighthood (in 1968) and two offers of the CH (in 1972 and 1976).

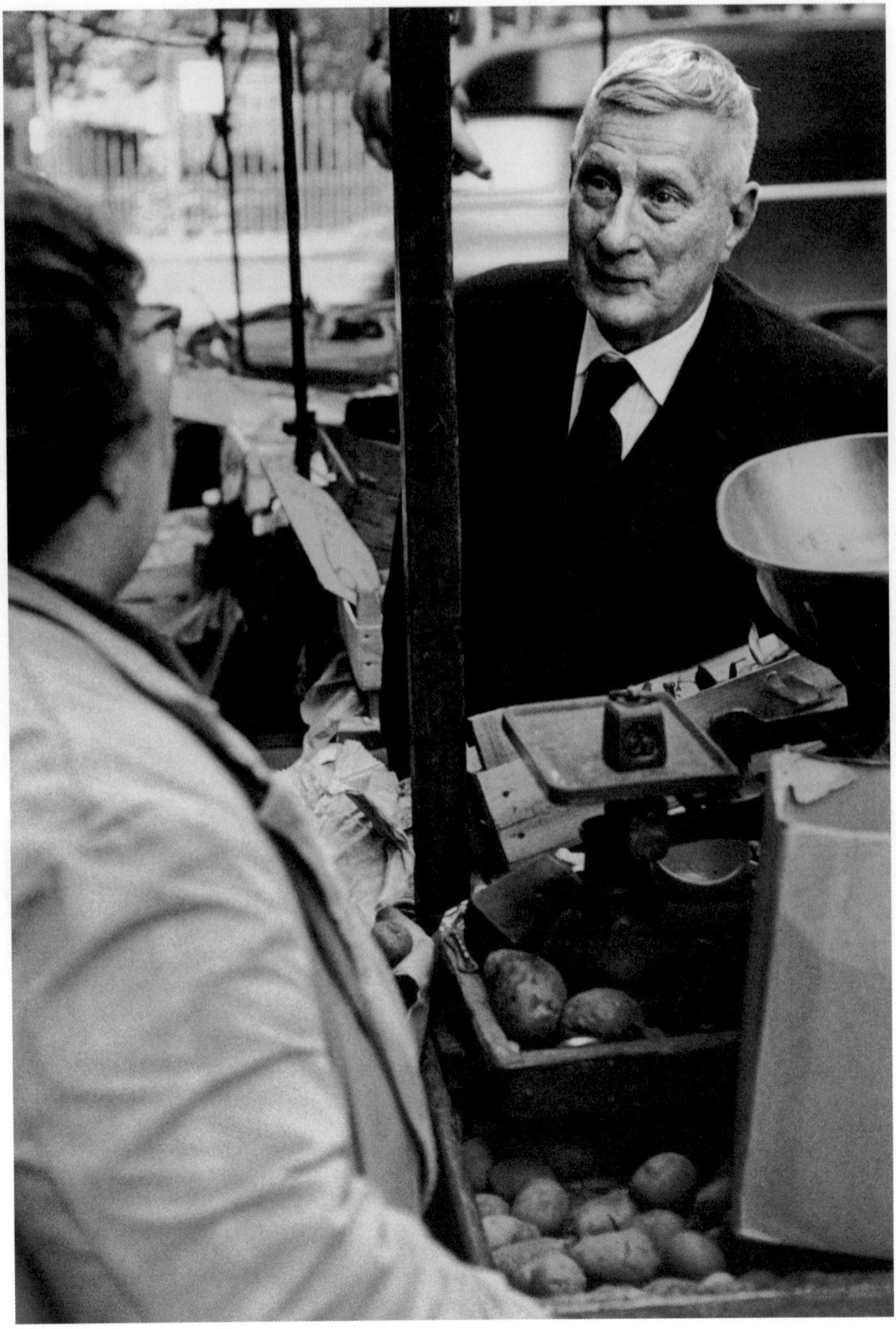

Anthony Blunt (1907–1983)

At the Courtauld Institute, 1963
Private View

During a long reign, it is said that the Queen has lost her equanimity just twice. The second time was on hearing, in 1979, that the Keeper of the Queen's Pictures had been revealed as the 'Fourth Man' of a ring of Cambridge-educated spies. Blunt was stripped of the knighthood she had bestowed on him in 1956. When Snowdon photographed him he was also Director of the Courtauld Institute, which, he had turned into a respected centre of learning. He was also a distinguished writer on seventeenth-century French and Italian painting. Though the pre-eminent authority on Nicolas Poussin, the sunlight falls here on his impassive mask of a face through a transparency of a Picasso painting.

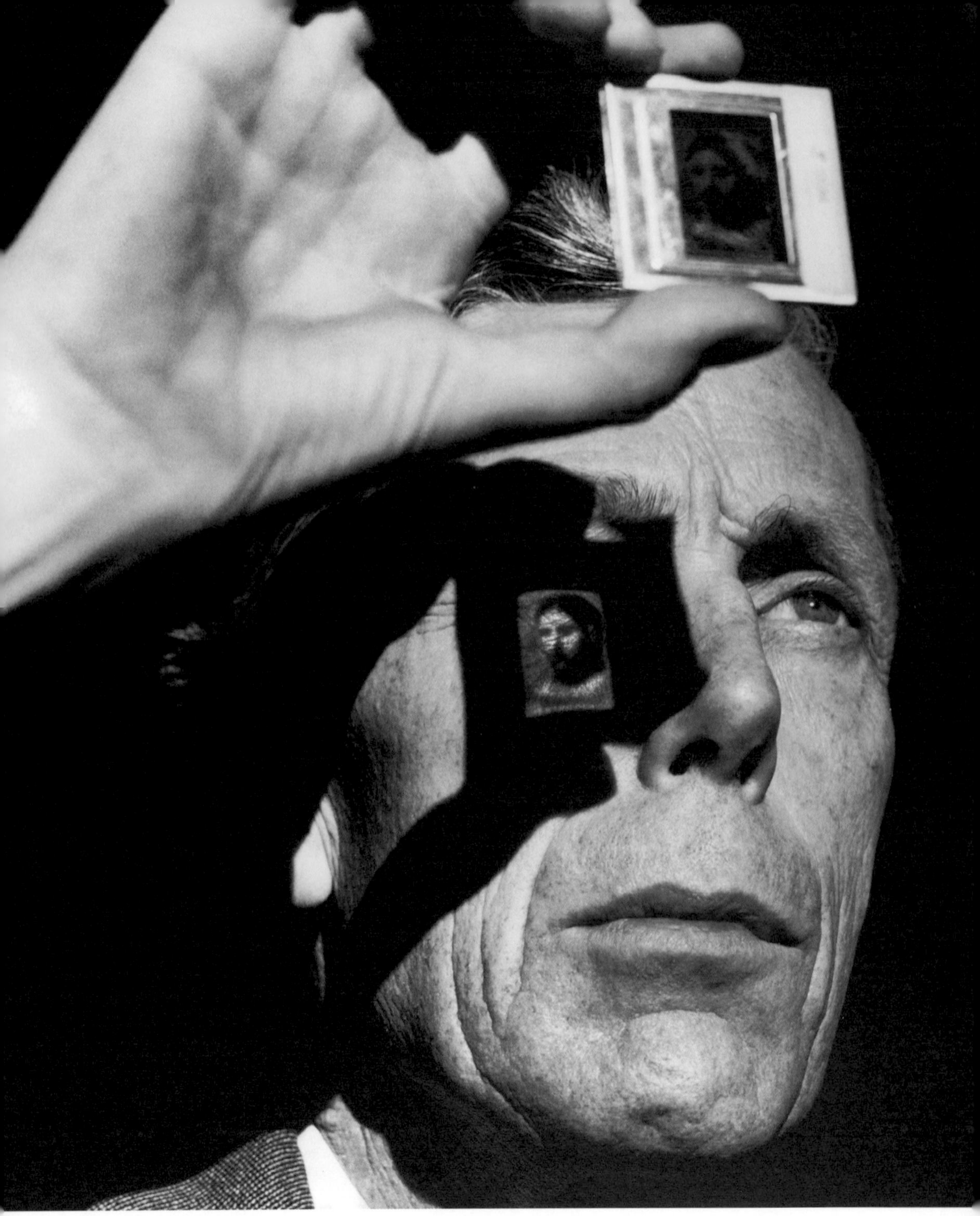

Peter Blake (b.1932)

In his garden, Chiswick, 1963
Private View

For *Private View*, Snowdon arranged the trophies in Blake's garden to mirror the arrangements found in his *On the Balcony* (1955–7). Like a shopkeeper setting out his wares, the painter shows the viewer the range and diversity of interests, influences and motifs that jostle for attention in his paintings. Blake's fascination with films and American popular culture is evident from the tailor's dummy with its stencilled face of Elvis Presley, and with Edwardiana and found objects, judging by another dummy decorated with military insignia. *The Knife-Thrower's Board*, between the two dummies, summed up these preoccupations perfectly; a *faux-naif* relic from a turn-of-the-century Vaudeville act decorated with an image of Brigitte Bardot taken from *Reveille* magazine. 'I still have the dressmaker's dummy', Blake said recently, 'It's now in the window of Mr Chow, the restaurant, but it's falling to pieces. It looks very decadent; the silk's all falling away, and I still have, of those things, the Lawrence of Arabia bust, but just the head of Mister Coffee...'

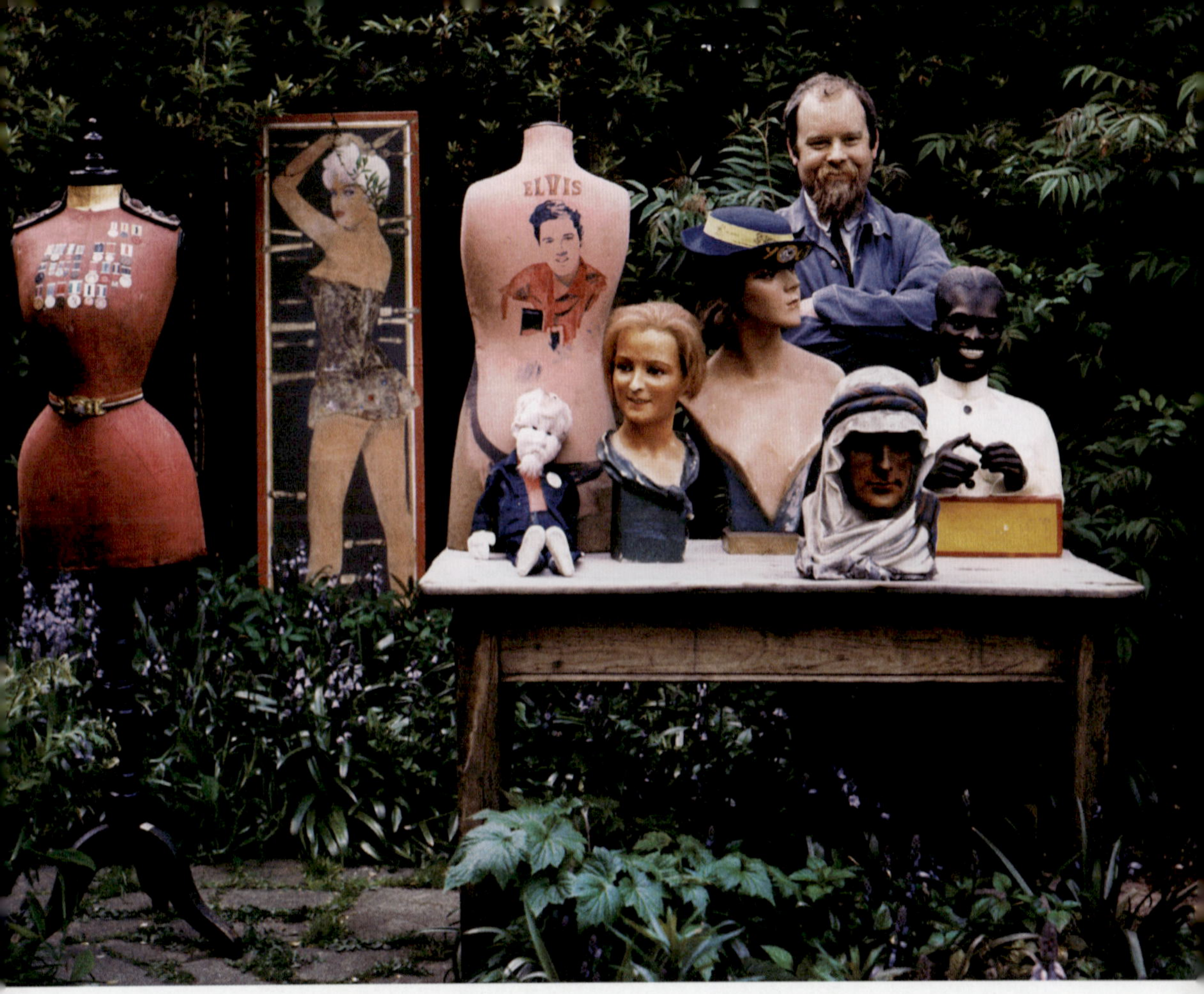
ELVIS

Derek Boshier (b.1937)

In his studio, Parson's Green, 1963
Private View

The walls of Derek Boshier's studio were collaged in paper, cut-outs, pin-ups and photographs (the artist Pauline Boty is in sunglasses to the left of the painter's head). Snowdon was keen to acquire the dentist's chair Boshier sits in. The striped barber's pole on the right would appear in various colours in the painting *Strike* (1964).
The assemblages hinted at a mixed-media *oeuvre* and over the years he experimented with 'shaped' canvasses, pioneered in the United States by Jasper Johns, Frank Stella and Kenneth Noland among others. America was a constant in his painting as earlier abstracts yielded to a more figurative Pop Art (he was a Royal College of Art contemporary of David Hockney, Peter Phillips and Allen Jones) and then back to a hard-edged geometric abstraction. He had studied the writings of Marshall McLuhan and his paintings developed a satirical, topical slant, broadly on themes such as the subsumption of human identity in the face of commercialism, all-pervasive advertising, the space race and the inexorable Americanisation of the rest of the globe.

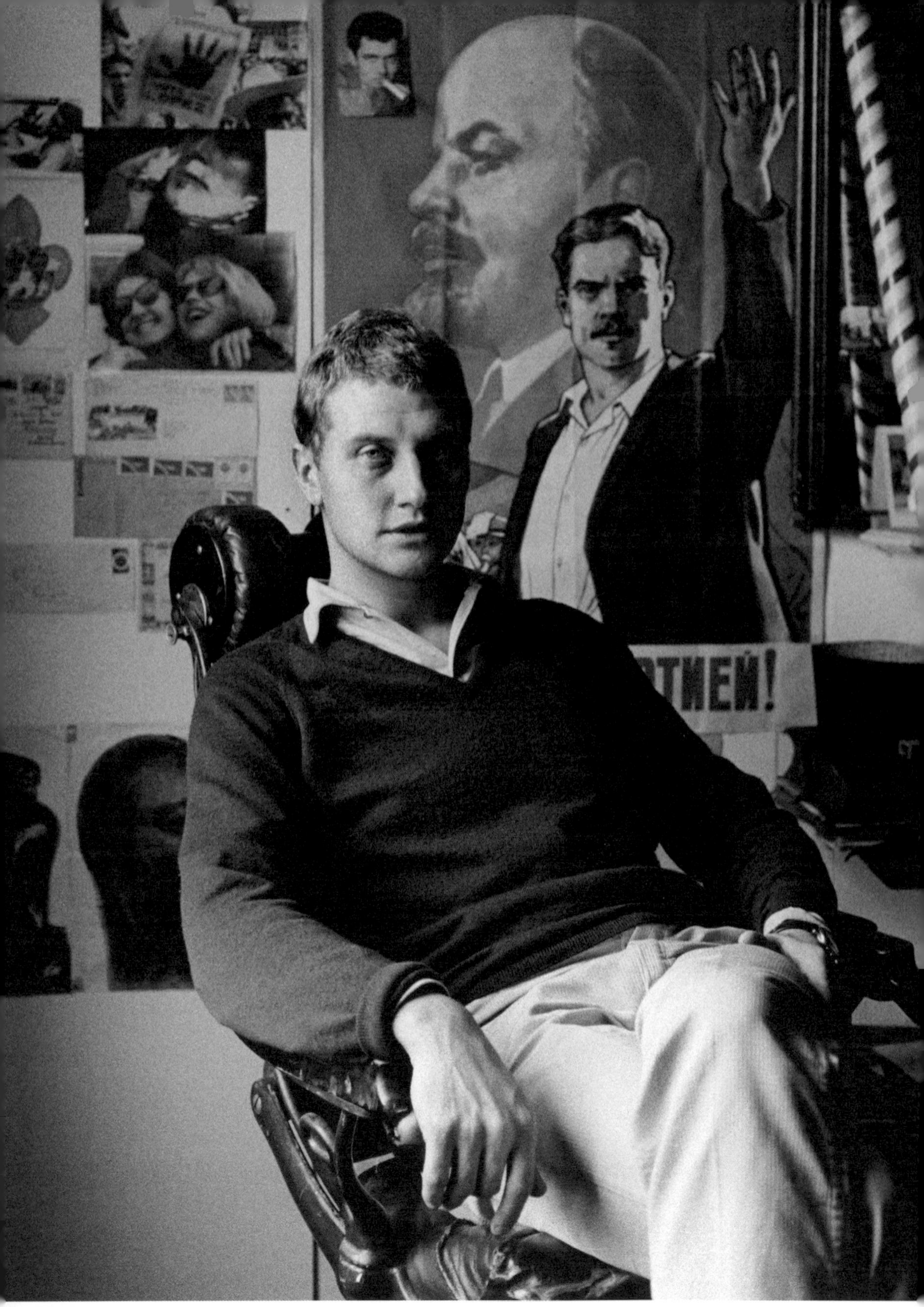
ТИЕЙ!

Prunella Clough (1919–1999)

In her studio, Fulham, 1963
Private View

The authors of *Private View* found Prunella Clough 'one of the best informed and most acutely intelligent painters in England'. On a personal note, they admired her 'instinctive elegance and sense of style, which are usually camouflaged behind a prosaic matter-of-fact manner and appearance'. Clough enrolled in the Chelsea School of Art in 1938 where her tutors included Julian Trevelyan, Henry Moore and Graham Sutherland, who would later acquire a house in the south of France, designed by Clough's aunt, the celebrated modernist designer Eileen Gray. Her first one-woman exhibition was held at the St Leger Gallery, London in 1947 and consisted mainly of Suffolk landscapes. Her next for the Leicester Galleries in 1953 was more sombre, concentrating on the realism of English working life. This led to gritty urban landscapes, sometimes literally so as she might add sand and ash to augment the subject matter. Ambivalent to money – she inherited considerable wealth – she was exceptionally philanthropic to art and design schools and other good causes. (One friend found a brand new estate car waiting for her at the garage to which she had earlier taken an irreparable wreck). As the trustee of her Aunt Eileen's estate, all licensing royalties went to fund design school bursaries.

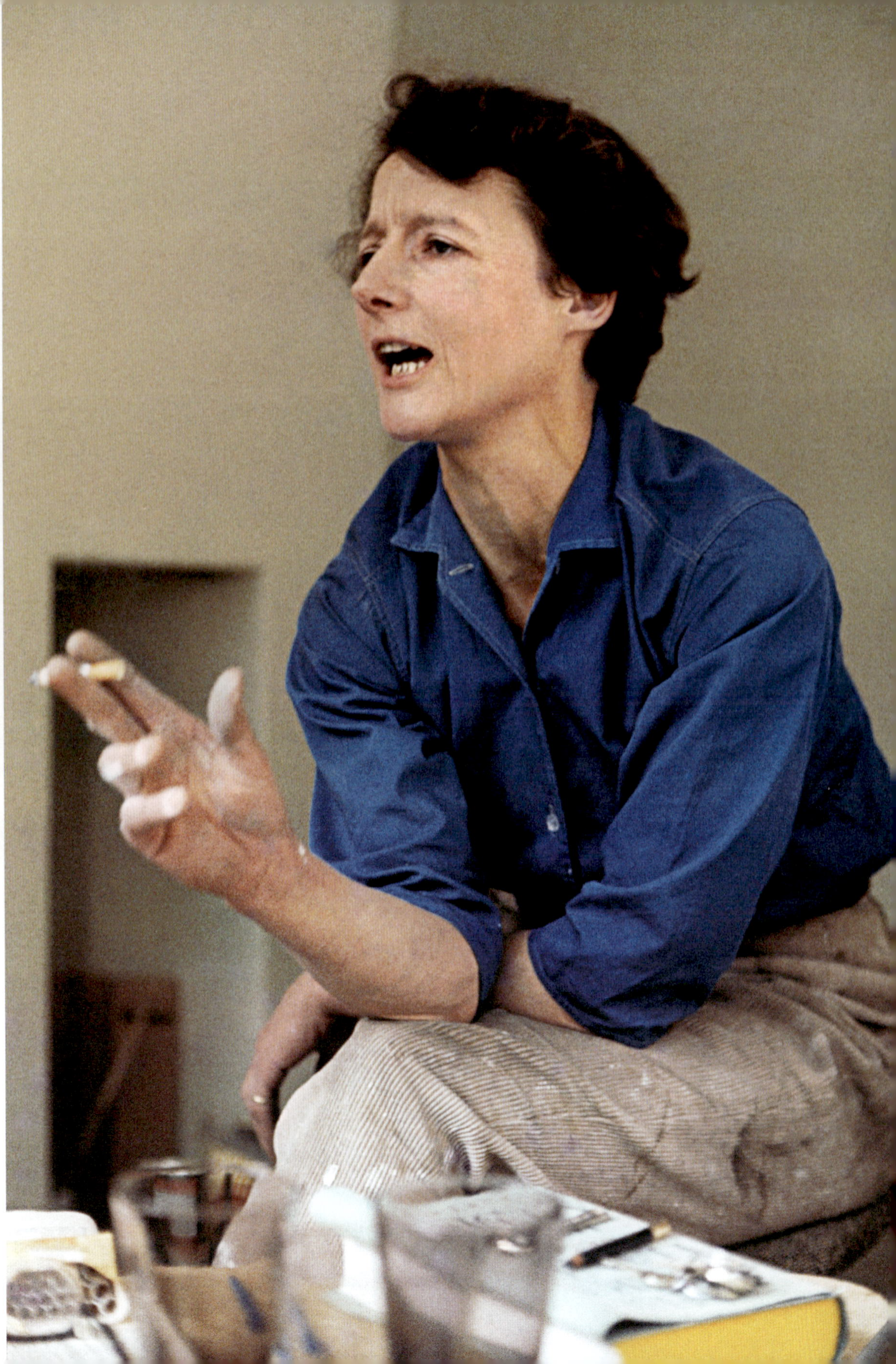

Elisabeth Frink (1930–1993)

In her studio, Chelsea, 1963
Private View

'Elisabeth Frink is that rarest of things in 1965', wrote John Russell in *Private View*, 'a full-blown romantic artist. Gifted with the looks of a young Boadicea, direct and downright in her turn of speech, she turns instinctively to the subjects which others evade, with irony or equivocation: helmeted warriors, a bird on the alert...' and as here, fallen heroes, the *Dying King* (1963). Other naturalistic themes included horses and dogs. *The Dying King* was a life-size representation, it is thought, of Richard III at Bosworth, arguably not much of a hero. Her bronzes were distinguished by the distressed and 'broken' form they took. Her etiolated, masculine, figures were idiosyncratic and recognisable: 'I have focused on the male because to me he is a subtle combination of sensuality and strength with vulnerability', she once remarked. The Tate Gallery acquired the menacing *Bird* (1952) while she was still a student at the Chelsea School of Art. Two years after Snowdon took this portrait, she had left Britain to 'cut myself off from the British art scene'. In 1985 she was the subject of a retrospective at the Royal Academy, London. Though mortally ill, she was able to watch her last public commission *Risen Christ* unveiled at Liverpool's Anglican cathedral in 1993.

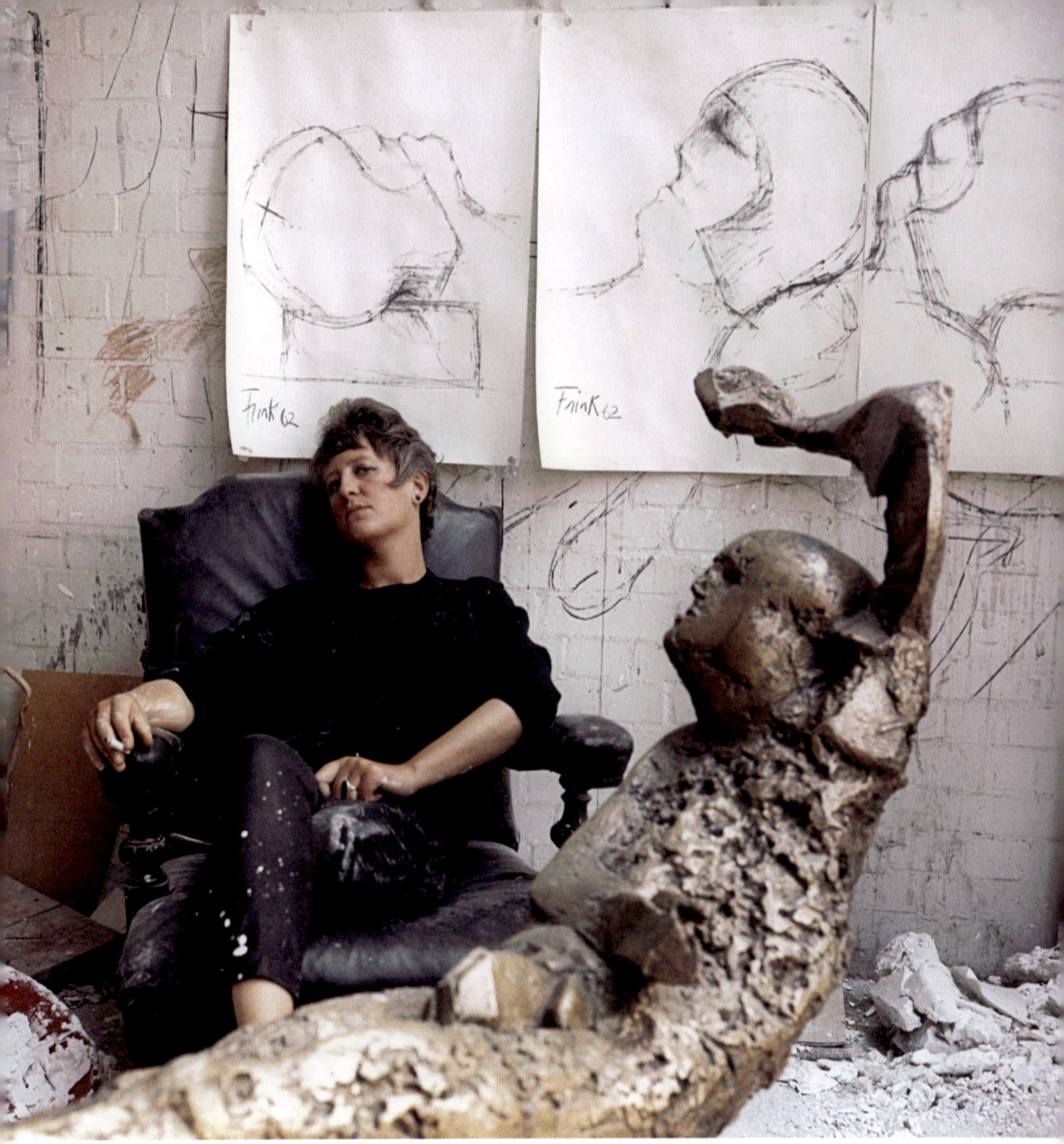
Frink 62
Frink 62

Patrick George (b.1923)

In his studio, Pimlico, 1963
Private View

Snowdon climbed to the top floor of the house opposite George's in Pimlico to observe the artist in one window and his model, the painter Natalie Bower, in the adjacent. The half-completed painting *Portrait of Natalie Bower* (1962–4) also visible, would turn out to be one of George's more swiftly rendered likenesses. Occasionally the painter, of the 'Euston Road School' of realism, might return to a canvas some twenty years after he started on it. As George wrote about his sittings with Dower, 'we sat for each other alternate hours ...the portrait Natalie Dower painted of me was abandoned'. George was appointed Professor of Fine Art at the Slade School in 1985.

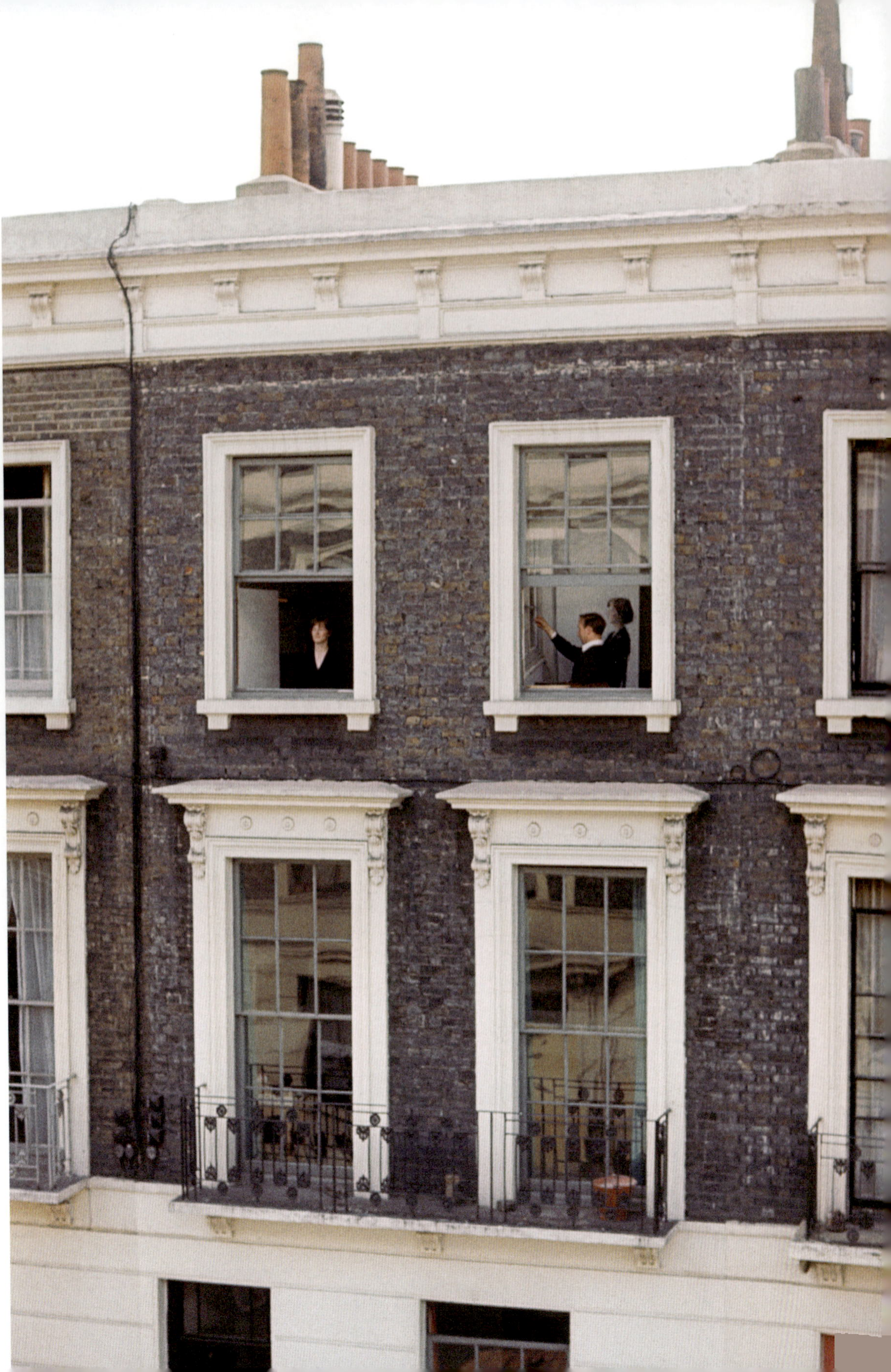

Ceri Richards (1903–1971)

In his studio, Fulham, 1963
Private View

The Welsh painter once wrote that 'I have to refer directly to nature for stimulus before I start my painting. Once I have transferred to canvas an expression of this stimulus, the painting grows on its own as an entity.' A close friend of Dylan Thomas, the poet's themes and imagery, often involving the fierce organiscism of nature, informed the painter's early work. After the Second World War, Richards began to experiment with the textural qualities of paint as well as with collage and the addition of *objets trouvés* into his work. John Russell was unsurprised that Richards' forward-thinking constructions, part Surrealist, part Picasso, part Welsh and mystic were for twenty years 'unsung, unbought, unrecognised'. An accomplished musician, an organist primarily, musical motifs and notation were often integrated into Richards' work. In Snowdon's photograph, the construction on the easel, part of the series *La Cathédrale Engloutie*, incorporates sheet music, a cowbell and a small approximation of piano keyboard. Sharp-eyed, regular visitors to Pallant House Gallery will recognise the painting decorated with silver bells held by the painter in his right hand, which was exhibited in the exhibition *Eye-Music: Kandinsky, Klee and all that Jazz* (2007).

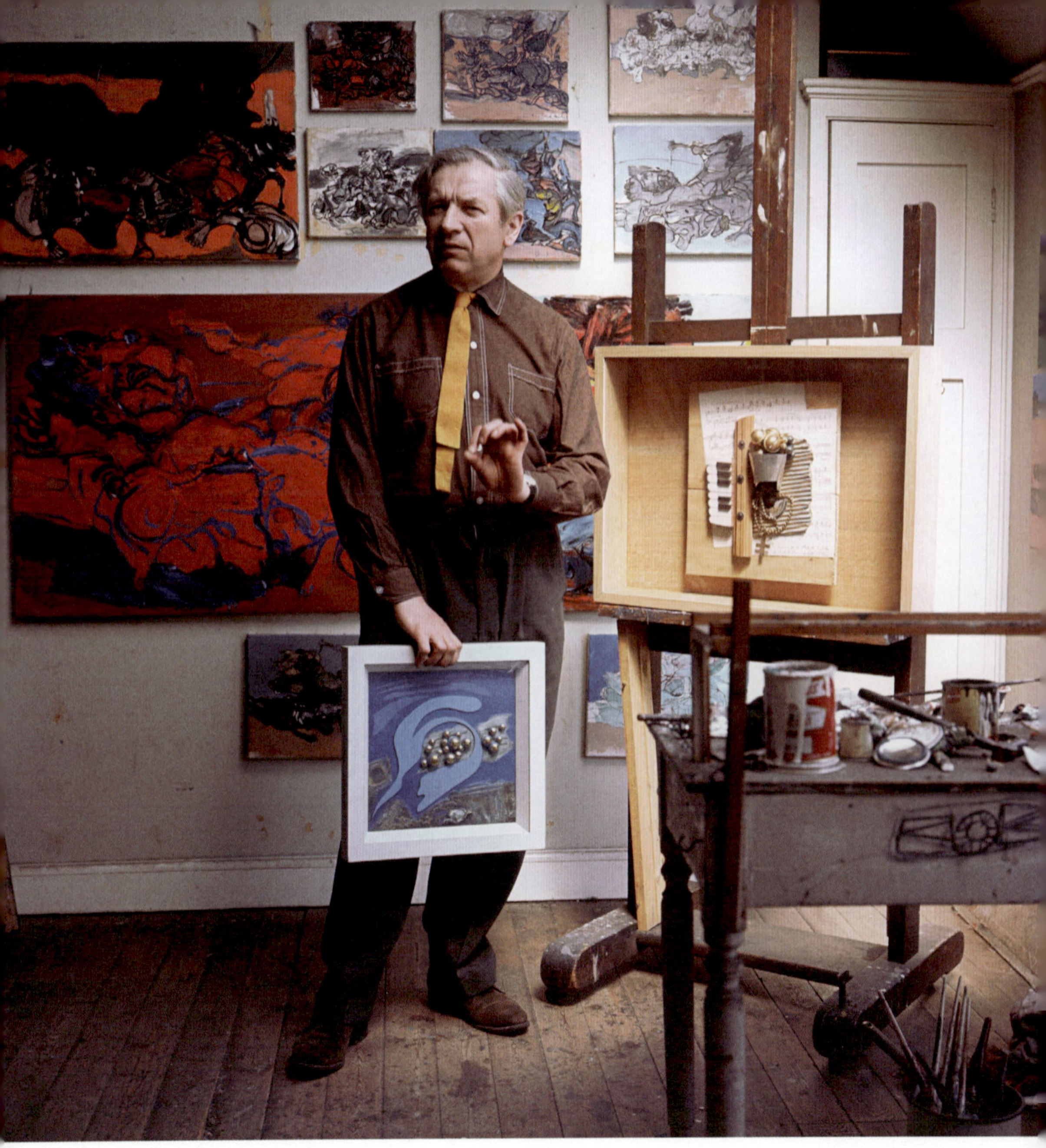

Bridget Riley (b.1934)

In her studio, Earls Court, 1963
Private View

Bridget Riley's paintings are among the most recognised of any modern British painter, but she remains, according to many observers, something of an enigma. 'I need to be on my own', she told *Vogue*, 'without interruptions. It is silence I like, exterior and interior'. Her 'Op art' paintings, often in black-and white, brought her to prominence in the 1960s relying for their effect on the shortcomings of the human eye to produce an impression of motion. But her pleasure in launching an art movement almost single-handedly was shortlived, as her clever geometric shapes and patterns were hijacked for 'high street' commercial purposes, with a deleterious effect on the originals.
Off the radar for some time despite a considerable auction house presence, a retrospective at the Serpentine Gallery, London and another at Tate Britain in 2003, which even its director agreed was long overdue, have re-established her as a British painter of integrity and enormous depth. This was apparent then as now. Writing in *Private View*, John Russell observed that 'nothing in British art prepared people for the impact of Bridget Riley's paintings...the experience they offer runs contrary to all ordinary ways of looking at a picture'.

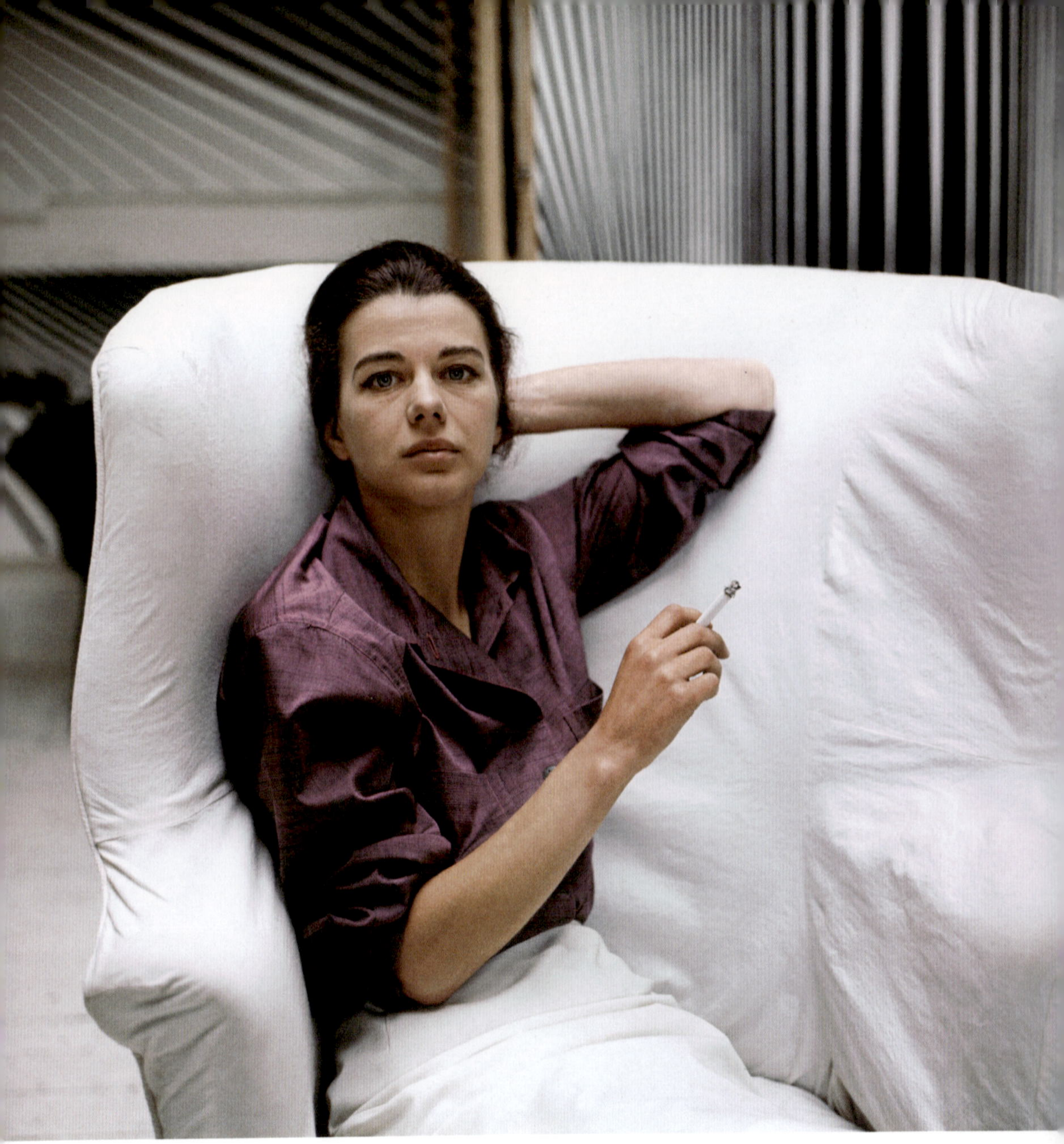

Keith Vaughan (1912–1977)

At home, Belsize Park, 1963
Private View

Before taking up painting full-time in 1938, Vaughan worked in an advertising agency. Encouraged by Graham Sutherland, he became part of the 'Neo-Romantic' movement in British art that flourished during the Second World War and in the immediate post-war years. Though at first he shared the movement's reverence for lyrical English landscape, Vaughan distilled his themes into virtually one constant: the male nude (though increasingly abstracted in his later years). He was held in high regard as a tutor at Camberwell College of Arts, Central School of Art and the Slade. Bryan Robertson admired the 'laconic, unused directness' of his work, which was he felt, characteristic of the man too.

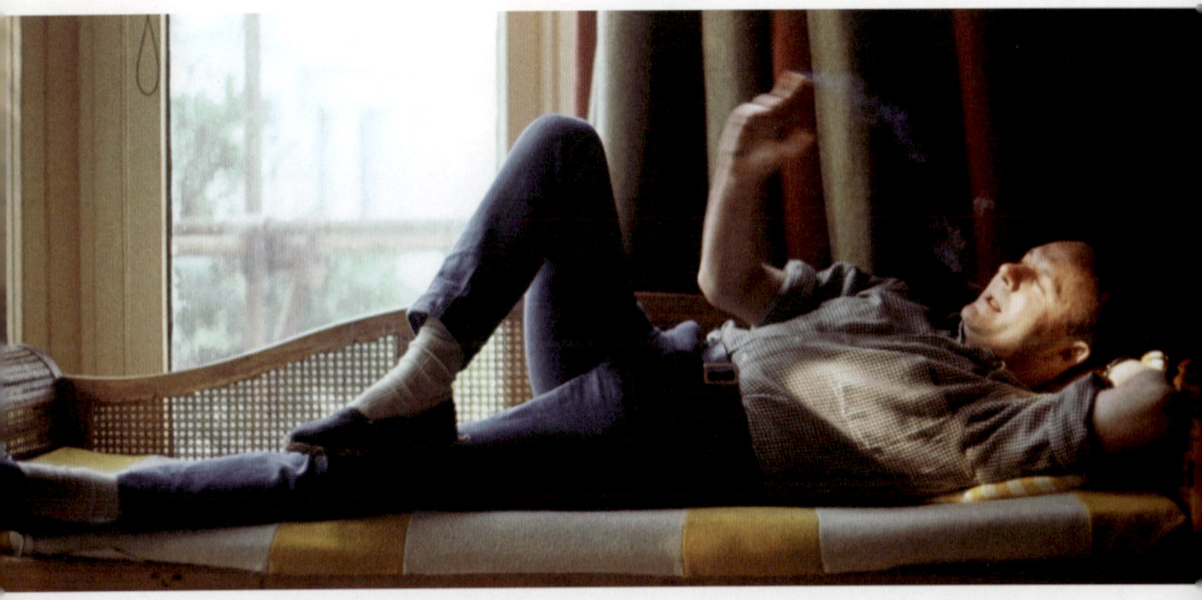

Roger Hilton (1911–1975)

In his studio, Cornwall, 1963
Private View

Bryan Robertson wrote of Hilton's work that it had 'maintained its own spiky integrity'. This was reflected in the painter himself, who took spikiness to new levels. Especially it seems in 1963, the year Snowdon visited for *Private View*. Then the painter was in a state of intoxication, but not enough to prevent him from recreating for his visitor, as far as possible, the animation contained in *Oy, Yoi, Yoi* (1963), a vigorous, sexually-charged leaping nude, recently completed (and now in Tate's collection). The exertion clearly intensified his thirst. The stories surrounding Hilton are the stuff of legend. His acceptance speech for winning the John Moores Prize, also in 1963, consisted of the words 'Give me the cheque, you look like a decaying oyster...' and at the dinner afterwards, an elderly alderman, already ill, was so shocked by Hilton's drunken rudeness that he collapsed and died at the table. Despite his best efforts, Hilton was hugely influential on a generation of painters, not least because his style eluded straightforward classification. In addition, he was a communicator who commanded rapt attention. Originally a figurative painter, he switched to St. Ives-style abstraction and back again to colourful, almost childlike nude work.

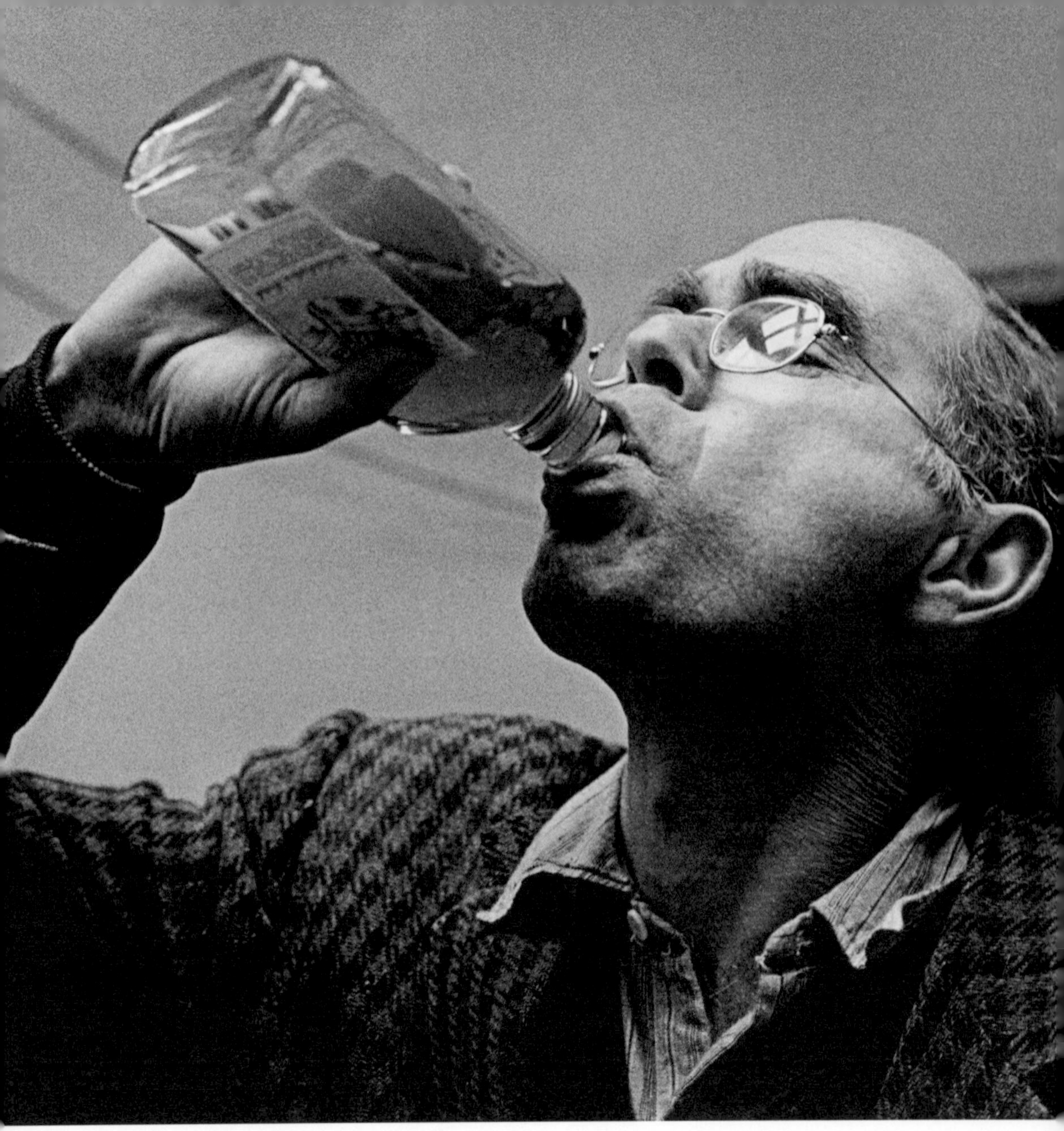

Richard Hamilton (b.1922)

In London, 1964
Private View

Snowdon's portrait of Richard Hamilton for *Private View* made reference not just to an American Pop art conceit of the faithful reproduction of blown-up comic book strips, but of the enlarged half-tone photographic reproduction that found its way into Hamilton's own collages. One of Hamilton's most famous pieces, which he explored in various painted and screen printed versions, was *Swingeing London* (1967–8) which was based upon a newspaper photograph of Mick Jagger and art dealer Robert Fraser handcuffed and on their way to Lewes Crown Court on drugs charges (the three dimensional piece is now in the Pallant House Gallery collection). As a coda to the hopes and dreams of the liberated, licentious sixties, it has few equals. Hamilton studied painting at the Royal Academy Schools in two brief bursts. The second was curtailed when it was considered that he was 'not profiting by the instruction given in the paintings school'. A leading member of the Independent Group, he came to prominence at the Whitechapel Gallery's *This is Tomorrow* exhibition in 1956 with his collage *Just What is it that Makes Today's Homes so Different, so Appealing?* which became emblematic of the show and of nascent British Pop art. He has experimented latterly with computer-generated artworks.

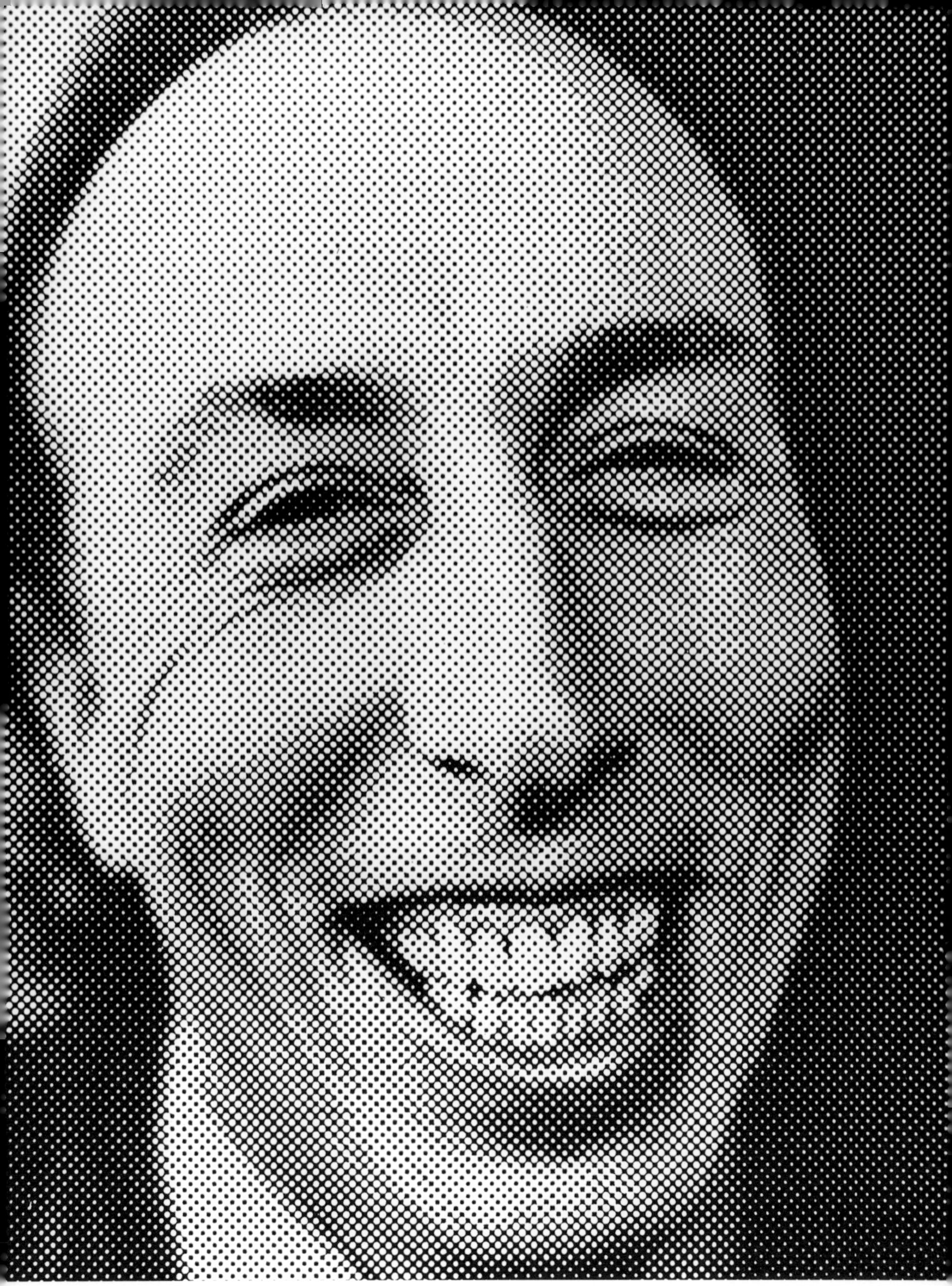

Graham Sutherland (1903–1980)

West Malling, Kent, 1964
Private View

'We must admit that our moments of vision are usually unpredictable', Kenneth Clark wrote. 'Mr. Graham Sutherland has described how on his country walks objects which he has passed a hundred times – a root, a thorn bush, a dead tree – will suddenly detach themselves and demand a separate existence; but why or when this should happen he cannot tell us, any more than a rider can tell us why his pony shies on a familiar road'. Influenced by Samuel Palmer and the landscapes of Paul Nash, Sutherland fixated on the incongruity of natural forms and the organicism of nature. Its inherent strangeness gave his work a surrealist inclination and he exhibited at the International Surrealist Exhibition in London in 1936. He had been greatly moved by his experiences as a war artist depicting the aftermath of German bombing raids on London's already impoverished dockland areas. *The Thorn Tree* (c.1945) merged nature with self-evident religious motifs and in 1946 he completed his *Crucifixion*. His imaginative landscapes influenced the emerging Neo-Romantic movement, but he was skilled too as a portraitist, though it was only an occasional preoccupation.

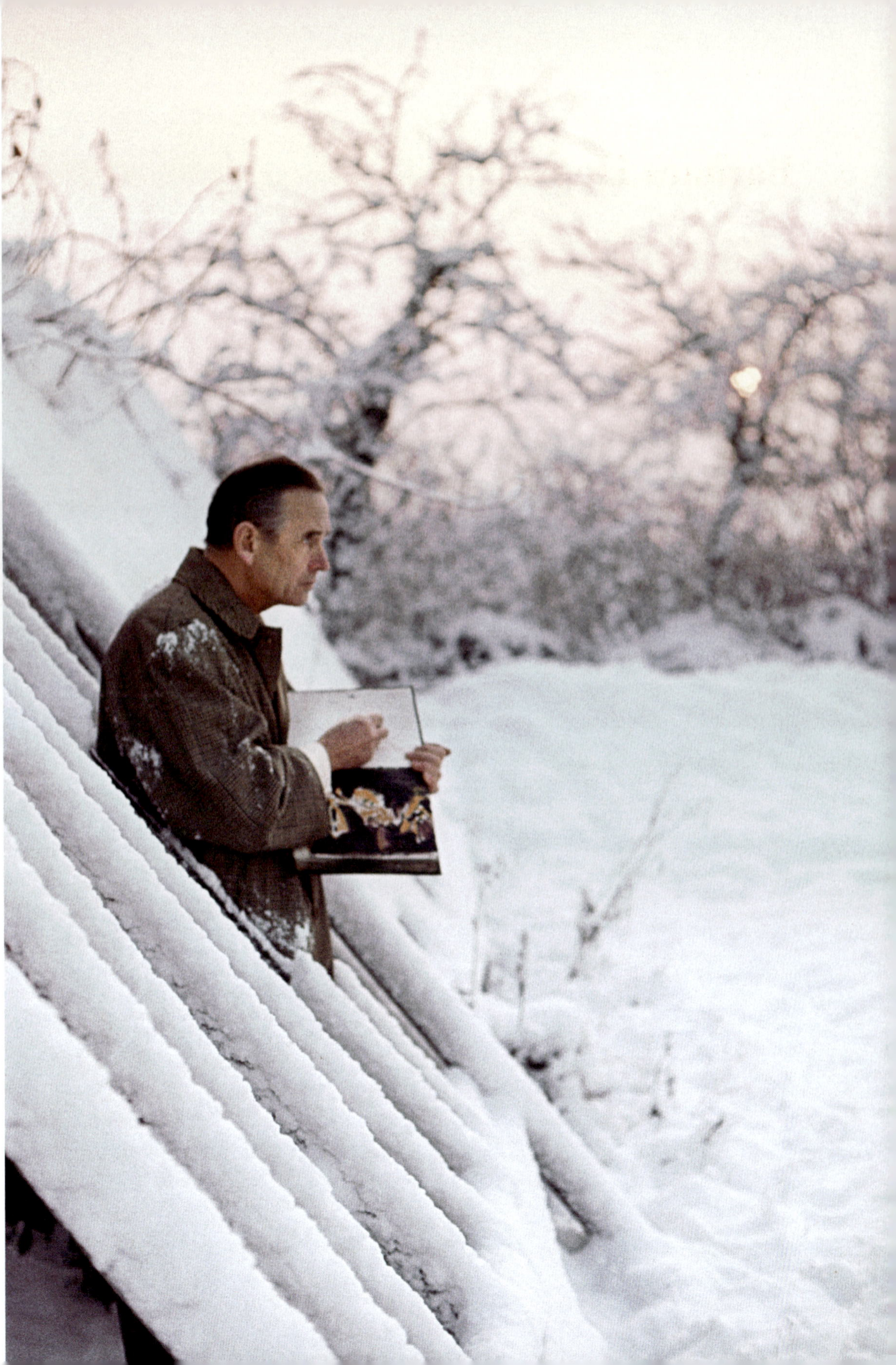

Barbara Hepworth (1903–1975)

On the beach, St. Ives, 1964
Private View

This portrait of the sculptress appeared on the cover of the *Sunday Times Magazine* and is the best known from *Private View*, where it was first published. She is shown on the foreshore at St. Ives where she then kept an apartment, and whose artistic community she did much to popularise. Described by one reviewer as 'something oddly marine', Bryan Robertson preferred a nautical analogy: 'Barbara Hepworth', he wrote, 'is rather like an extremely able Captain Ahab forever in search of a particularly alluring White Whale – in her case, the next sculpture.' By the time of *Private View*, she had been the recipient of two exhibitions at the Whitechapel Gallery (1954 and 1962), the CBE (1958) and in the year after this picture was taken she was made a DBE. Hepworth had settled in St. Ives during the Second World War and began to respond to what was around her, predominantly, the landscape.' Like Henry Moore, she was born in Yorkshire and both attended Leeds School of Art and the Royal College of Art, London. Like him, she remains one of the giant figures of twentieth century British sculpture.

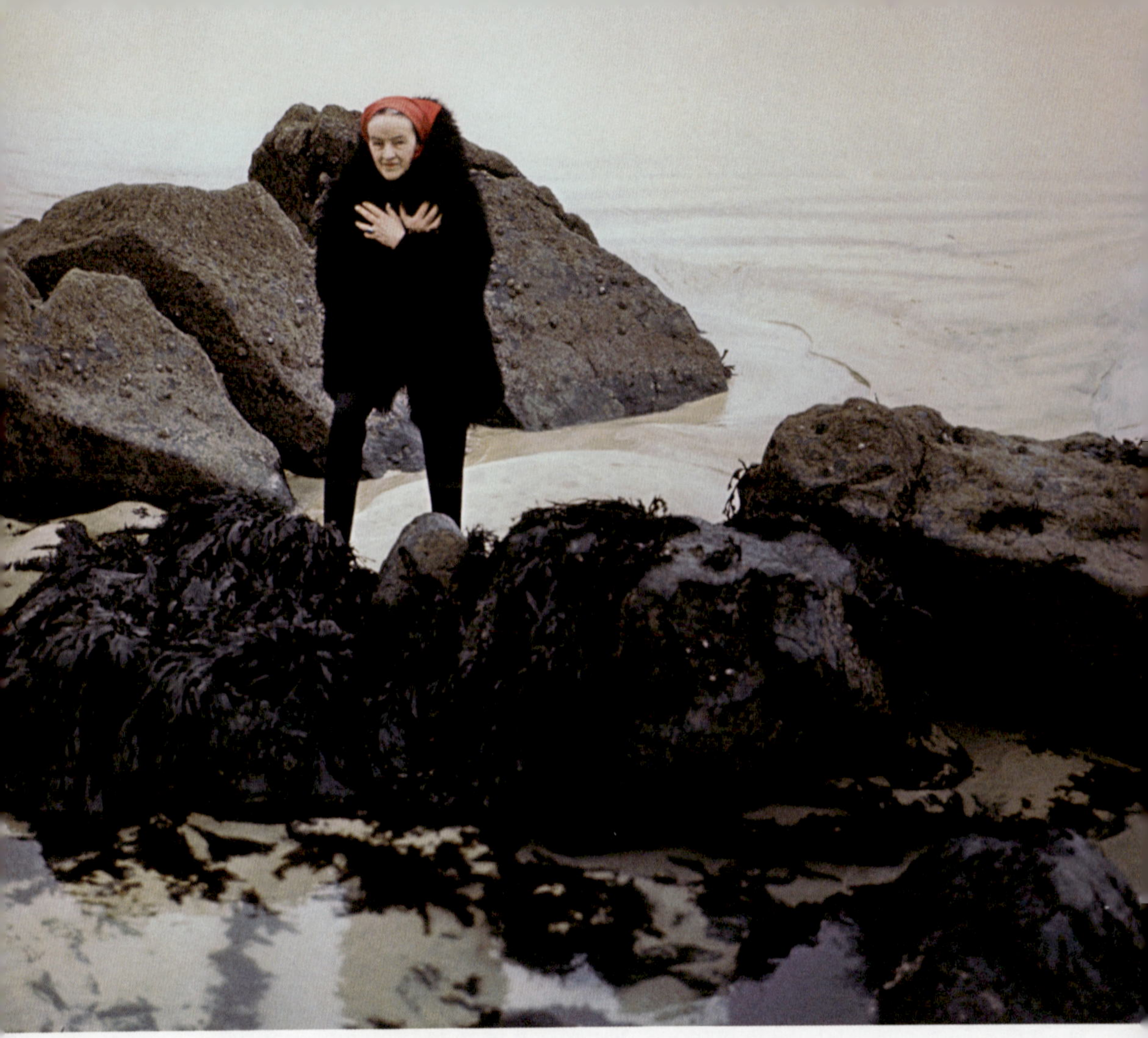

Alan Davie (b.1920)

In his studio, Hertfordshire, 1963
Private View

In the middle of executing a large-scale painting on the studio floor, Snowdon was able to catch Davie during a pause before bending over to recommence. John Russell and he marvelled at Alan Davie's studio, 'a huge white room, as big as a municipal swimming bath', which he had added to his house. As he frequently painted directly on to canvas, board or paper from above, this was almost a necessity. Influenced by Zen philosophy, much of his work is unstructured and unplanned and perhaps inexplicable anyway. Davie, born in Scotland, served with the Royal Artillery from 1940 to 1946 before briefly becoming a jazz musician and a jeweller. He had visited two vital exhibitions in London in 1945: Picasso at the Victoria & Albert Museum, and Paul Klee at the Tate Gallery. At Peggy Guggenheim's collection in Venice he saw the early work of Jackson Pollock. He would adopt Pollock's later *modus operandi* of painting rapidly and intuitively. When his work became increasingly abstract and symbolic (African, Aboriginal, Celtic) and with a reliance on intuition and improvisation rather than forethought, Davie appeared – unusually for British art – as an almost shamanic figure.

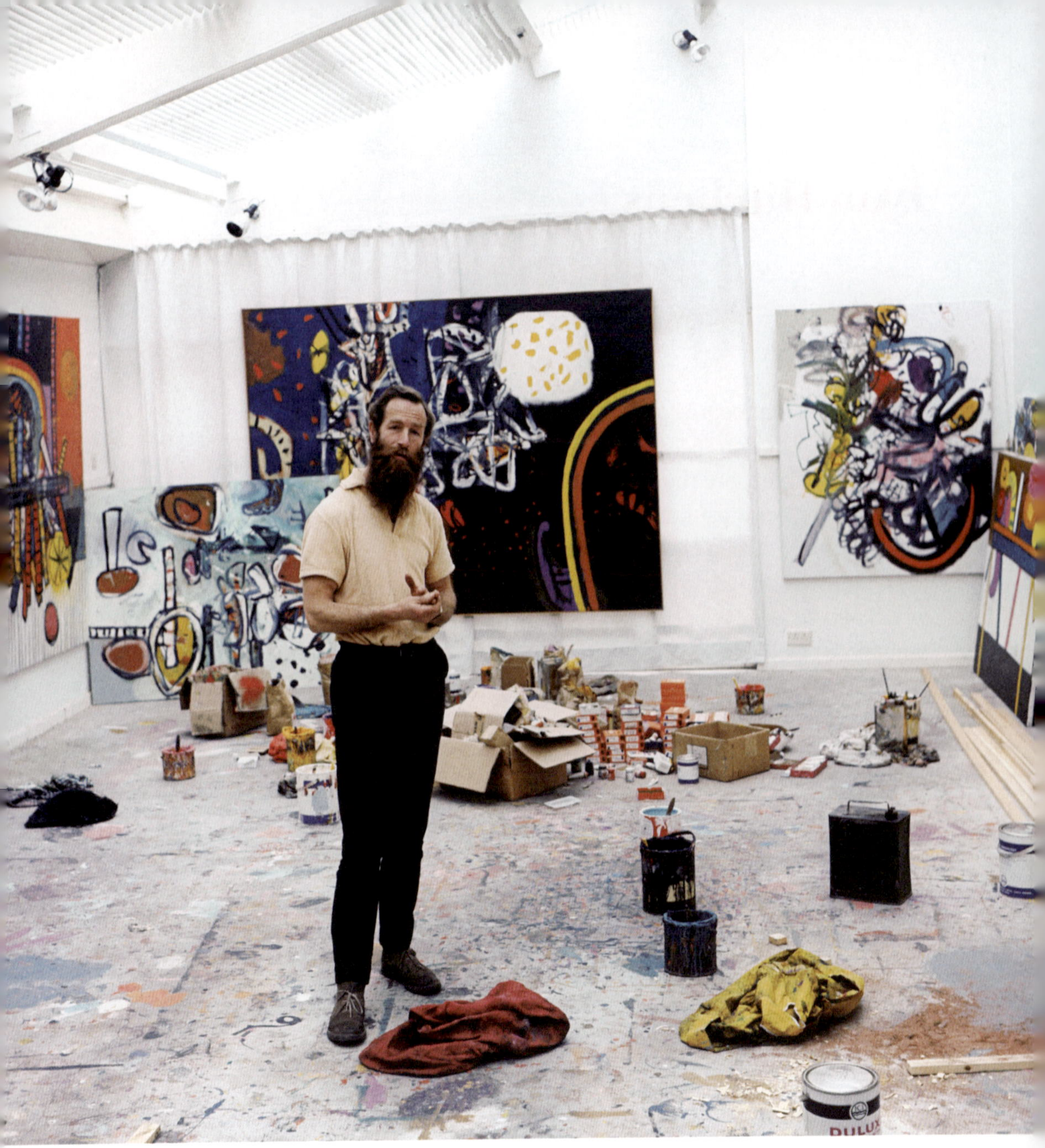
DULUX

Ivon Hitchens (1893–1979)

In his studio, near Petworth, 1964
Private View

Quoting Max Beerbohm's aphorism that living in the English countryside was akin to living inside a lettuce, Bryan Robertson in *Private View* lamented the slow decline of the English landscape tradition. The brightest hope and inspiration for a reversal was at 71, something of a 'Grand Old Man', who lived and painted around the Petworth area. A leading light of the experimental 'London Group', which also included Paul Nash and Ben Nicholson, Hitchens was primarily a painter of landscapes and nudes; the former loosely-defined and abstract but panoramic enough to suggest the flow of rolling landscape, and the latter figurative enough to retain an impression of the human form. At the height of the Blitz in 1940, his studio in northwest London was partially destroyed. He resolved to move to Sussex with his wife and four-month-old child where he had already acquired a caravan, driven deep into woodland at Lavington Common. Here, in rudimentary surroundings, without direct access to water or electricity, he made, with a broadly sweeping brushstroke, paintings bursting with colour. His pastoral subject matter reflected the safe and secluded Eden he had found for his family, totally at odds with their perilous urban life.

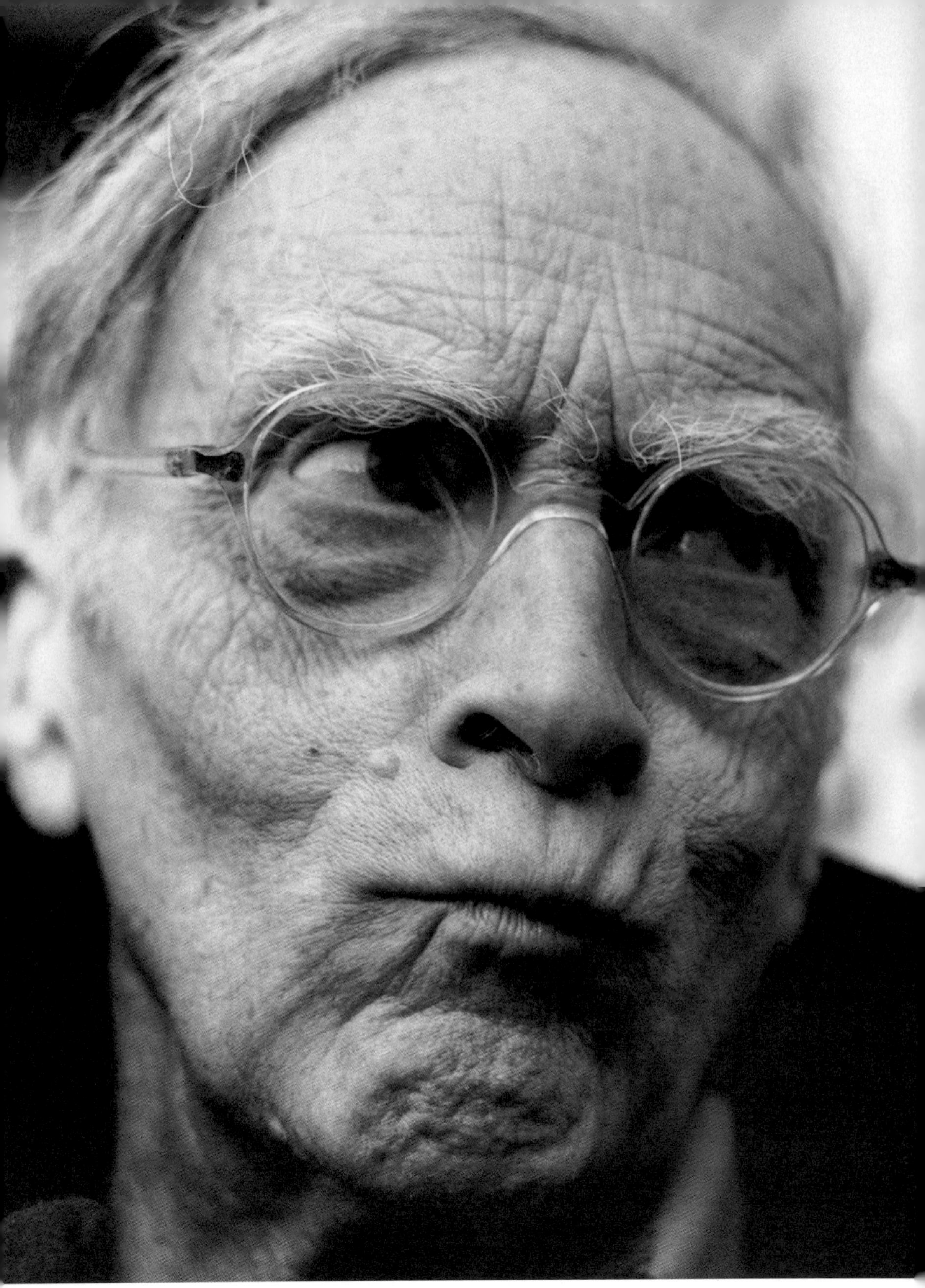

Robyn Denny (b.1930)

In his studio, London, 1964
Private View

The authors of *Private View* concurred that though Robyn Denny was 'not in the explanation business' he possessed a lucid grasp on what it meant to be a British painter in interesting times. His *Austin Reed Mural* completed in 1959 for the flagship Regent Street store of the firm of men's outfitters would become a 'Swinging Sixties' landmark (The Beatles were photographed against it) and a pulsating paean to the city in an exclamatory stream of consciousness: 'Great. Big, London. Biggest'. It was brought to the attention of a new generation as the cover image to the exhibition catalogue *The Sixties Art Scene in London* (Barbican Art Gallery, London, 1993). To curator David A. Mellor, it spoke 'the language of the new promotional culture that stood on every hand in the consumer boom...' In 1965 Denny represented Britain at the Venice Biennale as one of the *Five Young British Artists*. One of the great abstractionists working in Britain, he experimented with vertical, rectilinear forms and with an electrifying intensity that challenged the viewer's perception of colour.

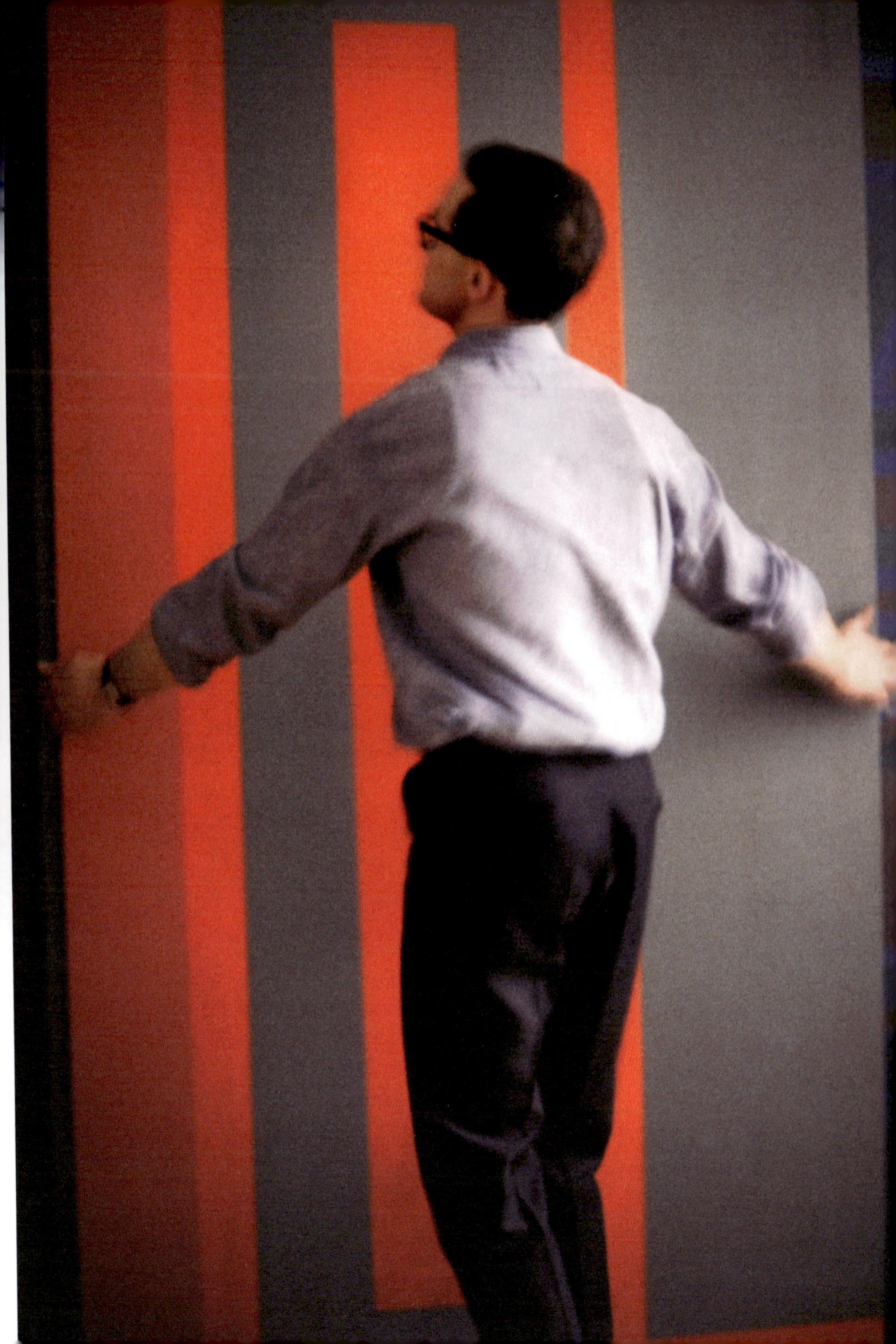

Phillip King (b.1934)

In his studio, West Hampstead, 1964
Private View

'King is the strongest figure in British sculpture after Moore, Hepworth and Caro', declared Bryan Robertson in *Private View*. He had studied under Anthony Caro at St Martin's School of Art (1957–8) and for a time had assisted Henry Moore. Though he held his first solo exhibition in 1964, the following year he came to wider public attention at *New Generation 1965*, an exhibition devoted to sculpture at the Whitechapel Gallery. He established a major international reputation for his use of non-traditional materials: fibreglass, plastic sheeting, wax and various forms of plastic. When *Private View* was published, one of the images used to promote it widely was King's gas-masked face (it protected him from the fumes given off by these new synthetic materials). *The Sunday Times Magazine* hailed him as the saviour of modern British sculpture, suggesting that with florid curves and full shapes, his sculpture had initiated a new movement: 'a kind of Modern Baroque'. King was President of the Royal Academy from 1999 to 2004, a troubled time in its history.

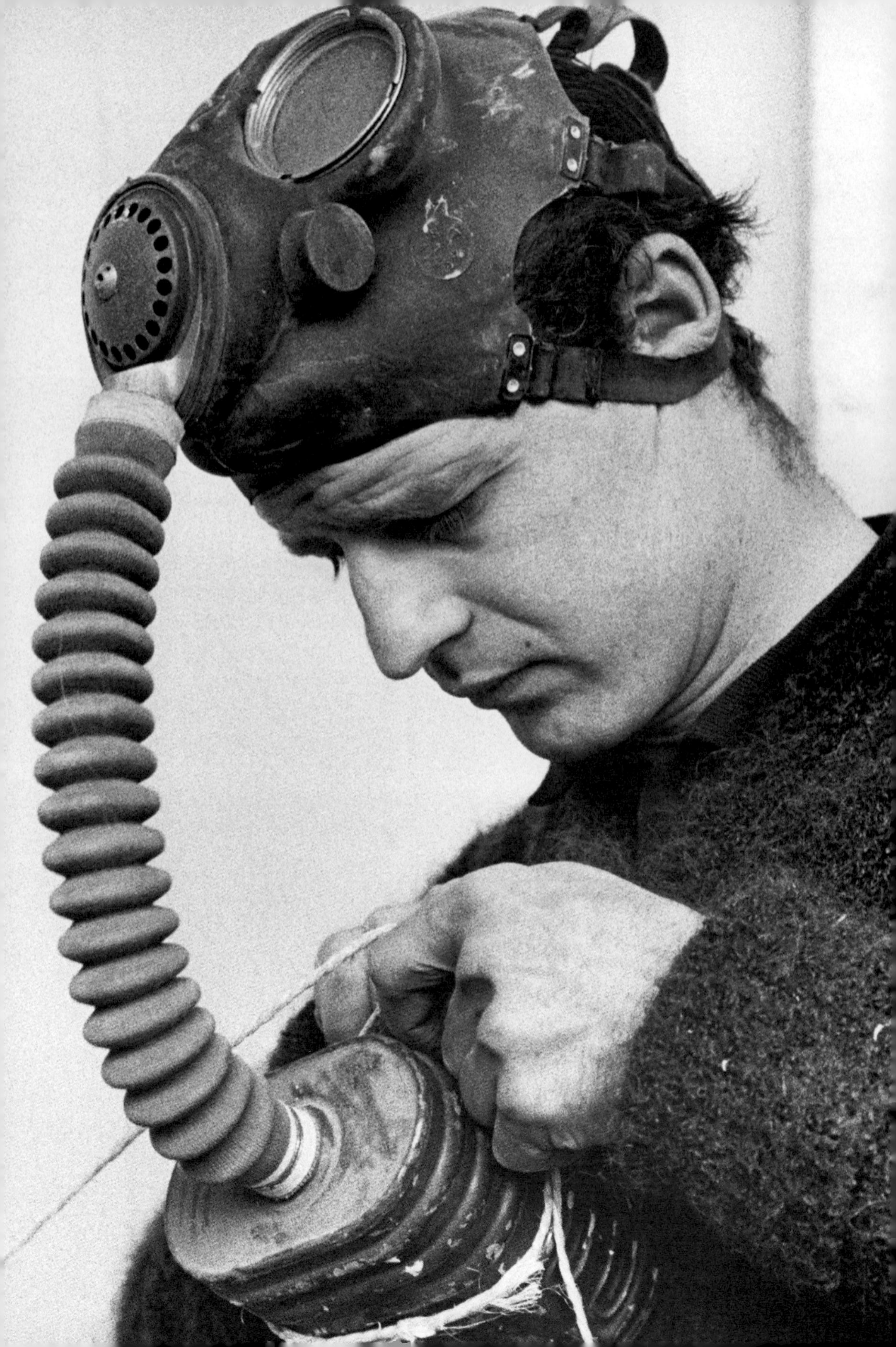

David Jones (1895–1974)

At home, Hendon, 1964
Private View

This stark portrait of David Jones, a poet as well as an artist, reveals a little of his innate modesty. His one-roomed bed-sit contained tea chests of books and his pictures were stacked in a corner. John Russell memorably described him as 'a man desert-islanded on the outskirts of London'. Born to a Welsh father, on the outbreak of war in 1914 he joined the Royal Welch Fusiliers and saw action on the Western Front – horrifically so at Mametz Wood in which 4000 Welshmen died. This was the basis for Jones' long prose-poem *In Parenthesis* (1937) hailed by T.S. Eliot and W.B. Yeats as a modernist masterpiece and it informed his paintings and drawings too. Because of his wartime experiences, his health was poor and he suffered two major breakdowns. After the second in 1947, he began to concentrate on calligraphic inscriptions borrowing as much from the Welsh language as from religious texts in Latin. These functioned as something of a bridge between his poetry and his graphic art. His paintings, to which he returned, alluded to his deeply-held religious beliefs and the visionary elements of the work of William Blake whom, as a poet and painter, he held in special esteem.

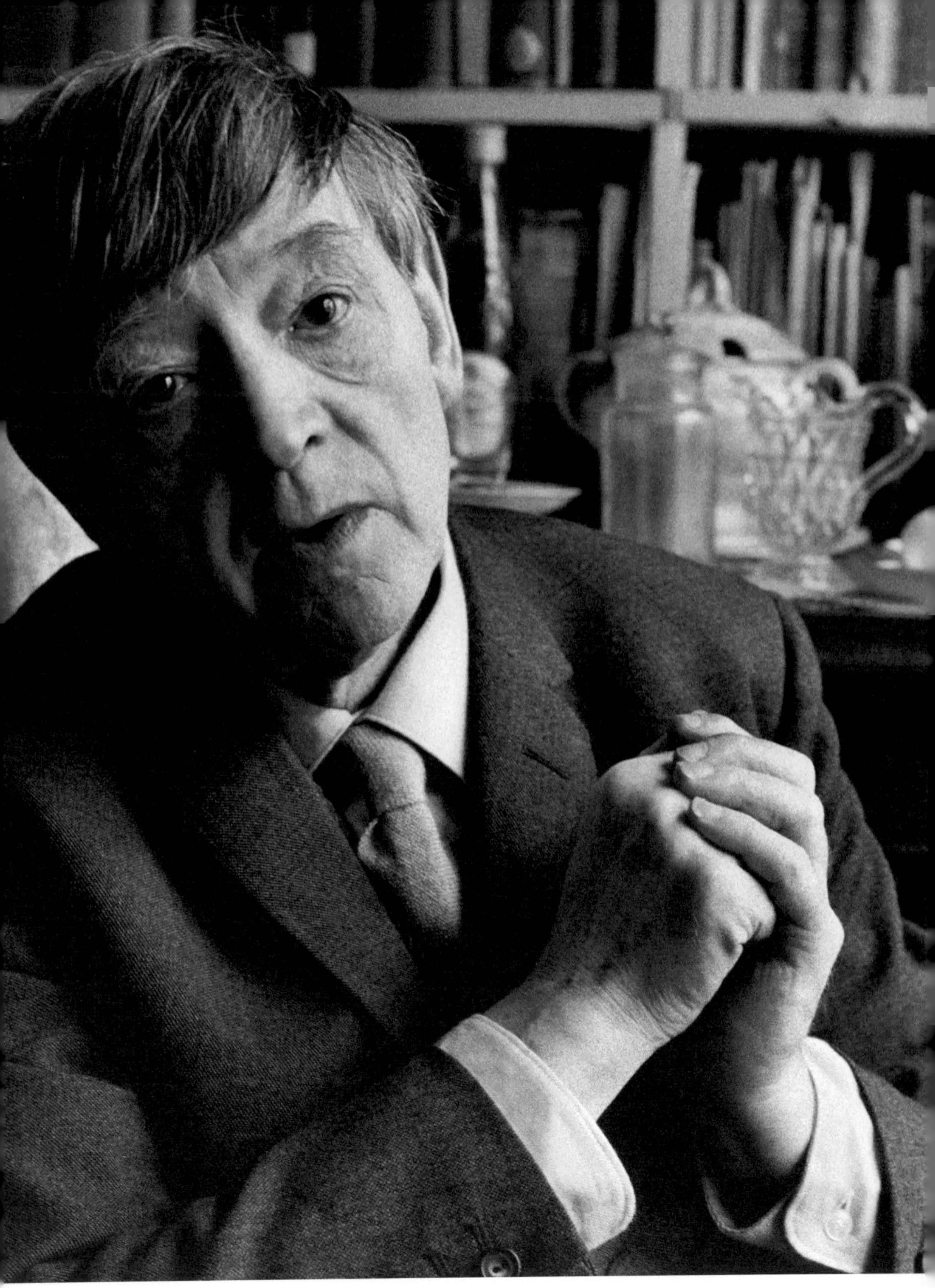

Roy de Maistre (1894–1968)

At home, Belgravia, 1964
Private View

Roy de Maistre was something of a curiosity not just among the new, exciting and distinguished of *Private View* but in the London art world itself. He was an Australian, born in New South Wales who lived in Belgravia in the grand manner of a late-Edwardian dilettante. Alone among the painters taken for the book he wore as his artist's 'smock' a pristine overall in a dashing pink. He was also anomalous for being one of the few painters who could not care if his work sold, possessing an inherited income and, as Bryan Robertson put it, 'a total incapacity for self-advertisement'. This had delayed major recognition of his geometric, Cubist-inspired paintings. That, and a propensity for commissioned portraiture that found its way into the private salon rather than the national institution. But if his work is still a little under-appreciated, his example as mentor and friend to Francis Bacon is not. He emerges in the younger painter's biography as an important early patron (he bought examples of Bacon's modernist furniture) and found him space in which to begin painting.

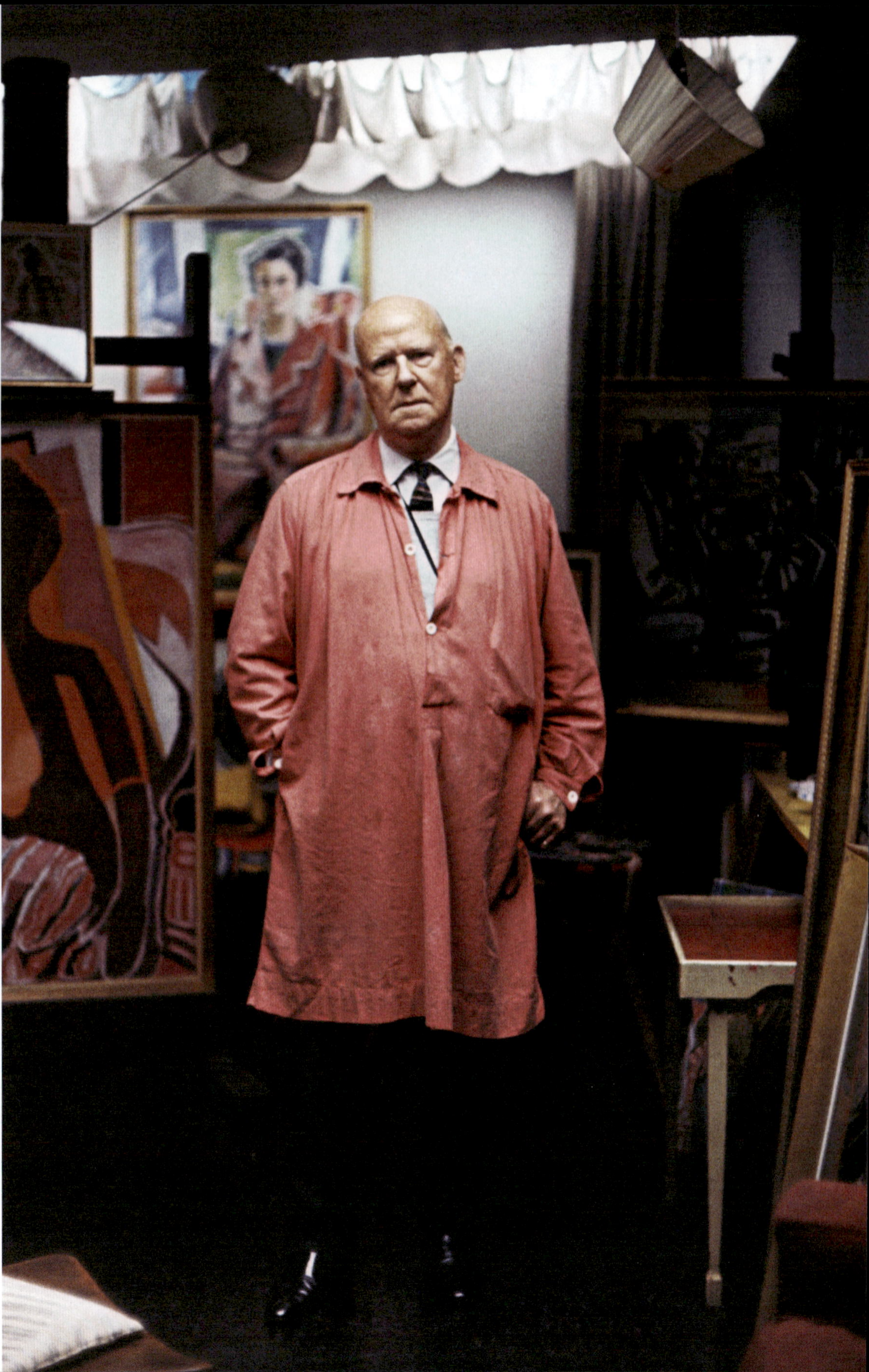

Reg Butler (1913–1981)

In his studio, Berkhamsted, 1964
Private View

In the mid-to late fifties, Butler became what was almost an anomaly: a British sculptor with an international reputation, something unheard of since Henry Moore's first successes in the pre-war decades. He had trained as an architect with a practice that won the commission for re-modelling the clock tower of Slough's town hall (completed in 1936). As a conscientious objector during the war, he worked as a blacksmith in West Sussex, which experience informed his early sculpture, a discipline he turned to in 1944 with no formal training. His first one-man show was held at the Hanover Gallery, London in 1949. With a growing reputation, he won the ICA competition to create a monument to 'The Unknown Political Prisoner'. The maquette for his composition of skeletal figures is with the Tate Gallery, the full version at 100 feet high never realised. By the time of *Private View*, Butler's sculpture had become more modest, at least in scale, he having discovered, as John Russell put it 'the sculptor's traditional subject: a beautiful girl, more or less undressed'.

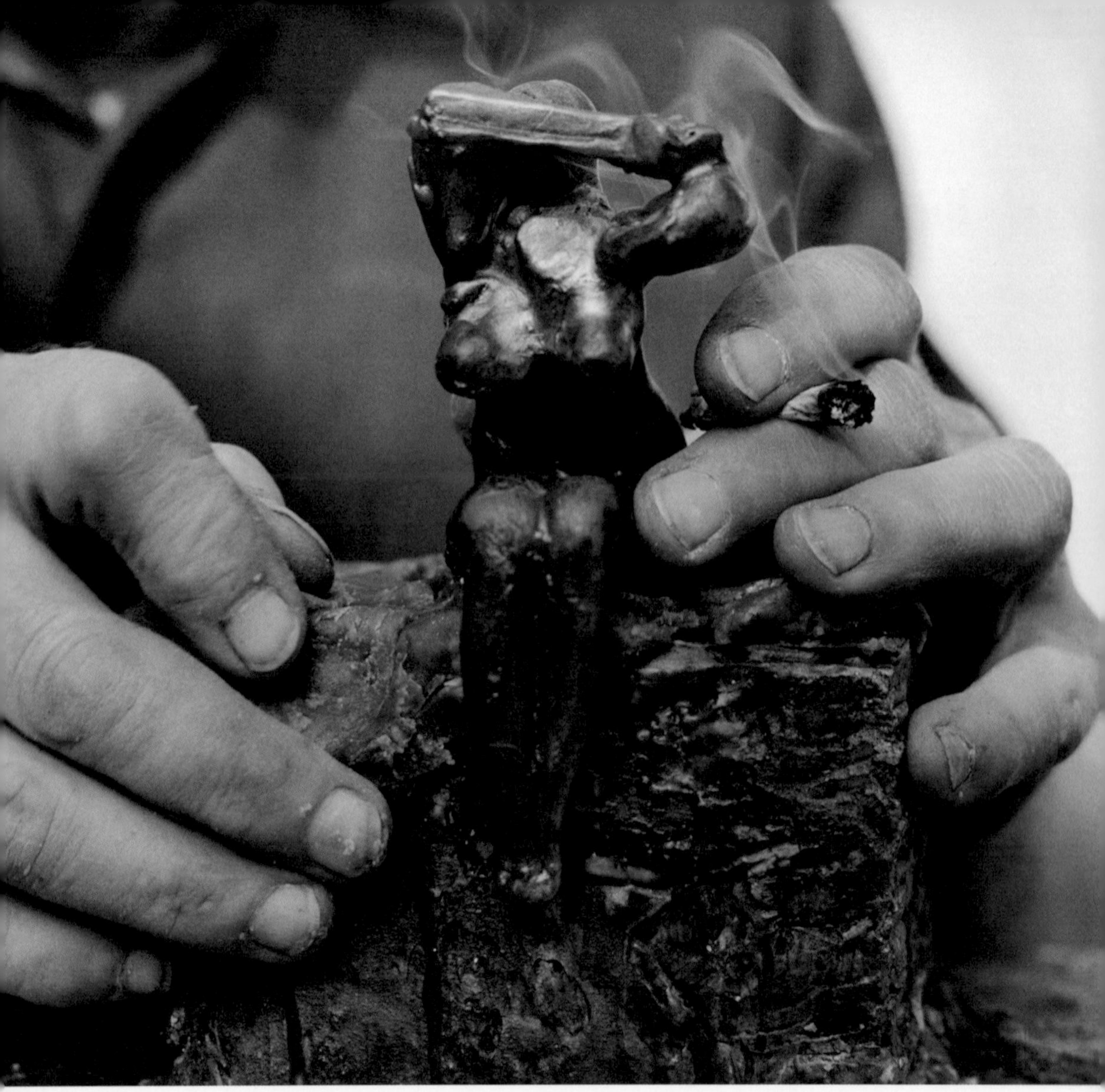

Patrick Caulfield (1936–2005)

At home, Primrose Hill, 1964
Private View

Patrick Caulfield's appearance at the front door of his home presented an apposite moment for Snowdon's camera, since many of his vivid, delineated Pop Art paintings took as their *mise-en-scène* objects from everyday domestic life: cheap table lamps, lightbulbs, mugs and beakers, fruit on a plate, water glasses. Stripped of detail, their flat readily-identifiable shapes hinted at the mass-consumerism at the heart of urban life. His eye often alit on what might be best described as discredited and sentimental subject matter: ships in the harbour, overblown classical or religious scenes or, as Bryan Robertson put it, 'occasionally plebeian, mass-produced tastelessness'. Beautifully rendered, though not in the painstaking detail that might have made them ironic, Caulfield has professed to celebrate the dimly-lit, artificial world of the plush-walled pub, the sterile hotel reception lobby and the suburban domestic interior focused around leatherette and polished wood. 'I have a lot of affection for things', he once remarked, 'like a wallpaper that I might have seen, which has a certain feeling for me...but I don't embrace kitsch, as such, it's just elements of life.' The painting on the left is now in the Pallant House Gallery collection.

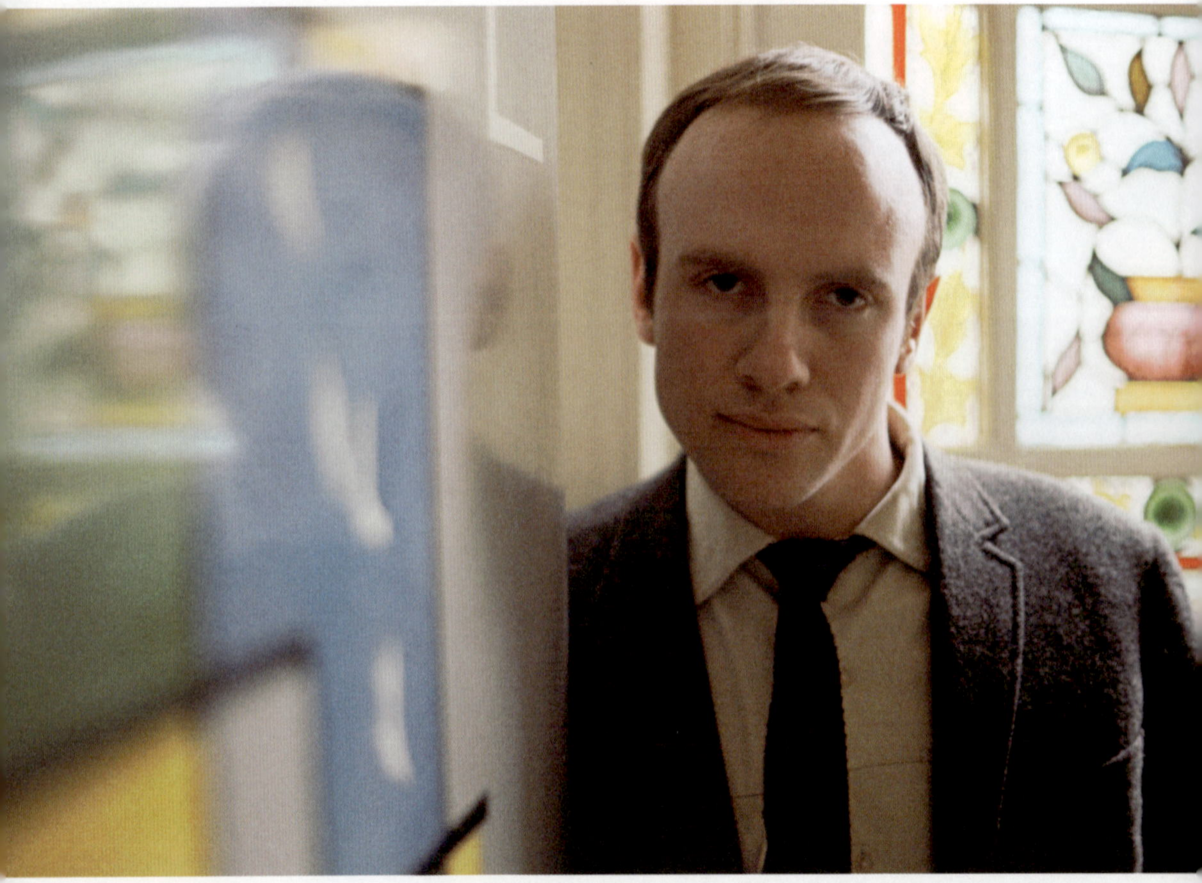

Sidney Nolan (1917–1992)

At lowtide, Putney, 1965
Private View

This portrait was taken on the Thames mudflats beneath Nolan's London house. A show at the Whitechapel Gallery included work that had prompted Kenneth Clark to suggest him as one of the major painters of the twentieth-century and for the sake of that, he should leave Australia. Born in Melbourne, he studied briefly at the School of Art attached to the National Gallery of Victoria. His war service saw him despatched to north-western Victoria and in painting its huge agrarian vistas, he almost single-handedly resurrected the tradition of Australian landscape painting. In 1945, he began a series of folkloric paintings on the exploits of the bushman Ned Kelly, with whose renegade exploits he had an affinity. A bold experimenter, he made another Ned Kelly series (1945–7) in enamel paint and landscapes with PVA paint on white board; a late mural was made in wax crayon and fabric dye. Nolan's subject matter was far-ranging: from the explorers Burke and Wills and the ANZAC's doomed Gallipoli campaign to frozen Antarctic landscapes and tropical African flora and fauna.

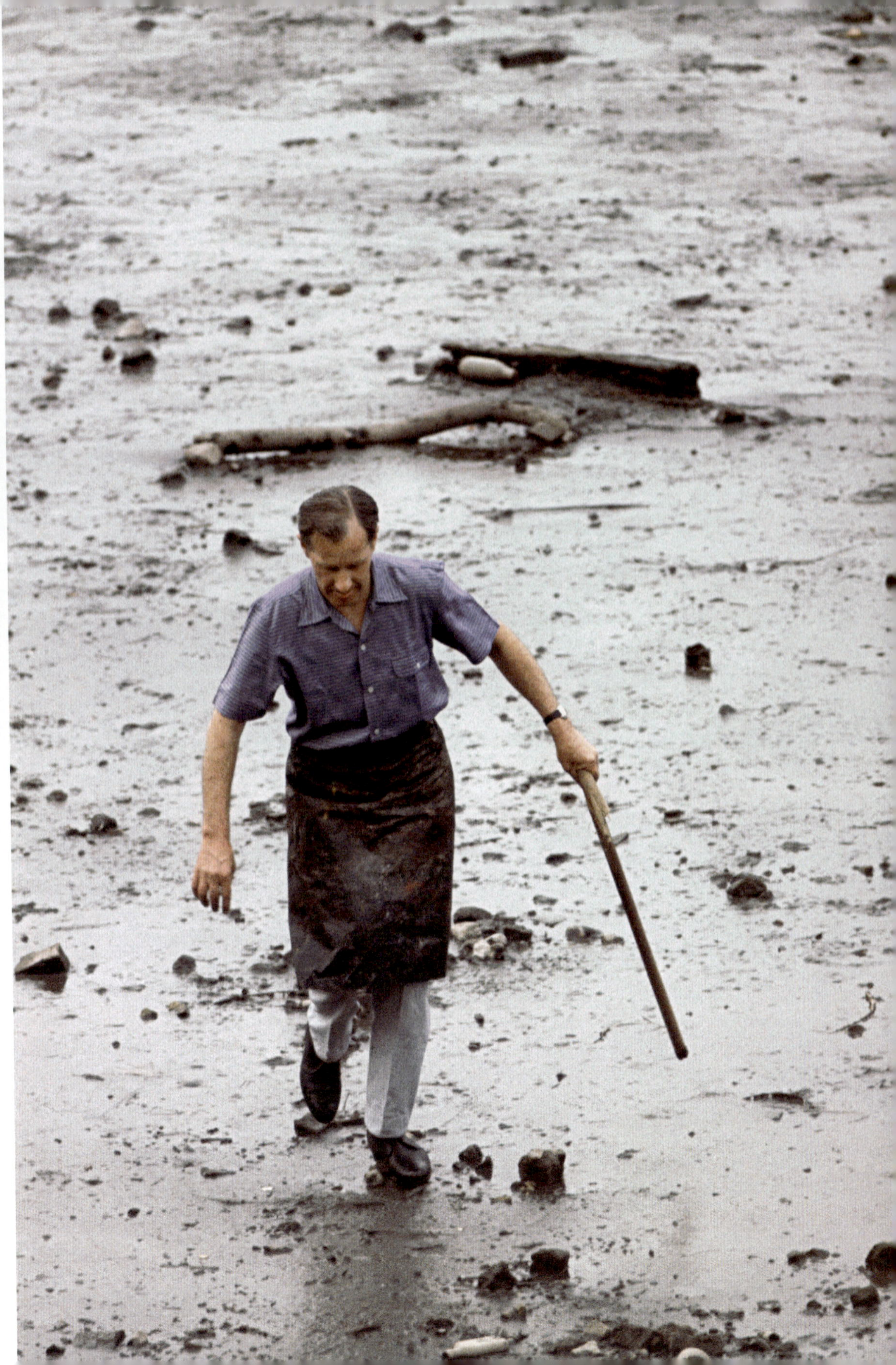

Gilbert and George

Gilbert Proesch (b.1943) and George Passmore (b.1942)

The Sunday Times studio, Holborn, 1970
The Sunday Times Magazine

Taken at face value, the colourful, conceptual art of Gilbert and George exists purely to shock. An interest in defining notions of male sexuality, especially in its working-class teenage manifestation, and predilection for 'taboo' subjects, serves rather to de-sensitize the public to the extent that it might grow to accept, perhaps even admire, what formerly it might have abhorred. Since leaving art college, Gilbert and George have made their lives their art as self-designated 'living sculptures'. When Snowdon photographed them they stood on a table in art galleries painted gold and singing a deadpan version of *Underneath the Arches*, an English music-hall classic, often for hours at a time. Always on show in immaculate tailored suits, they appear on the streets of London clad as quintessential English bachelors but with the inseparability and habitualness of old ladies at a seaside town. As 'living sculptures' they seem to welcome photographers at all times. It can be safely said that none have revealed anything about the artists that the duo did not want known. In interviews they speak as one and are richly ironical: 'We don't enjoy life, no. We already gave our life away for our art. We're the dead rabbit on the plate. We want to spill our blood, our brains, our seed for art'.

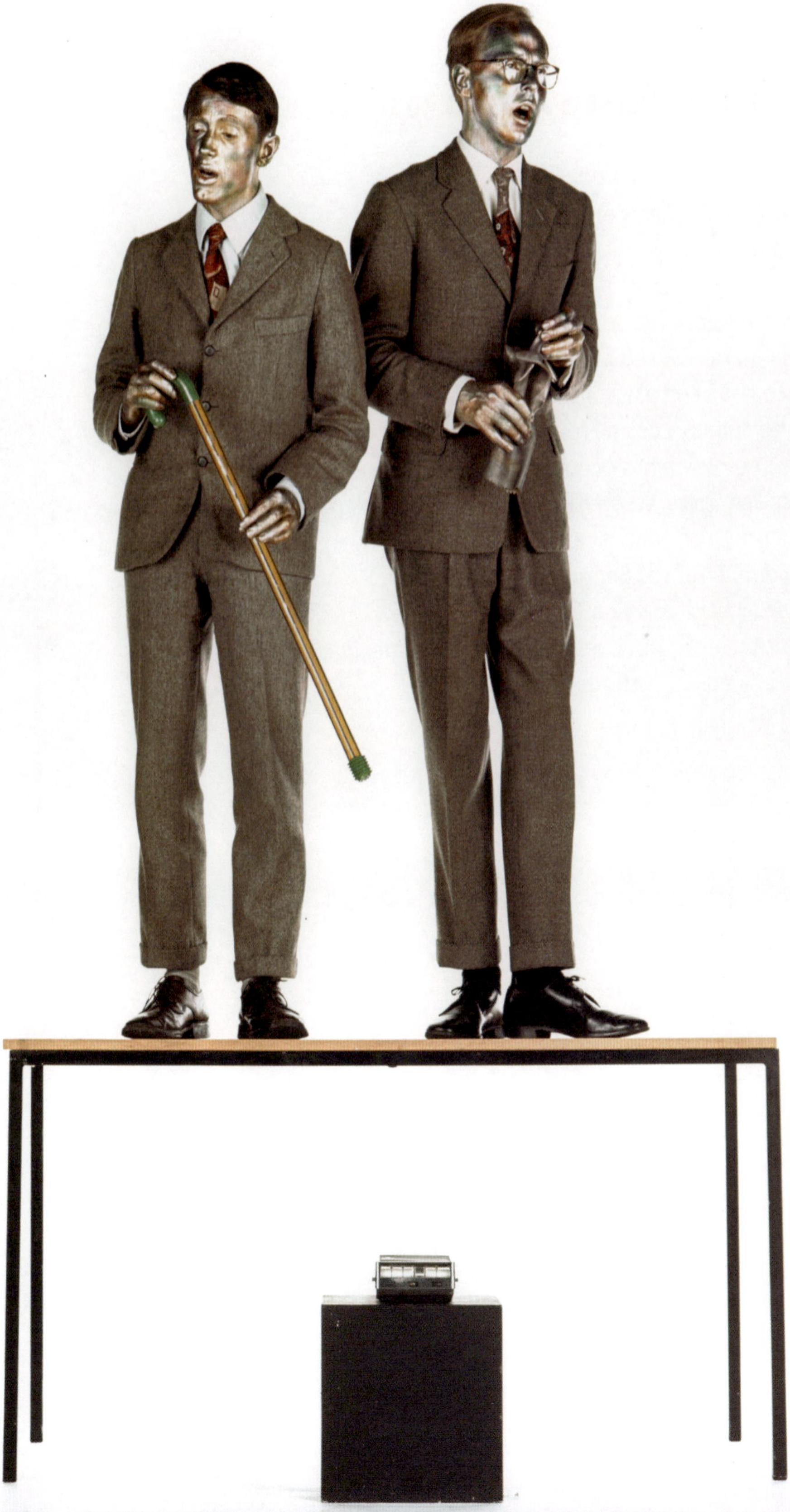

Frank Auerbach (b.1931)

In his studio, Camden Town, 1982
Vogue

Born in Berlin into a Jewish family, Auerbach was dispatched to England in 1939. He studied painting under David Bomberg and in the years since has been associated with a 'School of London' in the company of his friends Lucian Freud, Michael Andrews and Francis Bacon. Since 1954 Auerbach has occupied a small and self-contained studio in Camden Town, where he has for many years painted portrait studies of a group of people close to him and the nearby landscape of north London. This was Snowdon's second visit. He had photographed Auerbach 20 years earlier for *Private View* in virtually the same position – out of necessity not lack of imagination. Only a few of the pinned-up pictures had changed.

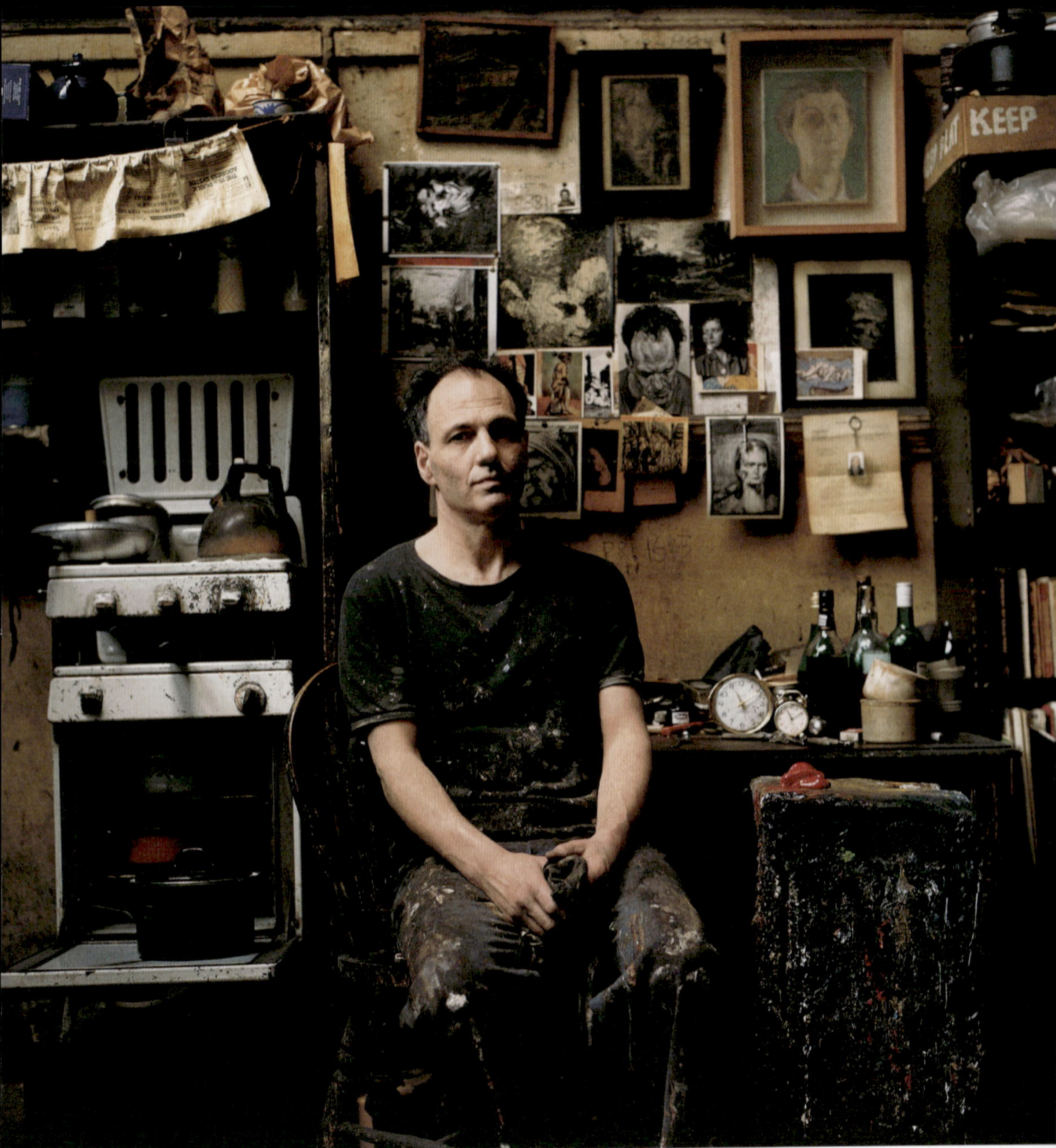
KEEP

Anish Kapoor (b.1954)

In his studio, Wapping, 1983
Vogue

'Because art can be about anything', Anish Kapoor told *Vogue* early in his career, 'it is very important that it should be about something'. Sitting with five works in progress, Kapoor emphasised the distinctions between painting and sculpture by fashioning shapes from the painter's prerequisite, paint, in the powdered pigment form from which it is made. These mounds of colour reflected the mounds of highly-coloured spices and pigments to be found in Indian markets (Kapoor was born in Bombay). Subsequent works, larger in scale and more solid and less transient, evoked the complementary, if contrasting dualities of India's spiritual and mystical heritage: earth and sky, life and the afterlife, permanence and insubstantiality. Kapoor represented Britain at the Venice Biennale in 1990 where he won first prize, and the following year received the Turner Prize. He received much acclaim both critical and popular for *Marsysas* (2002), a gargantuan installation created to fill the Turbine Hall of Tate Modern which challenged viewers' perceptions of space.

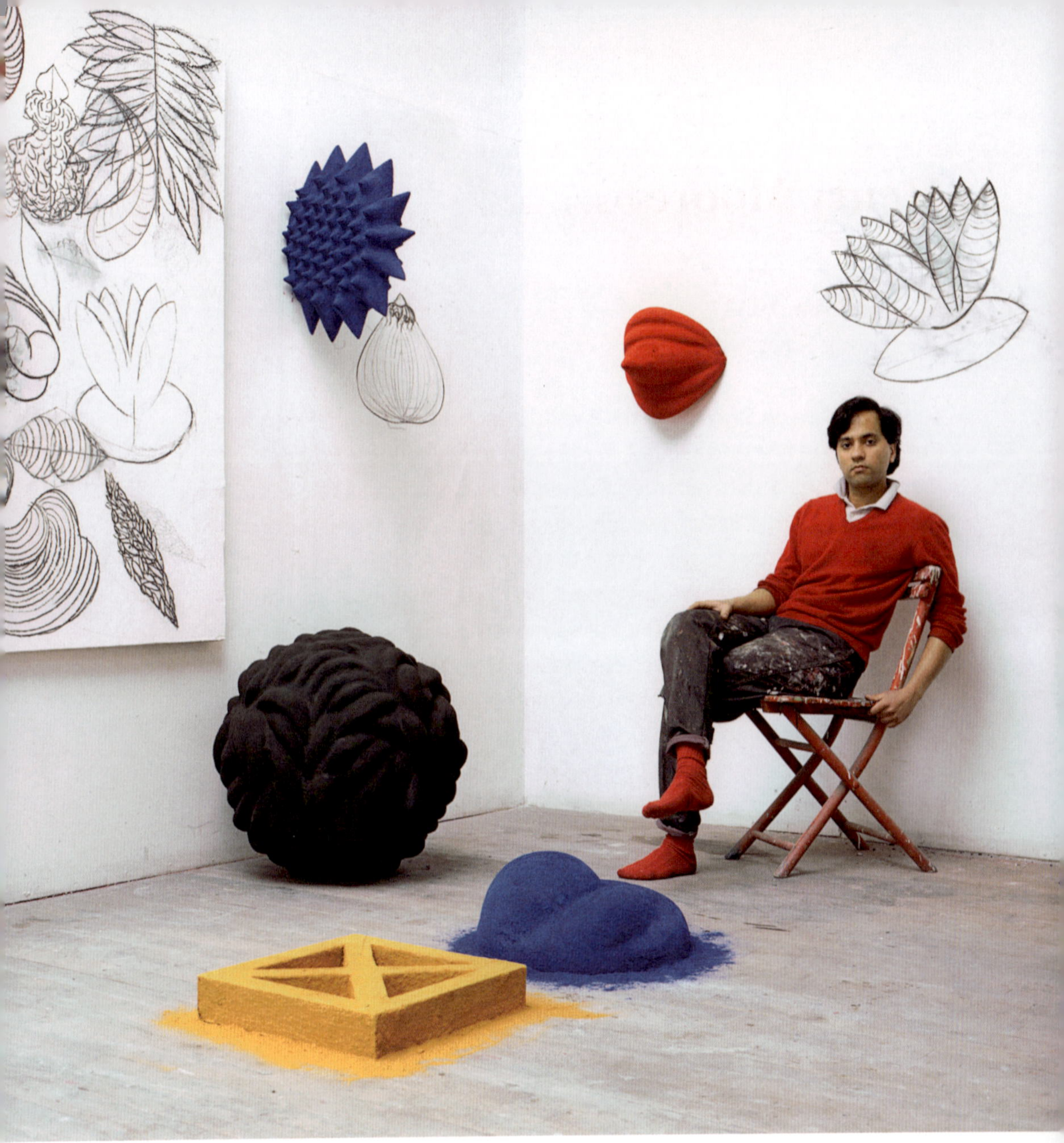

Henry Moore (1898–1986)

Much Hadham, 1983
The Sunday Times Magazine

This was taken on Snowdon's third visit to Moore's Hertfordshire home, Hoglands. The first and second, in 1963 and 1964, were for *Private View*. Of all the artists recorded therein, Moore is referred to the most, followed by Francis Bacon. For John Russell, both Moore and Bacon were, in their distinct ways, pivotal to the direction British art took in the twentieth century. 'We are aware', he wrote, 'that love and hate are inseparable, that the instinct of self-destruction plays a large part in human affairs, and that even the classic relationship of mother and child has within it elements of cruelty, and separation, and psychic warfare, and irreparable loss. Somebody has had to invent a valid imagery for these new concepts, and that somebody is Henry Moore.' In this close up of the sculptor's hand, he cradles a maquette of a mother and child which, Russell pointed out, was one of his recurring themes. Moore refused a knighthood in 1951 but became a Companion of Honour in 1955 and accepted the Order of Merit in 1963.

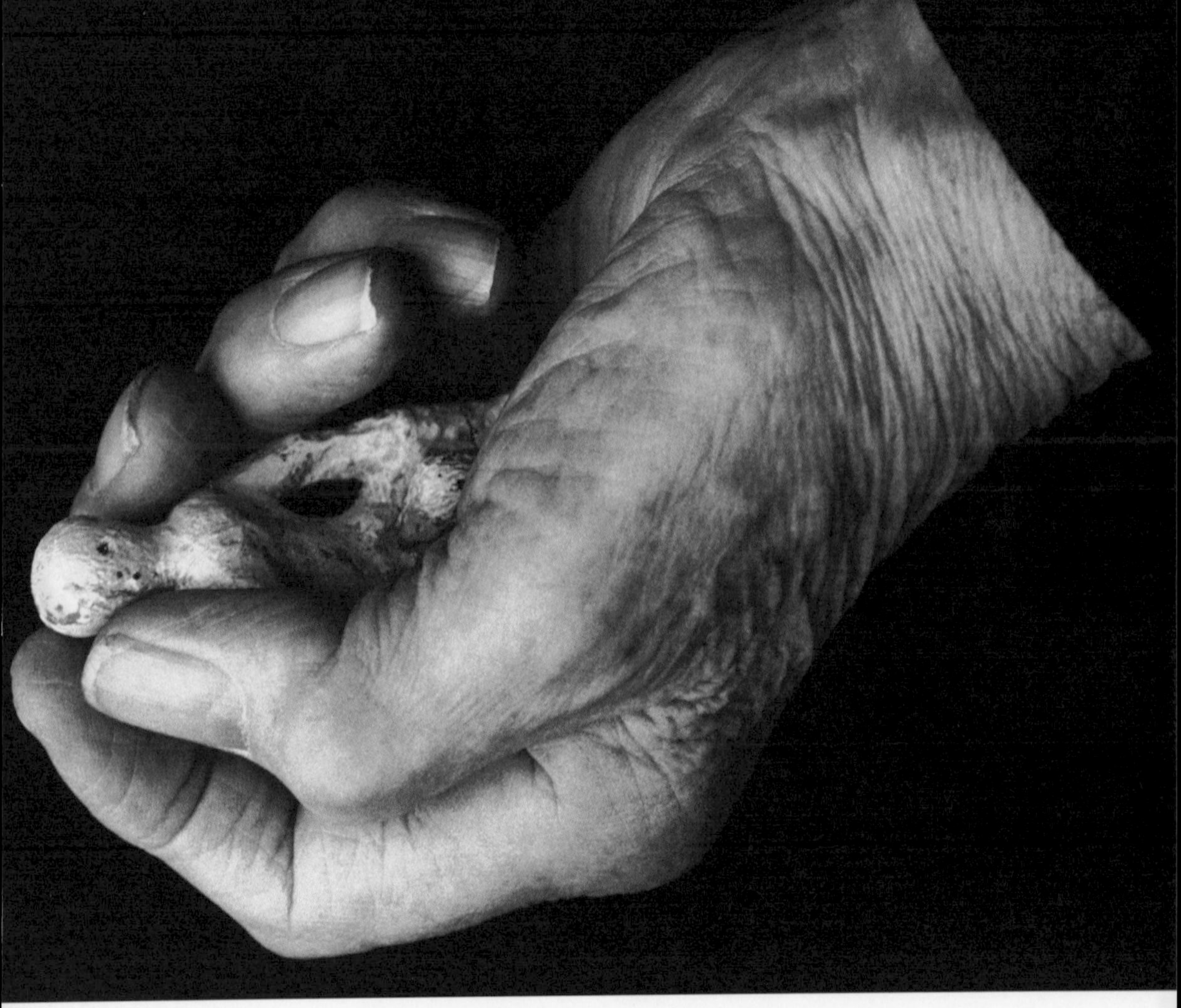

Bill Woodrow (b.1948)

Outside his studio, Clapham, 1983
Vogue

Woodrow emerged in the late 1970s along with sculptors Tony Cragg and Richard Deacon, but came to prominence in 1981 with his first set-piece made from re-activated junk. This was *Twin-Tub with Guitar*, which, to coin a well-worn consumer slogan, did exactly what it said on the tin: a guitar fashioned out of a discarded white-goods durable. Kettles became insects; bent ironing boards became tribal masks; a vacuum cleaner, old maps and car doors became a symbolic African elephant head. As the transformations became more *recherché,* the mother object reached a peculiar state of grace: still recognisable but unable to reassume again its original proportions. 'Car doors', William Feaver wrote in *Vogue*, 'serve as slabs of stuff as dreams are made on…' Woodrow's 'site-specific' installations are particularly alchemic. For a show at the Walker Art Gallery, he plundered the basements of the gallery itself for raw material; for New York, a panther out of a yellow taxicab; in Genoa, a tree out of olive oil cans. Snowdon photographed him outside his studio with the carcass of a Mobylette scooter found on the edge of a French motorway, 'which confused custom officials'.

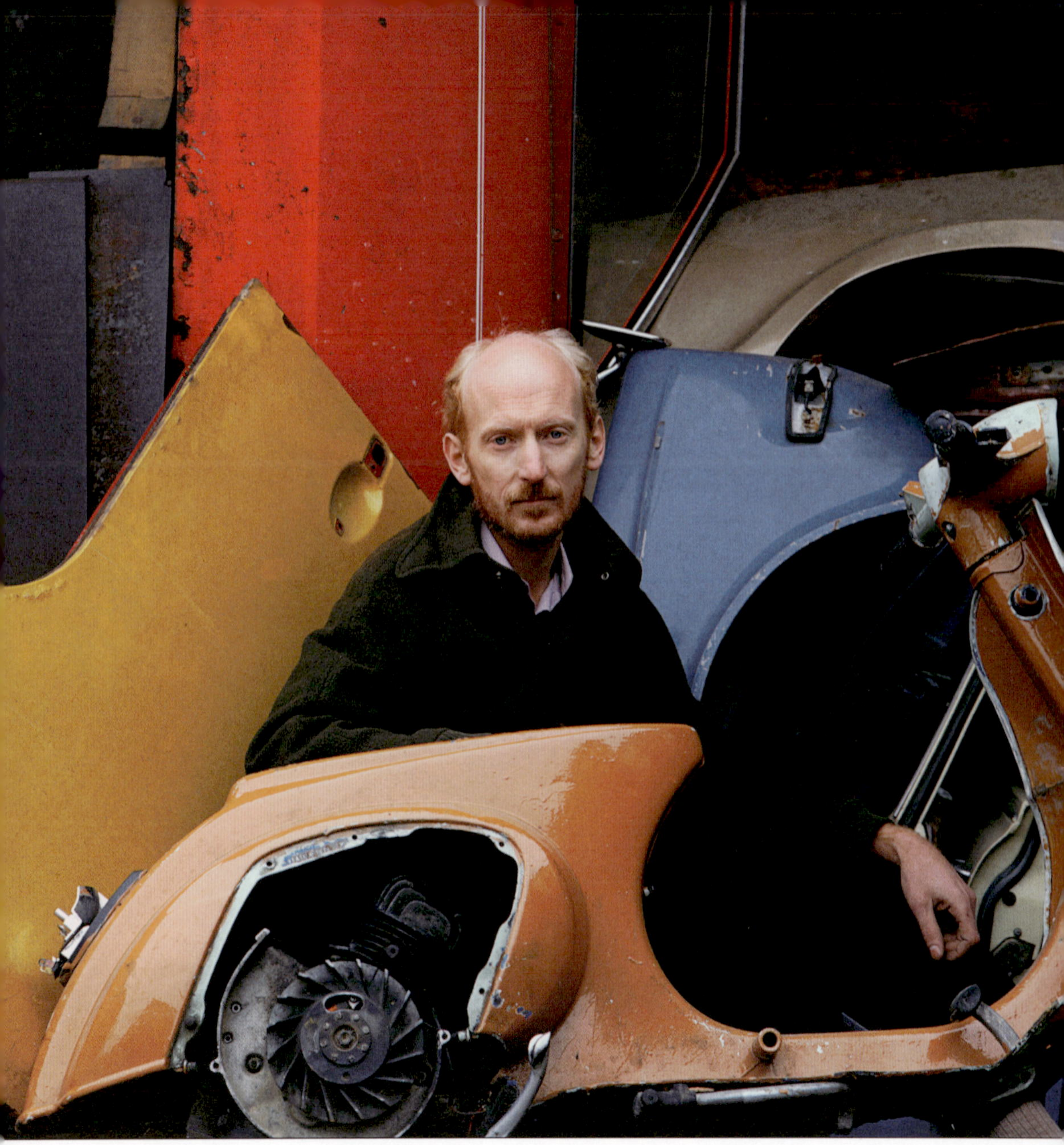

Craigie Aitchison (b.1926)

Outside his home, Kennington, 1984
The Sunday Times Magazine

The son of an eminent Scottish judge and former Lord Advocate, Aitchison came relatively late to painting, having first studied law at Edinburgh University and Middle Temple London. Though he briefly considered fashion design as a new departure, he enrolled instead at the Slade, London (1952–5). He was taught by William Coldstream whom he much admired, but found early inspiration in the landscape of rural Italy and childhood memories of the bleaker hills of the Isle of Arran. His much painted Bedlington terriers have found themselves set against both these landscapes, as well as next to simply rendered churches or beneath radiant Nativity stars, as objects of peaceable devotion.

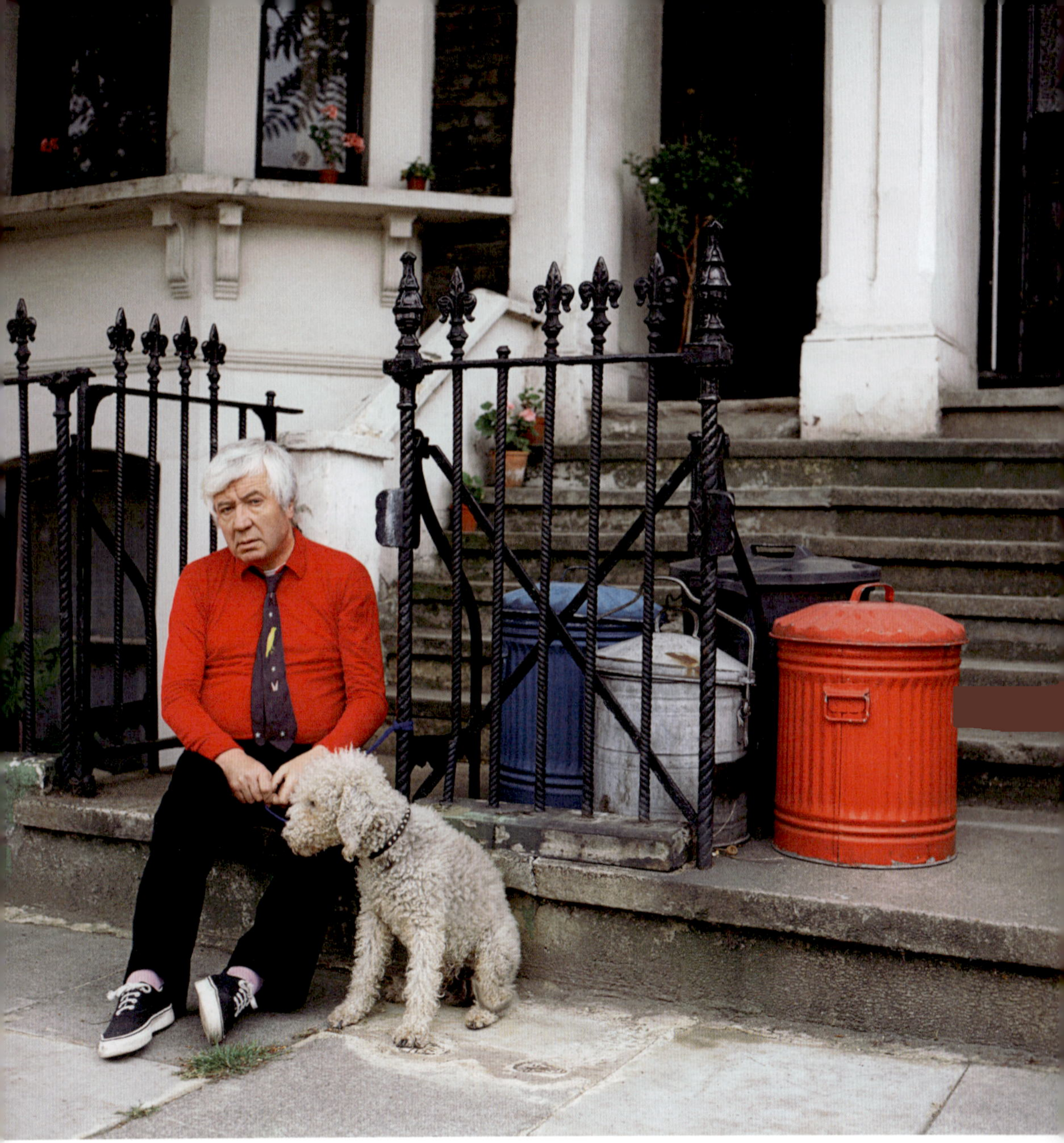

Ian McCulloch (b.1935)

Outside his studio, Glasgow, 1986
Vogue

One of Scotland's most distinguished artists, McCulloch studied at Glasgow School of Art and held his first one-man show after a year spent on a travelling scholarship. Apart from painting, he is known for his mural work at Glasgow's Italian Centre and for his designs for stained glass. He has also shown lino-cuts, woodcuts and ceramics, and has scavenged for found object constructions. In the mid-1980s, when a renaissance in Scottish art was evident, Snowdon made the trip north to photograph several artists for *Vogue*. McCulloch recalled his sitting recently: 'the photograph was taken outside my studio which was then situated in the basement of the School of Architecture in Strathclyde University in central Glasgow. Since the studio was windowless, Snowdon decided to take the photograph outside. At that time I was working on very large acrylic paintings and frequently applied the paint with my hands....'

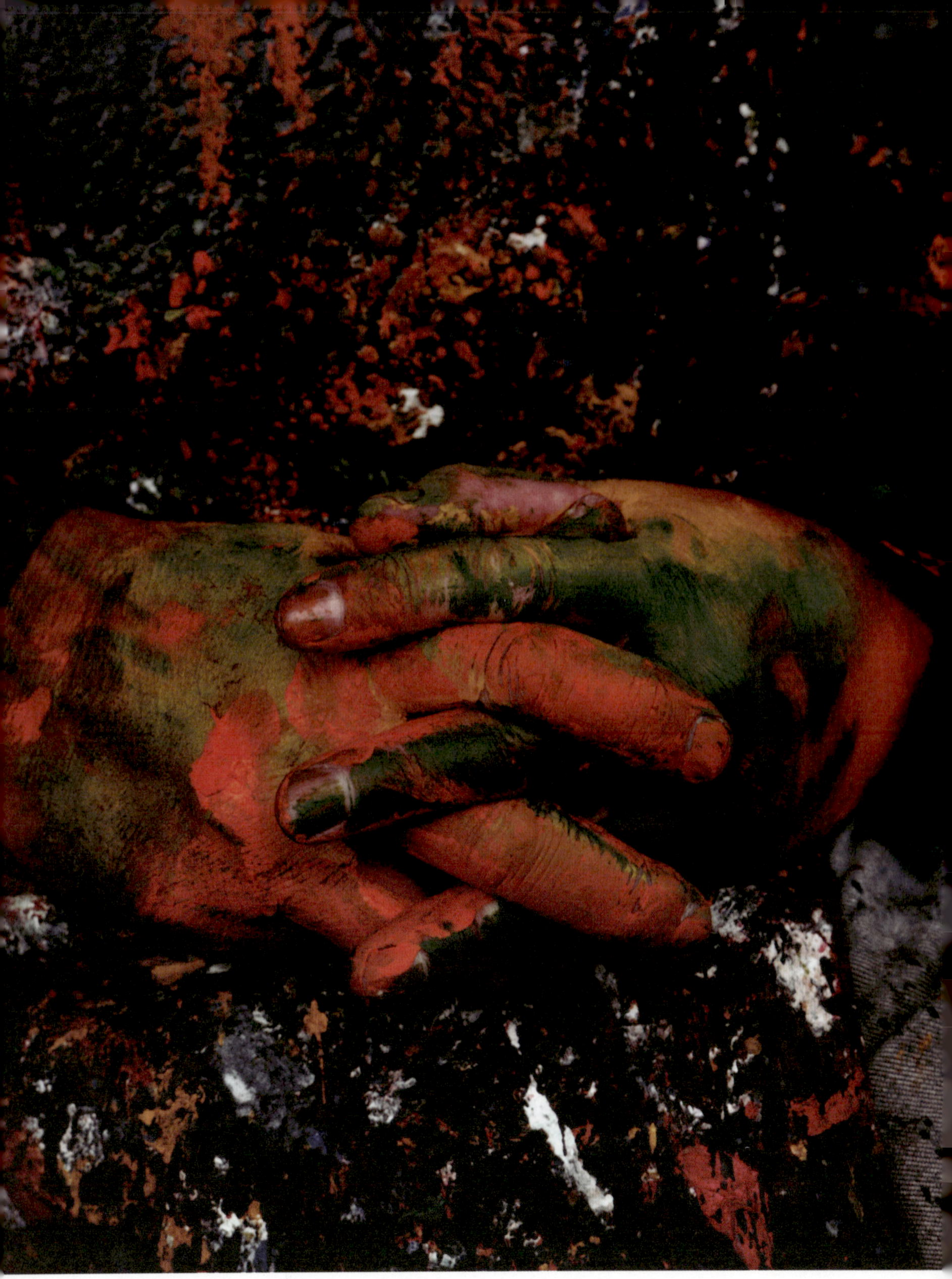

Sean Scully (b.1945)

In his studio, Dulwich, 1987
Vogue

Answering an interviewer who asked him why he made art, Scully replied, 'I think that I wanted to do something in my life that wasn't ordinary - which wasn't normal. I couldn't bear to live my life as a normal person, put another way: conventionally. So if I had a choice between living in suburbia and being dead, I would rather be dead.' A leading abstract painter, Scully, who was born in Ireland and based in England for 30 years, took American citizenship in 1983. His paintings, all variations on a thick stripe, are heavily worked and reworked and suggest the grid of his adopted New York's urban layout, or giant flags battered by heavy weather or the heat of battle. 'You paint the stripe', he told *Vogue*, 'and then you paint the stripe. And by doing that you reveal changes in yourself'. Shortly after this sitting, he was nominated for the Turner Prize (and again in 1993). He stands in front of the melancholic and washed out *Empty Heart* (1987) or rather, assumes a variety of karate poses. He is an enthusiast to black belt standard, a non-aggressive participant.

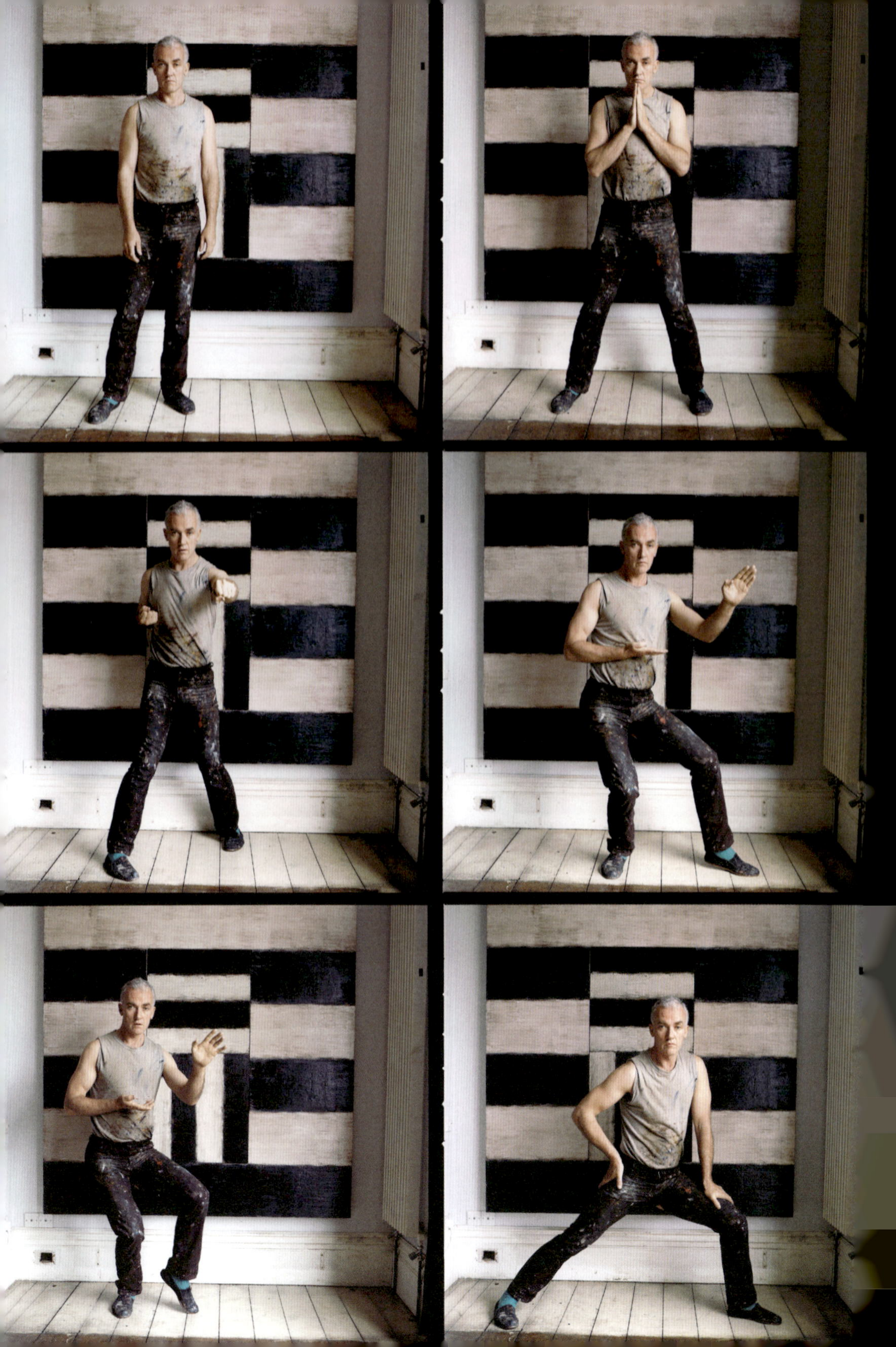

Cecil Collins (1908–1989)

In his studio, Chelsea, 1987
The Sunday Times Magazine

When Snowdon photographed Cecil Collins in his cramped London studio, the painter was mostly a forgotten figure. His mystical paintings, once compared to William Blake's, were dense with quasi-mythological allusion, arcane symbols, stylised views of the landscape and female figures that shared for nearly 60 years one face: that of his wife Elisabeth. Two years after Snowdon's visit, the Tate Gallery gave him a timely retrospective. He died within a month of its opening, impervious to the acclaim that had eluded him for most of his life. At his death, several hundred of his visionary paintings and drawings remained ceiling-high in his small apartment alongside scribbled *aides memoires* to quotidian tasks, such as 'Wash neck' and 'Take care of feet when crossing road'.

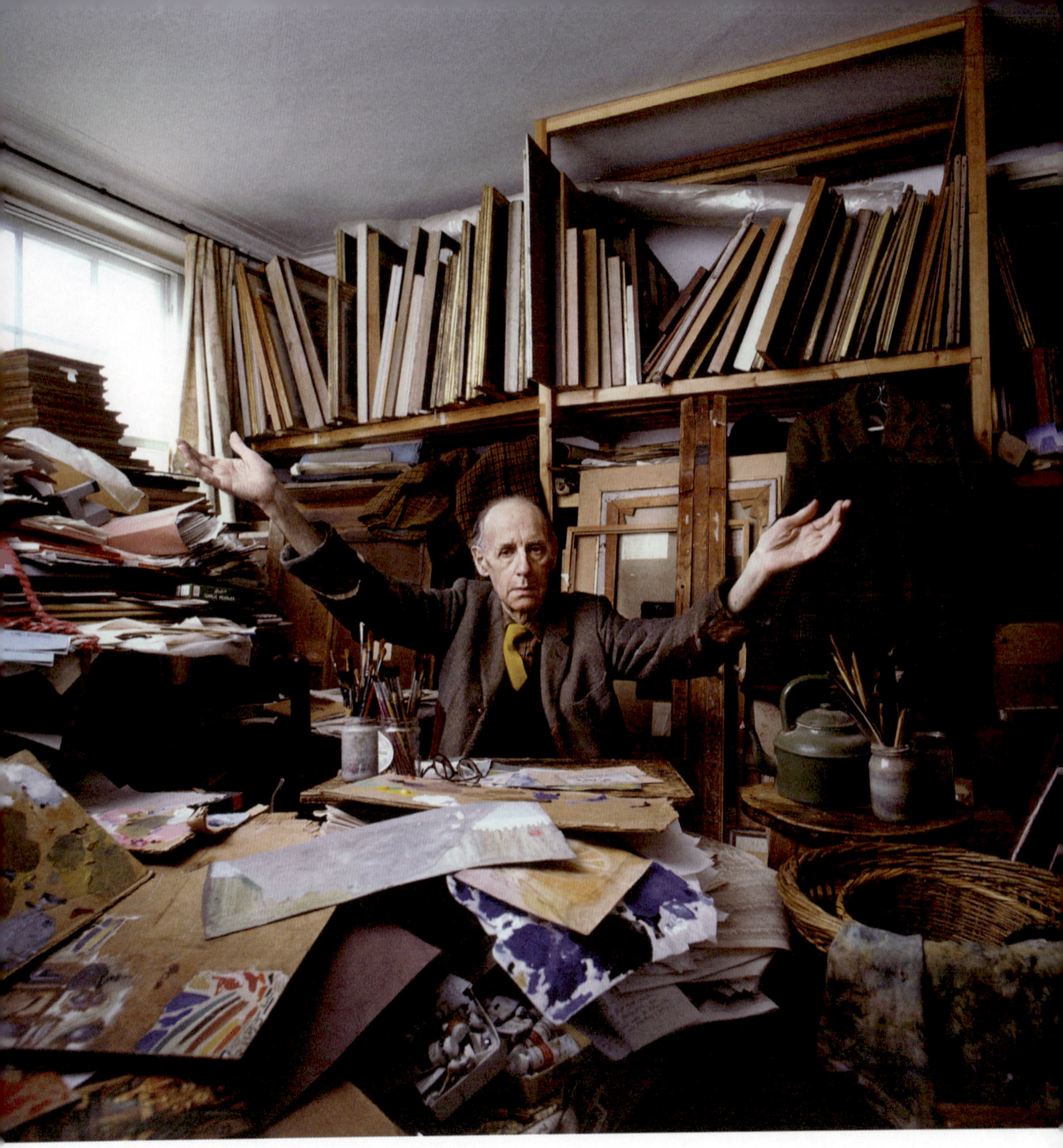

Richard Deacon (b.1949)

In his studio, Brixton, 1988
HG (American *House & Garden*)

The sculptor – though he prefers the term 'fabricator' – represented Wales in the 2007 Venice Biennale. He emerged in the 1980s, part of the new generation who worked with found objects and industrial materials rather than the constituents of traditional sculpture, and in the process, avoided carving or modelling in favour of welding and riveting. As such, his fabrications are often wrought from workaday materials, such as laminated wood and sheet and corrugated metals and do not attempt to hide their process of manufacture. The theme of containment recurs in Deacon's work as evinced by a piece in Tate's collection *Struck Dumb* (1988), a rounded organic form of welded steel. Deacon's first solo show was held in 1978 in Brixton where he kept his studio. This was followed in time by major exhibitions at the Tate Gallery (1985) and the Whitechapel Gallery (1998). Deacon was twice nominated for the Turner Prize which he won in 1987. He was awarded a CBE in 1999.

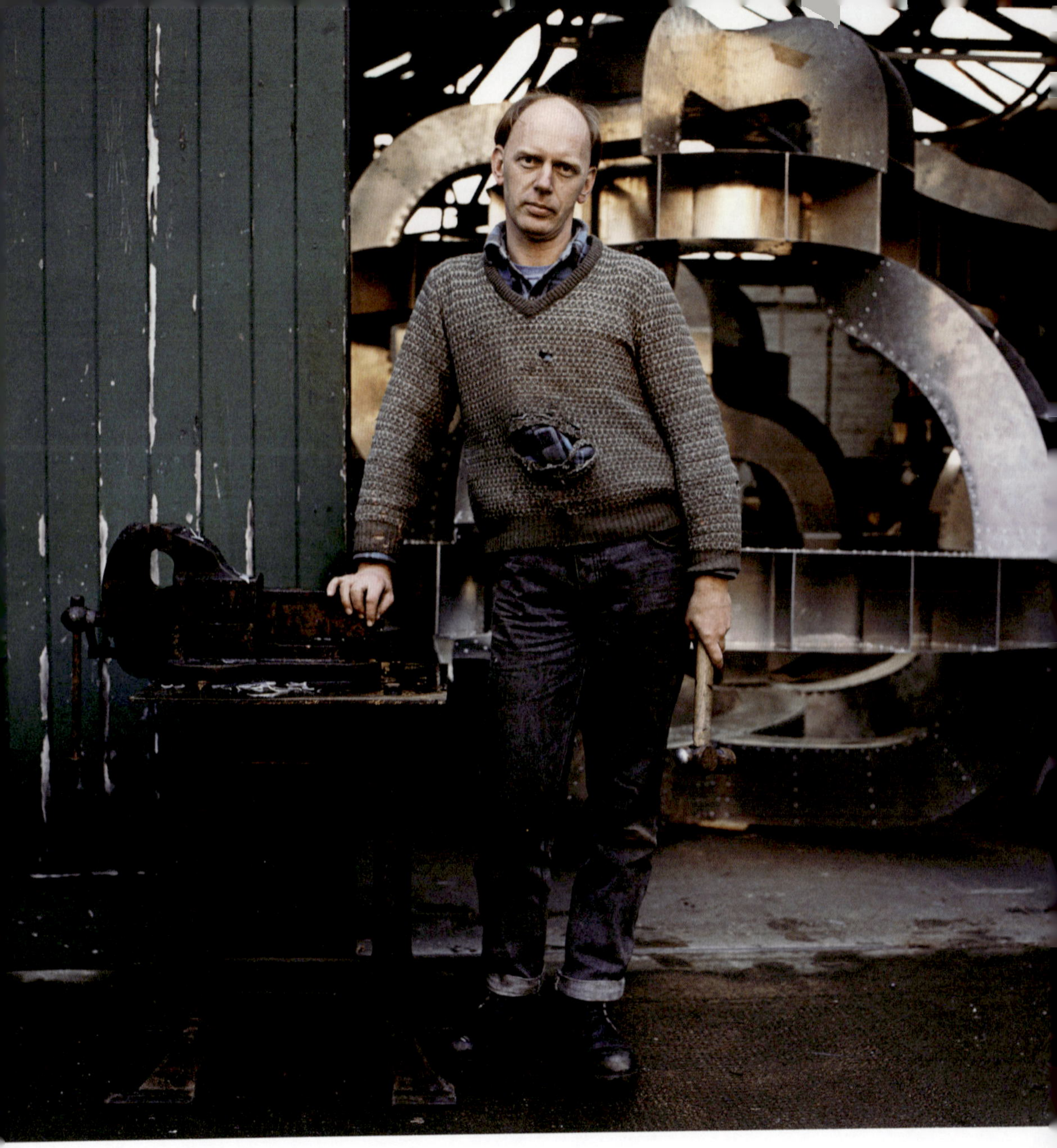

Michael Craig-Martin (b.1941)

At home, Kentish Town, 1988
HG (American *House & Garden*)

Craig-Martin is included in Snowdon's survey of British art by dint of his living and working in England since 1966. He was born an Irishman and spent his childhood in the United States, where he also studied painting. He is known not just for his striking conceptual art but also as a mentor to a generation of young artists, whom he taught at Goldsmith's College, London. The list of alumni includes Ian Davenport, Damien Hirst, Gary Hume and Lisa Milroy. Craig-Martin's early work referred to the contemporary American artists he then admired, such as Jasper Johns and Donald Judd. His first solo exhibition was held in 1969 and he was a vivid part of the groundbreaking show of British conecptual art, *The New Art* at the Hayward Gallery, London in 1972. His recent artworks have concentrated on a formal, though idealised, range of familiar, often domestic, motifs such as stools, chairs, tables and stepladders. These are boldly outlined and then more boldly coloured in.

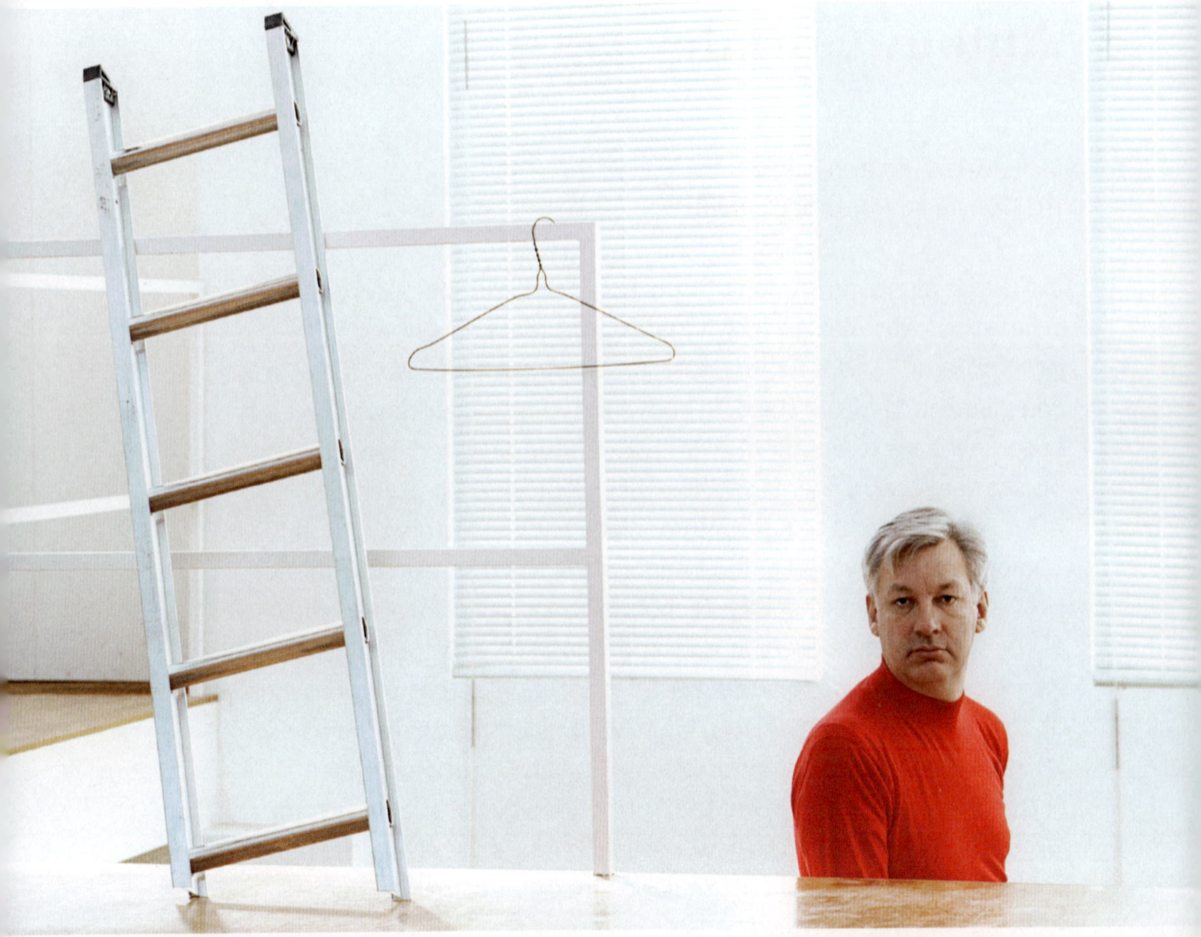

Antony Gormley (b.1950)

In his studio, Brixton, 1988
HG (American *House & Garden*)

'He is that rare thing', Antony Gormley's friend Will Self observed, 'a fine artist who makes highly visible works that connect with the general public'. This is not to understate it. *Angel of the North*, completed in 1998 and standing above the A1 near Gateshead, has become a place of unofficial pilgrimage, so too *Another Place* (1997), his seaward gazing figures on the beach at Crosby near Liverpool. After studying archaeology, anthropology and the history of art at Cambridge, he travelled to India and Sri Lanka and studied Buddhism. His Cambridge contemporary, Nicholas Serota, gave him a solo show at the Whitechapel Gallery in 1981, and in 1994 he won the Turner Prize for *Field for the British Isles* (1993), an installation of tens of thousands of terracotta figures. Invariably, his sculpture centres on the human form, usually his own but not exclusively. Snowdon photographed him in his former studio in Brixton, surrounded by fibreglass casts for works then cast in lead. His newer studio in King's Cross, has the feel, according to *Vogue*, 'of a science fiction medical centre. The human form is everywhere.'

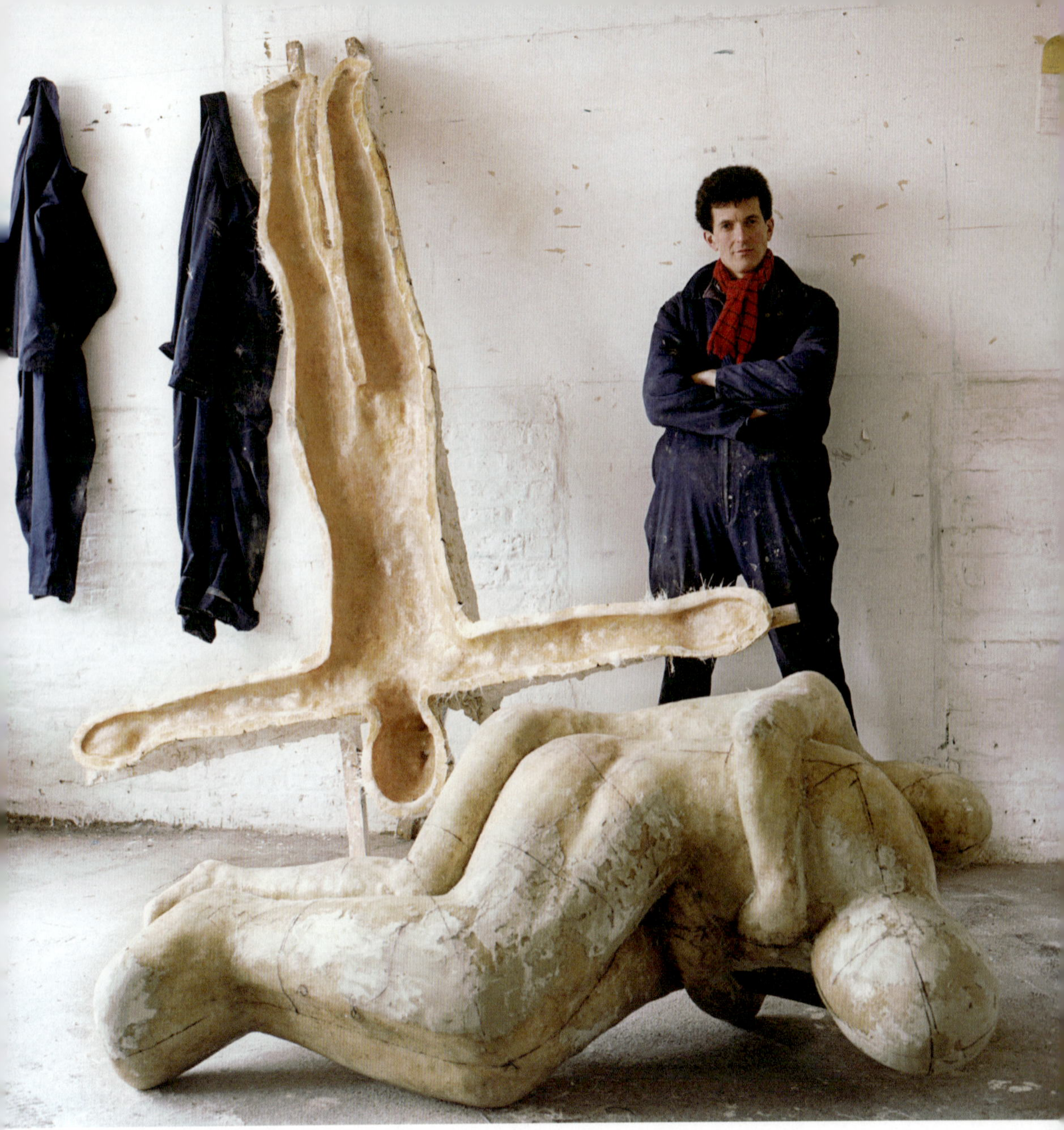

Eduardo Paolozzi (1924–2005)

In his studio, Chelsea, 1988
Vogue

By the 1980s Eduardo Paolozzi was something of an establishment figure. He began to accept public commissions, including a giant head for Euston Square and the now familiar tesserated mosaic designs for Tottenham Court Road tube station both in London. His four-metre high bronze of Isaac Newton cast in 1995 for the piazza of the British Library became a London landmark. Paolozzi had been awarded the CBE in 1968 and in 1989 was knighted. In 1994, The Dean Gallery, part of the Scottish National Gallery of Modern Art accepted his gift of many works in all media as well as his extensive library. The gallery recreated his working London studio and installed a giant robotic sculpture of the kind that cut through several gallery levels to touch the ceiling. In 1996, increasingly a presence in Edinburgh where he spent his childhood, Paolozzi was commissioned to make large-scale sculptures for its university and accepted the post of Visiting Professor at Edinburgh College of Art, where he had studied briefly.

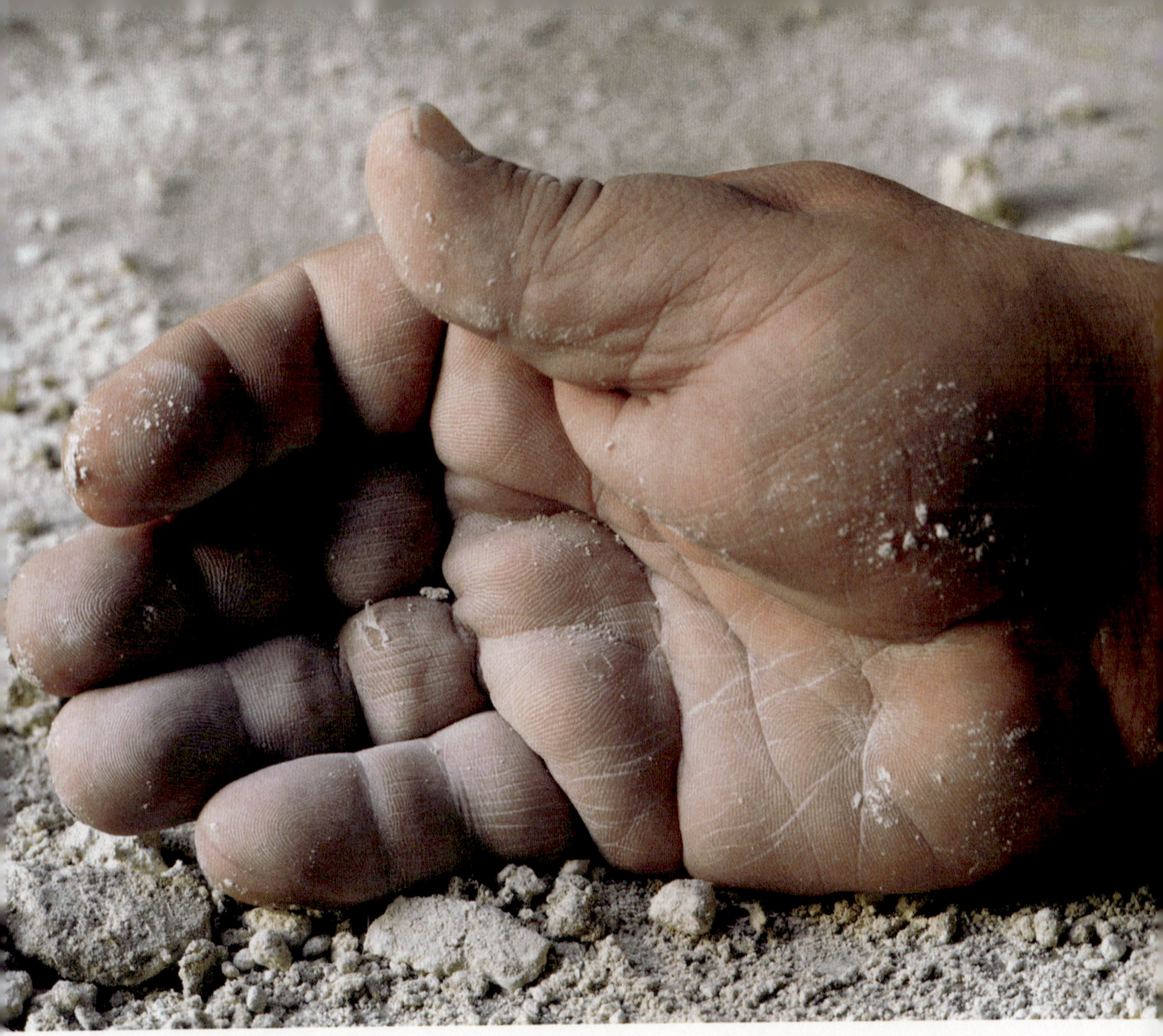

Damien Hirst (b.1965)

In Conran Studios, West London, 1991
Vogue

This portrait accompanied the first major profile of the artist to appear in a mainstream magazine. Styled by the late Isabella Blow, it incorporated motifs that have – like the plastic crabs on his profile – attached themselves to him ever since, at least in the popular imagination. The record £9.65million paid in June 2007 for *Lullaby Spring*, a trademark medicine cabinet installation, was the highest price then paid at auction for the work of a living artist. Snowdon's portrait was taken two years after Hirst had graduated from Goldsmith's College and shortly after Hirst had sold *The Physical Impossibility of Death in the Mind of Someone Living* (1991), a fourteen-foot shark preserved in a formaldehyde-filled steel and glass vitrine, to the collector Charles Saatchi. In the interview accompanying the portrait, Andrew Graham-Dixon observed of Hirst's spectacularly ambitious and impressive works of art that, 'they can seem wonderful, or they can seem spectacularly gauche and naïve. Whether Hirst is a genius, or just an extremely confident simpleton, is still open to debate. But whatever else he may be, he is persuasive...'

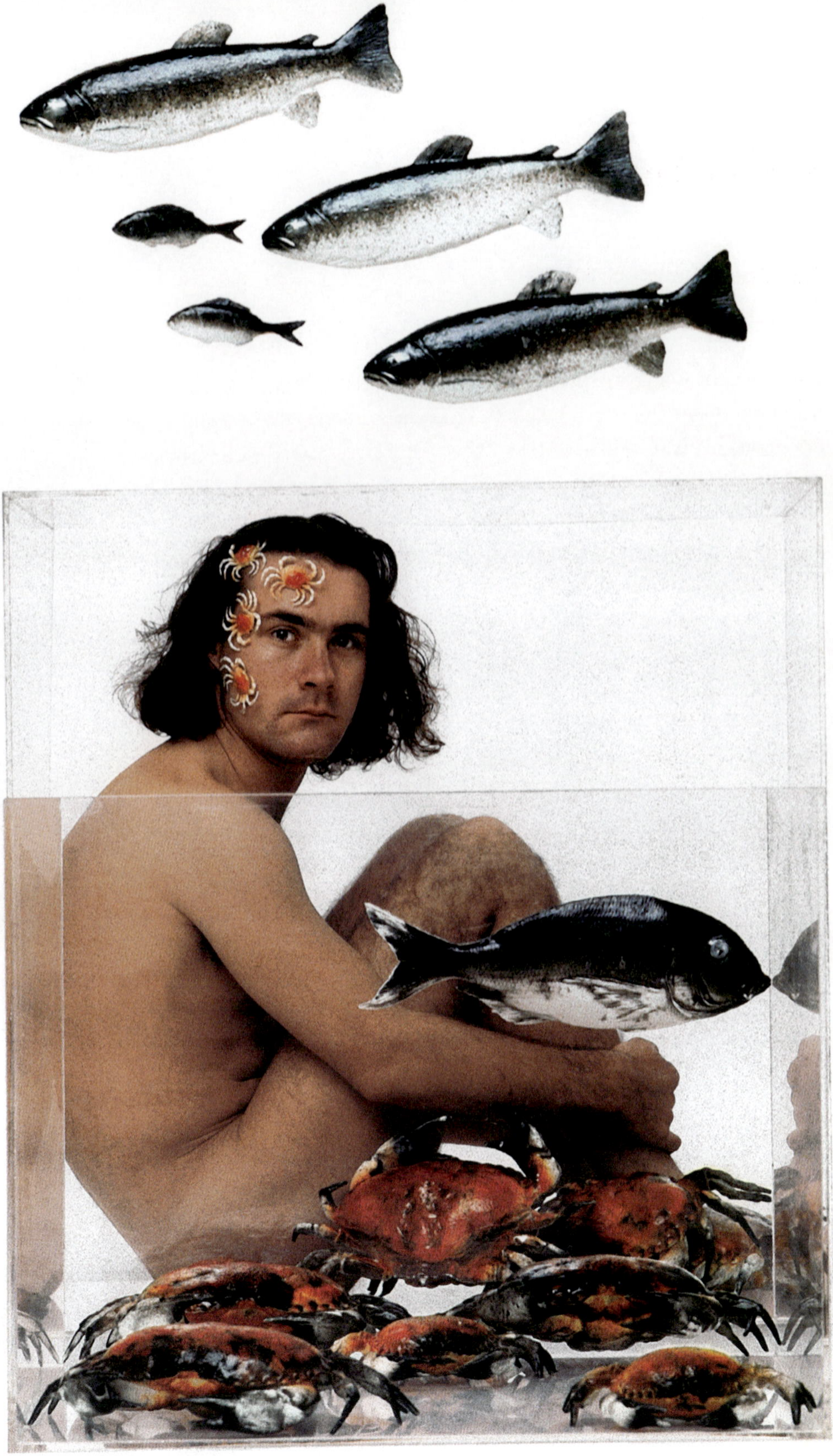

Carel Weight (1908–1997)

Wimbledon Common, 1994
The Telegraph Magazine

Carel Weight was appointed an official war artist in 1945 and dispatched to Italy. There he came to know Edward Bawden and Eric Ravilious well, and aspects of their English lyricism entered his own work. However, many of his early paintings were destroyed when his studio took a direct hit in a German bombing raid on London. A childhood spent mostly in down-at-heel Fulham with his godmother (both parents worked), had left him with an eye for the off-kilter urban vignette – a bus crash, buildings demolished, a minor human drama on the suburban street – and this informed his paintings. He contributed a mural to the Country Pavilion at the Festival of Britain (1951) and another *Christ and the People* for Manchester Cathedral (1962–3). He combined his teaching duties with portraits and landscape, the latter mostly in and around the suburbs of southwest London, and invariably populated his paintings with figures – even if none were apparent at the time of sketching: 'When I get back to the studio I always paint in figures; it would be too lonely without people', he once remarked. Snowdon photographed him on Wimbledon Common, a locale Weight knew well.

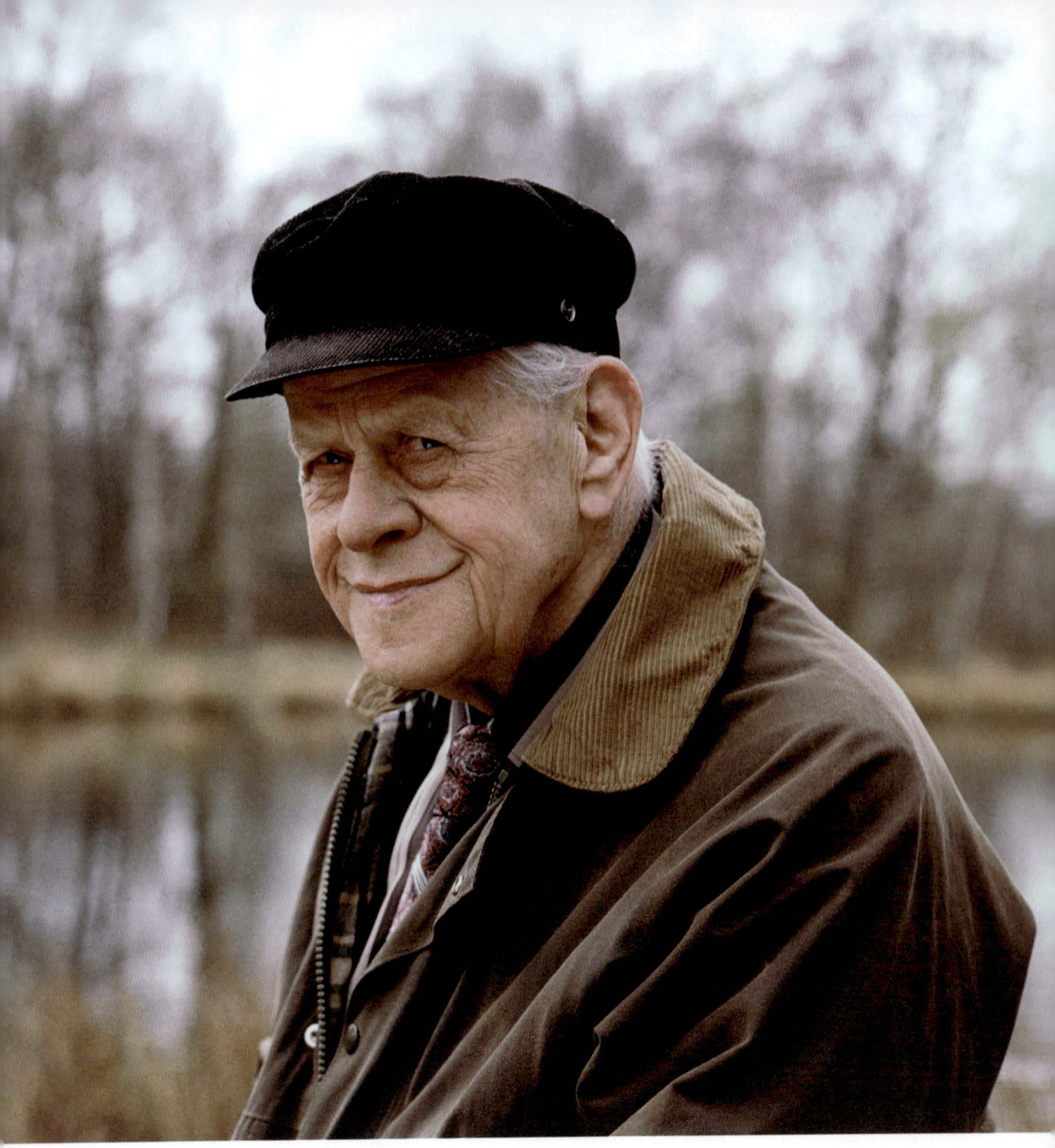

Mark Wallinger (b.1959)

In F45 Studios, Fulham, 1995
The Telegraph Magazine

The installation *State Britain* (2007), a painstaking recreation of Brian Haw's protest display at Parliament Square against the Iraq War, has led to Mark Wallinger's nomination for the Turner Prize 2007. This follows his first nomination in 1995, which owed much to *A Real Work of Art* (1994). This was a genuine thoroughbred racehorse, which he bought and re-named 'A Real Work of Art' with the intention of entering it at meets up and down the country. Thus art might, he hoped, reach a hitherto untapped audience of bookmakers' punters, race goers and armchair viewers of televised racing. Earlier work had also included meticulous life-sized paintings of racehorses, which along with *A Real Work of Art*, explains Snowdon's decision to clothe him in silks and be accompanied by a model horse. 'I take humour seriously as a way of getting a purchase on the subject. Some critics have trouble with this. They think I'm just a berk'. Whatever the critics thought, his concept for the empty fourth plinth in Trafalgar Square won him legions of admirers. This was *Ecce Homo* (1999), a statue of the Christ figure, barely life-sized, wearing a crown of barbed wire 'thorns'.

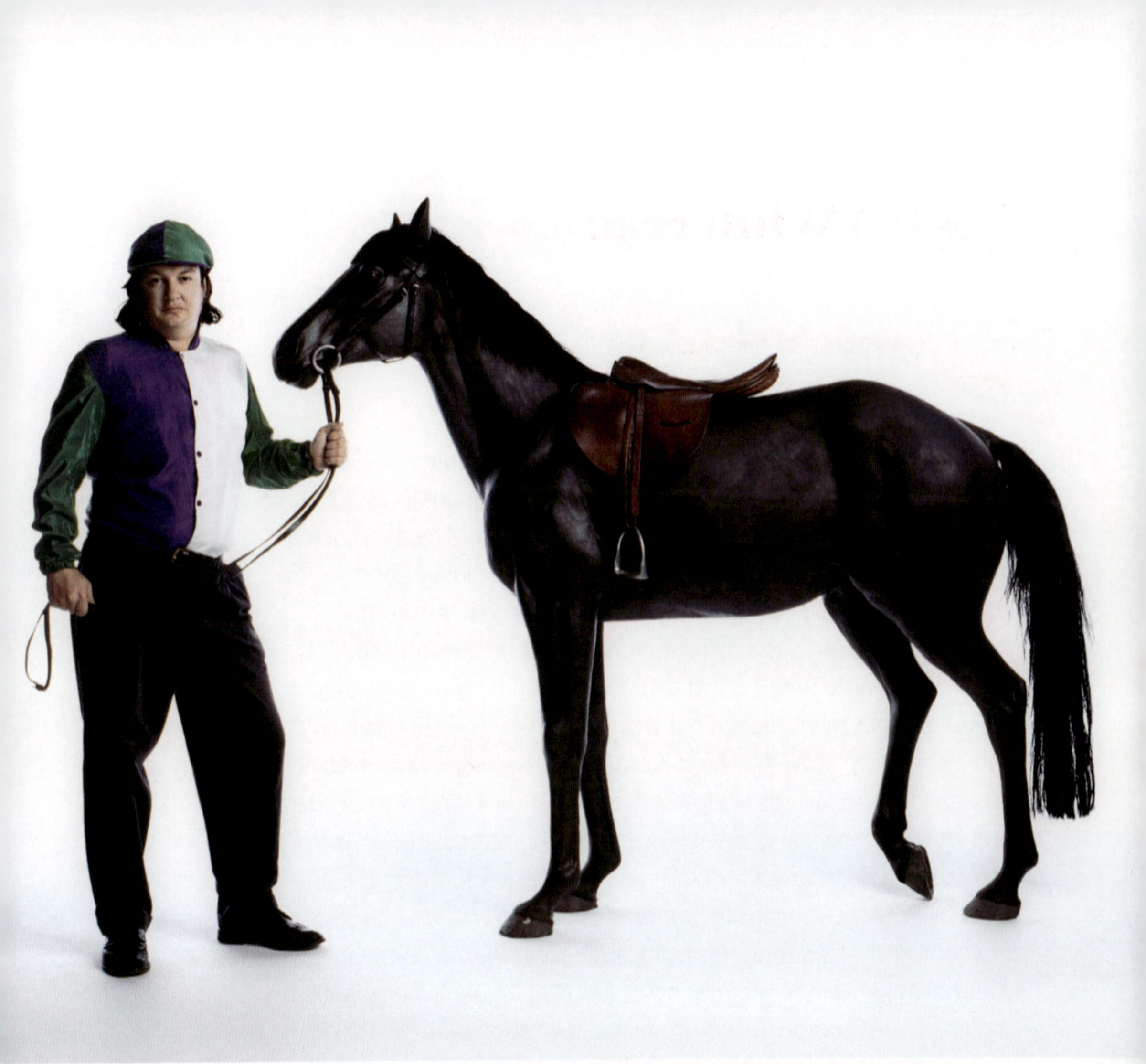

Rachel Whiteread (b.1963)

In the drying room of her studio, East London, 1997
Vogue

Rachel Whiteread's *Monument* (2001) briefly occupied the vacant plinth in the northwestern corner of Trafalgar Square. A 14′ 9″ high representation in transparent water-clear resin of the plinth itself, it stood inverted on top of the plinth as a mirror image of it. Greeted with approval and bewilderment in equal measure, it joined *House* (1993) as a striking, if transient, addition to the urban landscape. Winner of the Turner Prize for 1993, Whiteread's reputation has been fuelled not by hype or any willingly given self-promotion at all, but by the extraordinary regard given to her austere, frequently concrete-clad sculpture which resonates again and again around the globe. *House*, the concrete cast of an East End terraced house, is arguably her finest domestic moment, spawning in its brief three-month life, hundreds of press articles and tens of thousands of visitors. Her Holocaust memorial for Vienna's Judenplatz, a white concrete mausoleum, is arguably her greatest international triumph. Its controversial gestation was described by the artist as 'five years of sheer hell', the early stages of which she was embroiled in when Snowdon photographed her in her London studio.

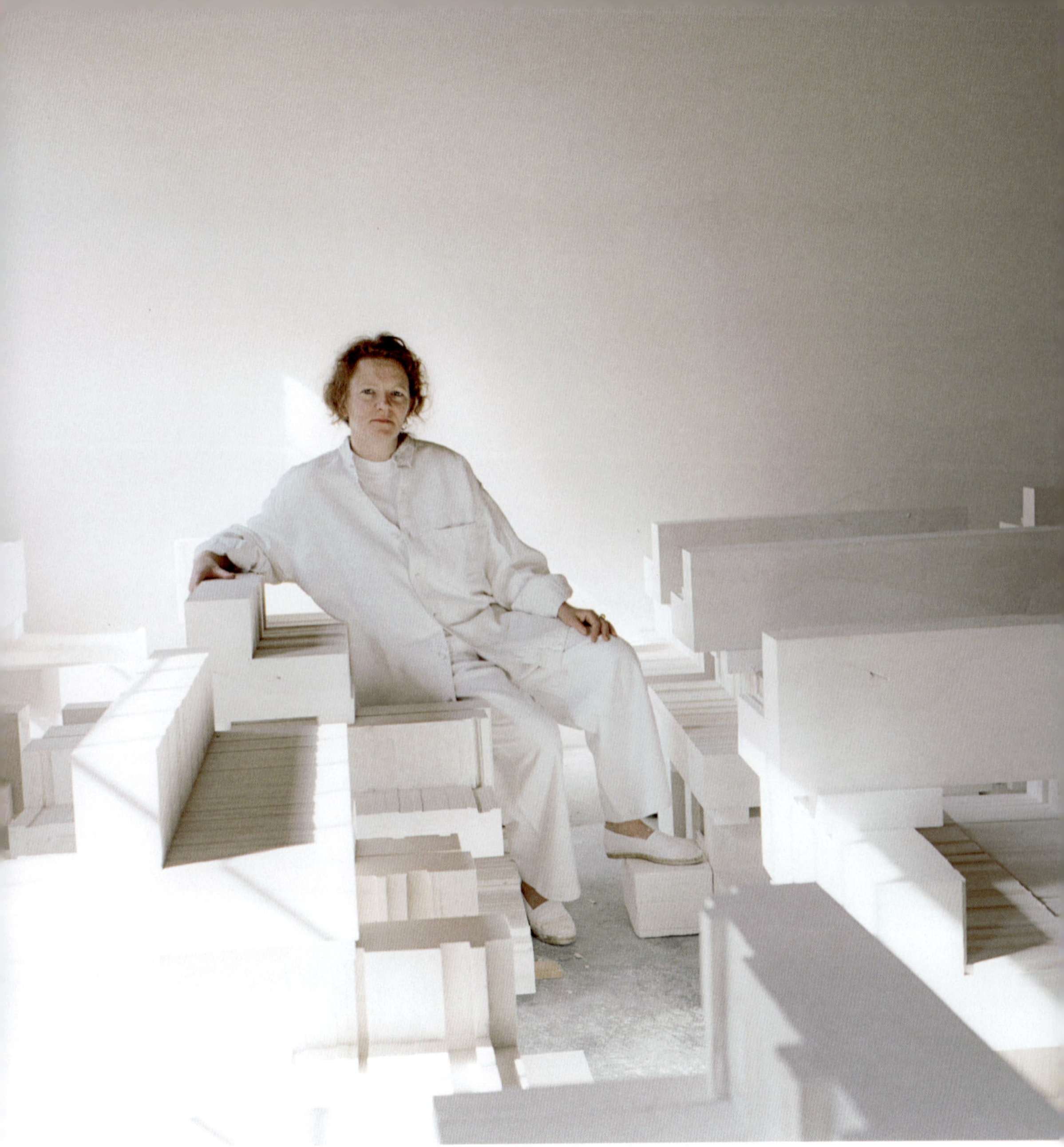

Chris Ofili (b.1968)

In his studio, East London, 1998
Vogue

Varnished elephant dung notwithstanding, the Nigerian-born painter has been no stranger to controversy which has occasionally overshadowed his bold and, almost literally, glittering work. In 1999, his iconographic painting *The Holy Virgin Mary* (1996) appeared in the Royal Academy of Art's *Sensation* exhibition and became the subject of a blistering obscenity debate between the Mayor of New York and the Director of the Brooklyn Museum. In 2005 many observers were troubled by Tate Britain's purchase of *The Upper Room* (1999-2002), a suite of thirteen paintings of rhesus macaque monkeys on elephant dung supports, while Ofili served as one of the gallery's trustees. 'Blaxploitation' films and African tribal ritual, as well as inner city 'hip hop' music have much influenced his vibrant work. In the year he won the Turner Prize, Ofili told *Vogue* 'I want people to look into the paintings as well as *at* the paintings – to pause, to rewind and to play them over and over.'

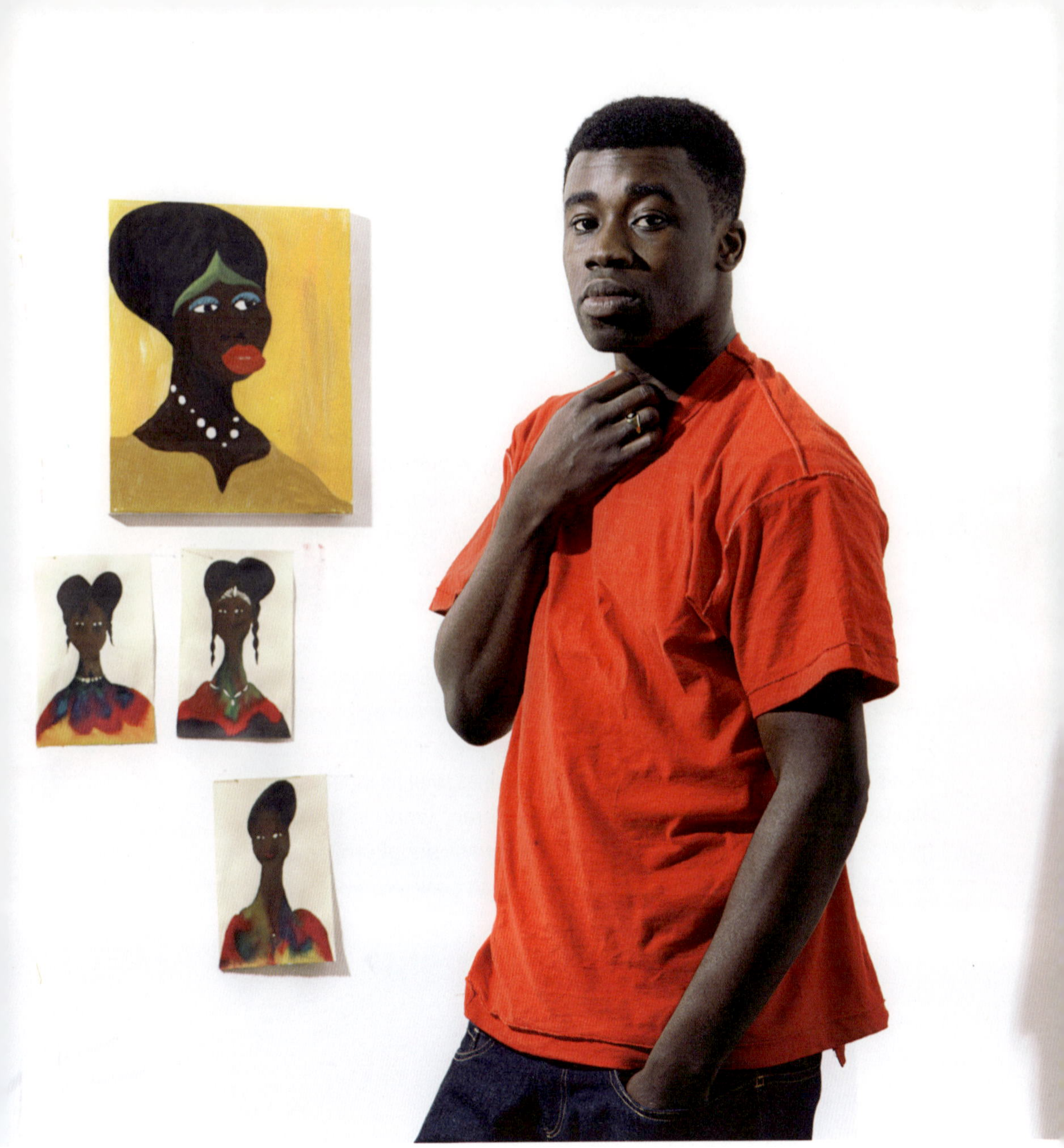

Wolfgang Tillmans (b.1968)

In his studio, East London, 2001
Vogue

In 2000, the German Wolfgang Tillmans was the first non-British artist to win the Turner Prize. 'It sort of put an official stamp on the very warm welcome I had already received here...' Born in Remscheid, Westphalia, he moved to London in 1993 and immersed himself in metropolitan life. His artworks – he is an artist who works with photography – range the parameters of the discipline in black and white, and colour: still life, portraiture, landscape and urban landscape, snapshot, giant blow-up. For a time he experimented with the camera-less photograph, that is, abstract images made purely in the darkroom, but his best known photographs are probably those of friends caught in quotidian moments. His gallery shows appear to revel in arbitrary sequencing, as if his pictures have been thrown against the white wall and tacked unframed where they hit it. These random, viewer-friendly arrangements take hours, however, to accomplish, and a closer inspection of his 'spontaneous' snapshots reveals their elaborate staging.

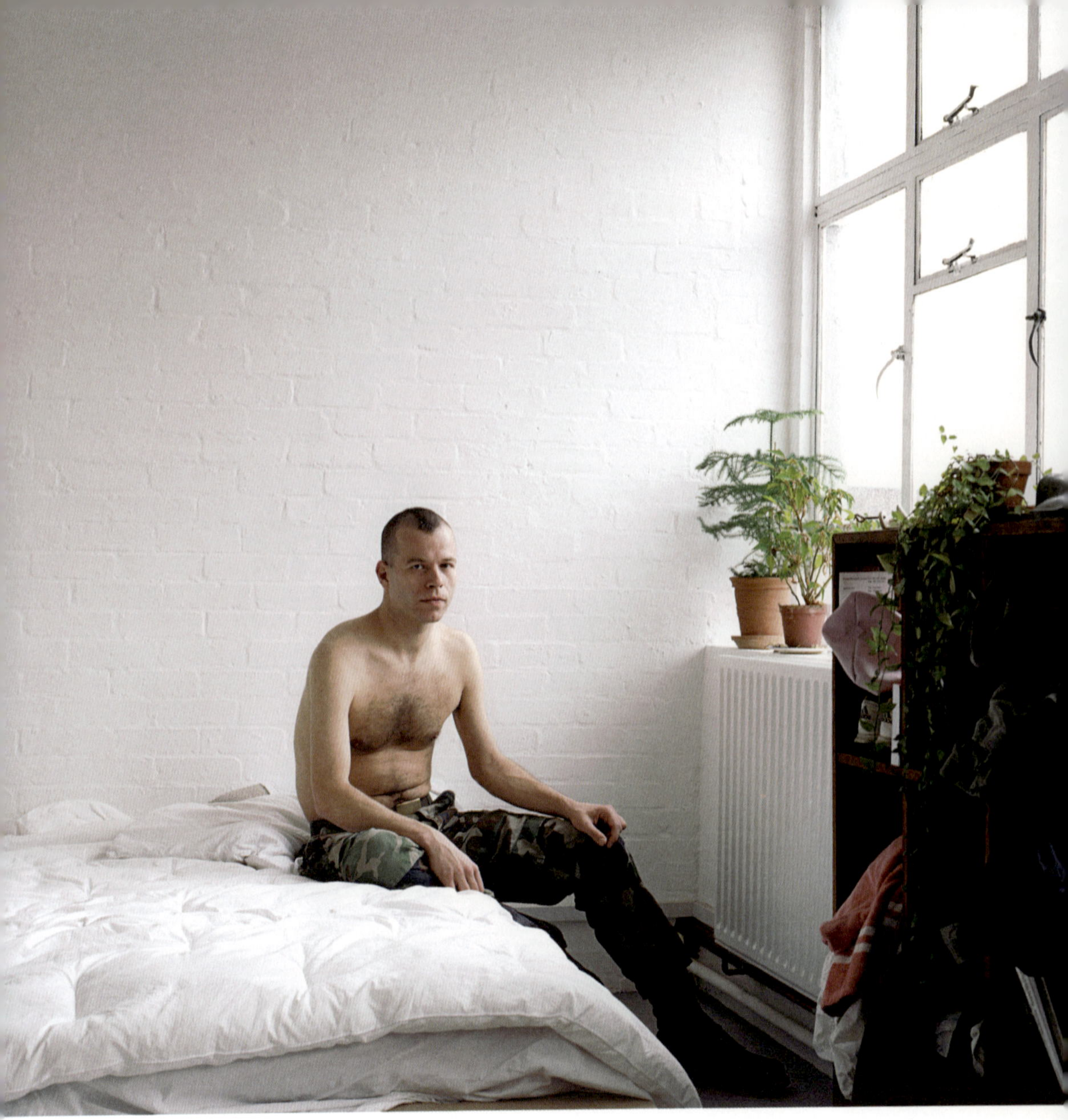

Jake Chapman (b.1966)
Dinos Chapman (b.1962)

In Snowdon's studio, Kensington, 2005
Vogue

The two brothers worked as assistants to Gilbert and George before making their 'terrorist aesthetic' public with a vivid diorama of limbless fibreglass figures, an interpretation of vignettes from Goya's series of etchings *Disasters of War*. They have continued to plunder from the history of fine art and marry it to their own taboo-shattering applied art. Goya was revisited for *Insult to Injury* (2003). The brothers acquired a series of extremely valuable, antique Goya etchings and reworked the surfaces with cartoons and colourful grotesquery. Though some considered it an act of cultural vandalism, overall it met with critical approval. They were nominated for the Turner Prize in 2003 and the following year a warehouse fire destroyed *Hell* (1999), an arrangement of miniature Nazi soldiers. Spotting Jake's tattoo, Snowdon asked the brothers to take off their T-shirts. 'And because he's royalty, we did' Dinos said. Jake added: 'That shows the true extent of our rebelliousness doesn't it?'

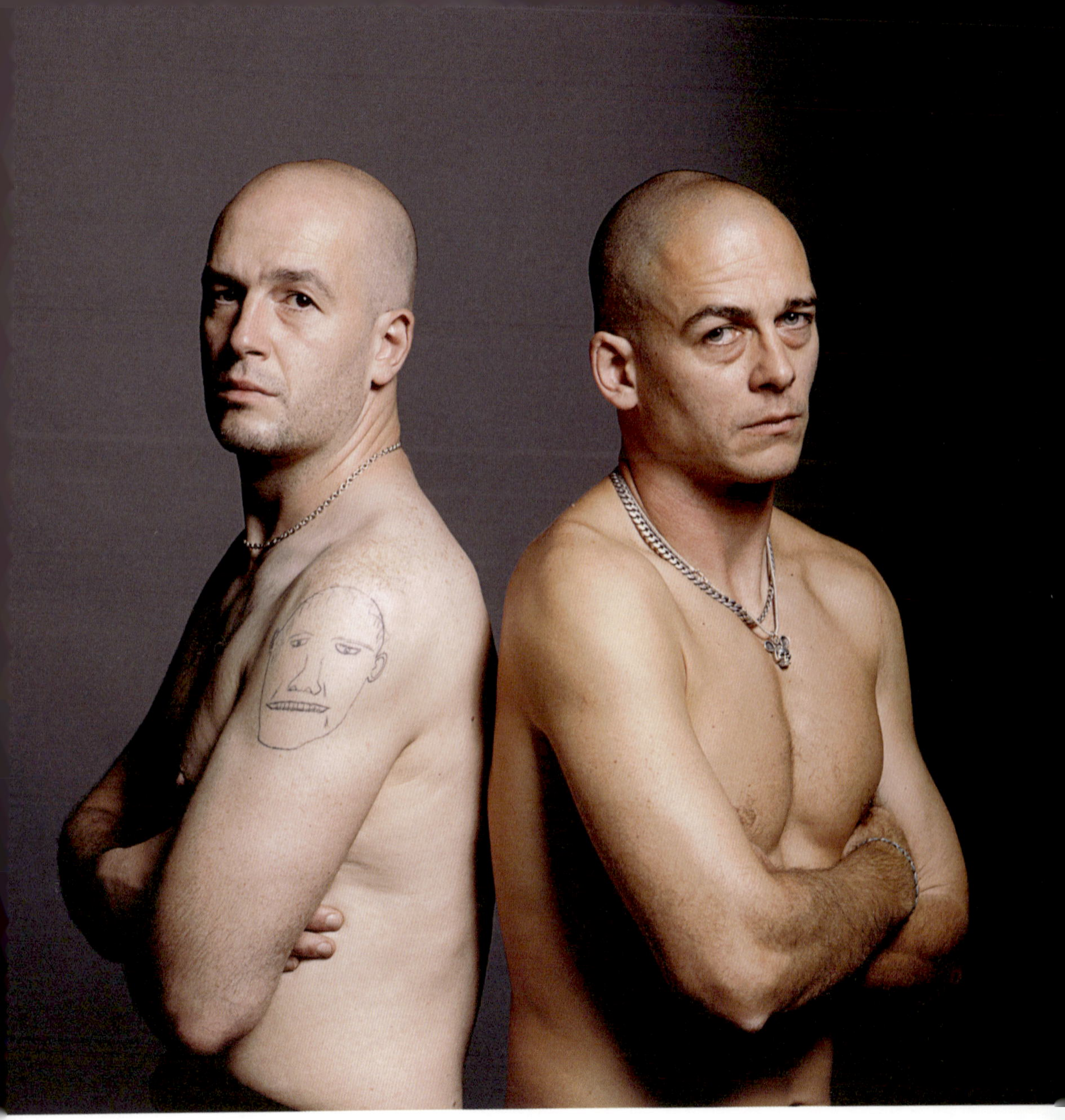

Grayson Perry (b.1960)

In Snowdon's studio, Kensington, 2005
Spoon

In 2003 Grayson Perry became the first transvestite ceramicist to win the Turner Prize. *The Guardian* decreed him 'the hottest potter the British art world has ever known.' Snowdon's portrait shows him in the 'Little Bo-Peep' guise of his transvestite alter-ego, Claire. Perry's classically-shaped but artisanal decorative vases and amphorae are often brightly hued and glazed but even cursory inspection reveals a hard-edged subject matter. This has much to do with his upbringing – he was born in suburban Essex – and his on-going inquiries into the nature of masculinity and cultural stereotypes. The vase *I was an Angry Working Class Man* (2000) dealt specifically with the latter point with a series of vignettes of motorbikes and pit-bull terriers, while other ceramics dealt with domestic child abuse and wider political issues. But it is 'Claire' that tends to remain in the popular imagination, allowing Perry to meditate upon the place of the 'gentle' sex in a harsh world, and to recreate tableaux of a domestic suburban world now slightly slipping from view. Her 'Coming Out' dresses are often the highpoint of a dull cultural gathering. Having experimented with photography and video, Perry has also pushed the boundaries in polemical embroidery.

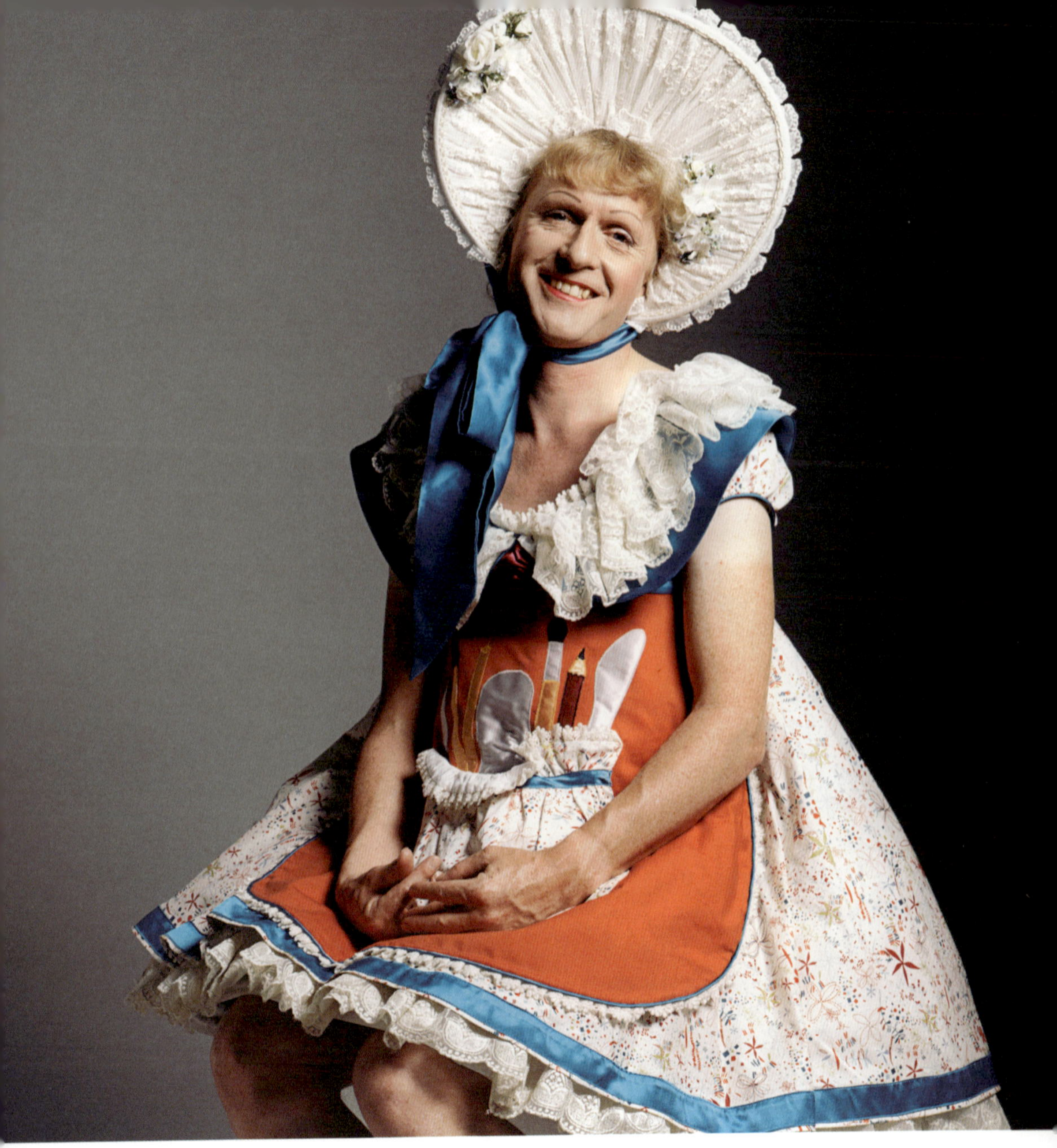

Conrad Shawcross (b.1977)

In his studio, Clapton, 2006
Vogue

As is often the case with young unknowns, the collector Charles Saatchi put the sculptor/machine inventor Conrad Shawcross on the map. 'To his credit', recalled the artist, 'he bought this massive unwieldy structure that was prone to breaking down. I owe him a great debt, Saatchi, it was a big thing, a difficult thing to buy...' This was *The Nervous Systems* (2003), a titanic spinning machine. Difficulty and engineering aside, the sheer size of Shawcross' mechanical timber contraptions is daunting. As he has pointed out, they don't have to 'do' anything but assume the guise of something that might turn around, flap its wings or ignite into motion should the correct lever somewhere be depressed. If they don't creak into life then so much the better, for it forces the viewer down a more philosophical path. Shawcross is reminiscent of an artist-scientist-alchemist of the Renaissance age, questioning meaning when metaphysics and practicality collide.

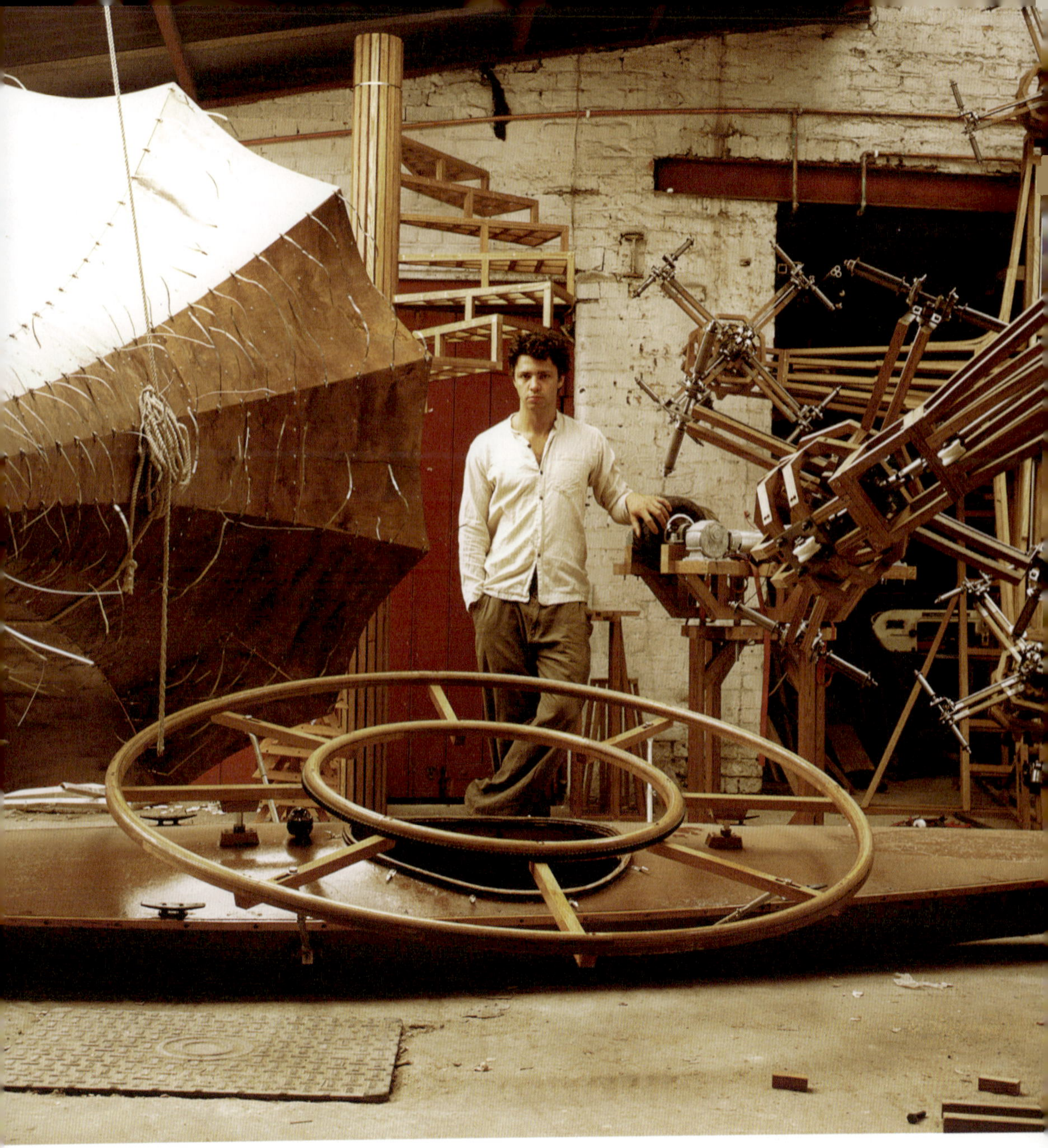

Chronology & Publications

Chronology

1930 Tony Armstrong-Jones born 7 March, son of Ronald Armstrong-Jones KC and Anne (neé Messel). Great-grandson of Linley Sambourne, political cartoonist for Punch; and nephew of the legendary theatre, ballet and opera designer Oliver Messel.

1936 Played Peter Pan (three performances). Designed costumes out of laurel leaves.

1943 Left prep school with report from headmaster, 'Armstrong-Jones may be good at something, but it's nothing we teach here'. Went to Eton. Revived the Photographic Society. The Eton *Chronicle* said of his photograph of Upper School after bombing: 'This photograph would have been more lively if there had been people in it'. One year spent in the Royal Infirmary, Liverpool with polio.

1948 Went up to Jesus College, Cambridge. Read Natural Sciences for ten days before changing to architecture.

1950 Contributed photographs to *Varsity* magazine. Coxed Cambridge in the Boat Race. Won by three and a half lengths. Failed exams.

1951 Started three-year apprenticeship with society and ballet photographer Baron for which his father paid £100. Left after six months. Worked with David Sim, in Shaftesbury Avenue basement in London, taking actors' portraits for *Spotlight*. First picture published in *Tatler*.

1952 Opened studio (in converted ironmonger's shop) in Pimlico. First spread in *Picture Post*: flamenco dancers at an Oliver Messel party.

1953 A regular contributor to *Tatler* and *The Sketch*. Made an underwater camera for *Tatler* feature.

1954 First theatre photocall: Terence Rattigan's *Separate Tables*. Used miniature cameras for theatre pictures rather than accepted plate camera. First assignment abroad (to Madeira for *Tatler*).

1956 First photographs for British and American *Vogue*, *Harper's Bazaar* and the *Daily Express*. Large blow-ups used for the first time as theatre front-of-house display. Rented a room on the river at Rotherhithe to research *London*.

1957 First exhibition *Photocall* at Kodak House, Kingsway. Began regular contributions to Jocelyn Stevens' *Queen* magazine.

1958 Designed high-key photographic sets for John Cranko's *Keep Your Hair On* (closed after two weeks). Designed collection of women's ski-wear.

1960 Married Princess Margaret.

1961 David Linley born. Began work on the Aviary at London Zoo with architects Cedric Price and Frank Newby. Joined staff of Council of Industrial Design. Editorial adviser to *Design* magazine (until 1987). Honorary Fellow of the Royal Photographic Society. Retained by *The Sunday Times*, mostly for the new colour supplement edited by Mark Boxer.

1962 Joined the Arts Council and the Council of the National Fund for Research into Crippling Diseases. First feature for *The Sunday Times Magazine* on social issues ('Old Age', published in 1965).

1963 Appointed Constable of Caernarfon Castle, Wales.

1964 Sarah Armstrong-Jones born.

1965 Aviary opened. Completed the Isle of Man TT course on a Triumph 650cc motorbike in 44 minutes (the then record was 21 minutes).

1966 Issue of *The Sunday Times Magazine* devoted to Indian coverage - arrested for photographing a bridge. Fourteen-page essay on the English theatre, with text by Penelope Gilliatt, initiating the phrase 'Swinging London'.

1967 Photo-essays on Venice and Japan for *The Sunday Times Magazine*. Came fourth out of 55 in the two-way cross-Channel water-ski race (lasting three and a quarter hours, only seven finished).

1968 First TV documentary (with Derek Hart) *Don't Count the Candles*, about aspects of old age. Wins two Emmys, the St. George Prize at Venice, and awards at Barcelona and Prague film festivals; and is shown in 22 countries. Designed 'chairmobile', a motorised platform (5000 sold).

1969 Responsible for overall design of the investiture of the Prince of Wales at Caernarfon Castle, Wales; worked with Carl Toms as co-designer. Art Director's Club of New York Certificate of Merit.

1970 Started work again for British *Vogue*. TV documentary *Love of a Kind* about the incongruous British attitude towards animals, with Derek Hart (who worked on the next two documentaries as well).

1971 TV documentary *Born to be Small* about the problems facing people of restricted growth (Chicago Hugo Award).

1972 *Assignments* exhibition opened in Cologne. Subsequently shown in London, the US, the Far East and Australia. Maiden speech in the House of Lords on mobility for disabled people.

1973 TV documentary *Happy Being Happy*. Fellow of the Society of Industrial Artists and Designers.

1974 Two historical documentaries for the BBC: *Mary Kingsley* (in Gabon) and *Burke and Wills* (in Australia). Fellow of the Royal Society of Arts.

1976 Snowdon Report on Integrating the Disabled. Gained access for wheelchairs and guide dogs to the Chelsea Flower Show.

1977 TV documentary *Peter, Tina and Steve*.

1978 Married Lucy Lindsay-Hogg. Conferred Royal Designer for Industry (RDI). Royal Photographic Society Hood award for 'promoting concern for children, the disabled and the generally underprivileged.' Member of the Council of the English Stage Company (until 1982). Design and Art Directors' Association Silver Award.

1979 Frances Armstrong-Jones born.

1980 Founded Snowdon Award scheme for further education of disabled students.

1981 President (England) 'International Year of Disabled People'. Presented *Snowdon on Camera* for the BBC (BAFTA nomination).

1984 Took stills of *A Passage to India*, directed by David Lean. Outstanding Achievement Award of the American Society of Magazine Photographers.

1985 Silver Progress Medal, The Royal Photographic Society.

1986 Appointed Senior Fellow, The Royal College of Art. Photographed the Paris Collections for French *Vogue*. Designed (with Jeremy Fry) the 'Squirrel', a wheelchair with four-wheel drive and power steering.

1987 Highly publicised interview with Simon Hornby, Chairman of the Design Council. Resigned as Honorary Adviser to the Design Council.

1988 Patron of Polio Plus. Another highly critical interview, with Sir Robert Reid, Chairman of British Rail, highlighting the company's attitude to disabled passengers.

1989 *Serendipity* exhibition at the Royal Pavilion in Brighton, in Bath and the National Museum for Film, Photography and Television, Bradford. Honorary Doctorates, University of Bath and University of Bradford.

1990 Contract to photograph for the *Telegraph Magazine*. Designed a series of prism clocks. 'Natterjack Toad' included in *Life* magazine's 'World's Best Photographs 1980–90'.

1991 Designed 'The Link', a hearing device based on infra-red communication rather than amplification.

1994 Honorary Doctorate, University of Portsmouth.

1995 Provost, Royal College of Art. President of ADAPT (Access for Disabled People to Arts Premises Today). Contributed eighty-eight photographs to 'British Theatre' issue of *Vanity Fair*. Completed *Telegraph Magazine* contract, having photographed 223 pages and 19 covers.

1996 *Snowdon on Stage* exhibition at the Royal National Theatre.

1997 Edited special 'London' edition of *Country Life*. Official portrait of the Queen and Prince Philip to mark their golden wedding anniversary, subsequently adopted for use as a postage stamp (his twelfth since 1957).

1998 Aviary at London Zoo given Grade II* listing.

2000 *Photographs by Snowdon – A Retrospective* exhibition at the National Portrait Gallery, London, City Arts Centre, Edinburgh and KunstHausWien, Vienna.

2001 *Photographs by Snowdon – A Retrospective* exhibition at the Yale Center for British Art, New Haven. U.S.A.

2002 Exhibition at Dimbola Lodge, Isle of Wight and at Linley, London. Retrospective exhibition at The Kuskovo Museum and 18th Century Estate, Moscow.

2005 Spent a month in India for the book *Snowdon India*.

2006 *Snowdon* exhibition at Chris Beetles Gallery, St. James', London. Assignment on Berlin for *Stern* magazine.

2007 *Iconic Snowdon* at the Plymouth Arts Centre, Plymouth. *Snowdon in New York* exhibition at Godel Fine Art Gallery, New York.

Publications

Malta (with Sir Sacheverell Sitwell), Batsford, 1958

London, Weidenfeld & Nicolson, 1958

Private View (with John Russell and Bryan Robertson), Nelson, 1965

A View of Venice, Olivetti, 1972

Assignments, Weidenfeld & Nicolson, 1972

The Sack of Bath (with Adam Ferguson), Compton Russell, 1973

Hong Kong, 'Portraits of Power', Weidenfeld and Nicolson, 1975

The Inchcape Review, Inchcape & Co., 1976

Personal View, Weidenfeld & Nicolson, 1979

Pride of the Shires (with John Oaksey), Hutchinson, 1979

Tasmania Essay, R.T. Banks, Australia, 1983

Sittings 1979–83 (introduction by John Mortimer), Weidenfeld & Nicolson, 1983

My Wales (with George Thomas), Century Hutchinson, 1986

Israel – A First View, Weidenfeld & Nicolson, 1986

Stills 1983–87 (introduction by Harold Evans), Weidenfeld & Nicolson, 1987

Serendipity (introduction by Carl Toms), Royal Pavilion Art Gallery and Museums, Brighton, 1989

Public Appearances (introduction by Jocelyn Stevens), Weidenfeld & Nicolson, 1991

Wild Flowers (foreword by Roy Strong), Pavilion, 1995

Snowdon on Stage (introduction by Simon Callow), Pavilion, 1996

Wild Fruit (foreword by David Attenborough), Bloomsbury, 1997

London Sight Unseen (with Gwyn Headley), Weidenfeld & Nicolson, 1998

Photographs by Snowdon, A Retrospective, National Portrait Gallery Publications, 2000

The Snowdon Collection, The Kuskovo State Museum and 18th Century Estate, Moscow, 2001

Snowdon Russia, Mentatron Publications, Moscow 2003

Snowdon on India, The Khemka Foundation, New Delhi, 2007